I0005670

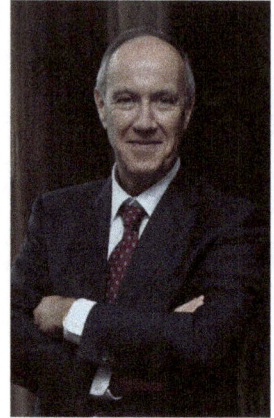

This new report aims
to shed light on the
trends in innovation in
AI since the field first
developed in the 1950s.

WIPO Director General, Francis Gurry

Preface

I am pleased to present the first report in a new flagship series, *WIPO Technology Trends*. This first edition features artificial intelligence (AI) as the theme. It is a fitting topic for the launch of the series as AI is a cutting-edge technology with impacts on a wide range of businesses and activities.

AI is fast becoming part of our everyday lives, changing how we work, shop, travel and interact with each other. Yet we are only at the beginning of discovering the many ways in which AI will have an impact on – and indeed challenge – business, society and culture. There are numerous misconceptions and misgivings about the nature of AI, and in particular the challenge it poses to humankind. Given these widely held reservations and concerns, it is essential to have a factual basis for policy discussions about innovation in AI. Through this report, we hope to contribute evidence and bring clarity to this important area of debate.

Based on a detailed study of patents and other information, this new report aims to shed light on the trends in innovation in AI since the field first developed in the 1950s. Research has involved the analysis of patent data related to AI inventions, as well as data on scientific publications, litigation filings and acquisition activity. These data findings are discussed in detail and accompanied by commentary and industry perspectives from more than 20 of the world's leading experts in AI; more complete datasets, patent search methodology and expert contributions are openly available on the WIPO website. We hope that this report will prove an invaluable resource for businesses, researchers and policymakers in the field, as well as for those general readers who want to find out how AI research has so far developed – and where it is going.

The analysis offers unique insights into trends in AI techniques (i.e., the different approaches used in AI, such as machine learning and fuzzy logic), AI functional applications (such as natural language processing, speech processing and computer vision) and AI application fields (i.e., those industries and other sectors in which AI innovation is being put into practice). One of the most striking findings of the report is that 50 percent of all AI patents have been published in just the last five years – a remarkable illustration of how rapidly innovation is advancing in this field.

This report identifies the key players in AI from both the corporate and public sectors across different research areas and industries. Furthermore, the analysis of the data and the inputs from AI experts address many of the policy issues raised by AI, such as the regulation and control of data, the incentivization of further research, the role of intellectual property (IP) protection and the development of human-centered and ethical AI to benefit all.

Together, the analysis of technological trends presented in this report and the voices of AI experts collected here are a valuable new addition to a growing knowledge base on AI.

I hope that this contribution will help to shift debate away from speculative interpretation and toward evidence-based projections, thereby informing global policymaking on the future of AI, its governance and the IP framework that supports it.

Francis GURRY
Director General

Foreword

Andrew Ng
CEO, Landing AI
and deeplearning.ai

I remember watching the final chess match between Deep Blue and Gary Kasparov while I was a graduate student at MIT in the 1990s. When Kasparov resigned, I jumped out of my chair in excitement – the AI community had finally triumphed over the human chess champion!

This moment stands out for me, among many milestones in the development of AI, such as the rise of deep learning, lessons in scalability and the DARPA Grand Challenge. AI is automation on steroids, and we had "automated" the process of playing chess. I was once captain of my high school chess team and used to play competitively, but at that moment I was happy to retire and leave it to the computers. This was not a sad event for me; on the contrary, I was thrilled to give up chess this way.

As AI continues to develop and transform industry after industry, I hope it will create many more similarly joyful experiences. We have a duty to address serious issues relating to unemployment and inequality, but we should also never lose sight of the value and possibility that AI brings.

This report illustrates some of those possibilities and where they are arising. One of its findings is that deep learning is the biggest and fastest growing technique in AI. When I was at Stanford in the 2000s, my PhD student, Adam Coates, came into my office with a chart showing that the more data you fed to a neural network, the better the neural network performed. We started looking for the biggest computers we could find. That discovery, and the idea of using distributed computing to scale up neural networks, led to the creation of Google Brain in 2011. Since then, deep learning has made great progress as we've collected more data and created the powerful computers to make it work.

But we still have a long way to go in the field. For example, a toddler can usually recognize a cat after just one encounter, but a computer still needs more than one example to learn. We need to find ways to train computers on training datasets as small as 100, or even 10. Manufacturing lines, for example, use computer vision to check for defects in parts but hopefully they will never have a million examples of defects to train on. Effective "unsupervised learning" – learning without labelled data – remains a holy grail of AI.

Even without this "holy grail," AI is already creating massive economic value in the world today. In covering AI, the media tends to focus on images, speech and natural language processing because those types of data are very human. Everyone can understand what it means for a computer to identify a cat or recognize your speech. But a lot of the economic value today is driven through deep learning on "structured data." Think of this as machine learning applied to massive Excel spreadsheets (only bigger than the biggest Excel spreadsheet in the world). This data – for example, what trucks should be dispatched when, what products to recommend to what user – is more specific to individual companies and industries. Structured data gets less attention because it's not as visual or intuitive. But it is driving massive value today and will continue as incumbent companies across all industries transform themselves with AI.

With this potential to transform every industry and create so much economic value, AI presents just as great a technological shift as the Internet did. In the Internet era, companies including Microsoft and Apple saw the Internet trend early, and their leaders made strategic decisions to become true Internet companies.

This meant investing in the right technology, building teams, developing a digital strategy and adapting how they communicated about their products.

We are seeing a small number of incumbent companies undergo a similar transformation in the AI era. Google and Baidu were leaders in hiring AI talent and building pilot AI projects; they are now fully AI-driven companies. But AI transformation is not limited solely to Internet search companies. The biggest untapped opportunities today lie outside of the software industry in industries such as agriculture, healthcare and manufacturing.

Every organization can leverage its data and domain expertise to build pilot AI projects. They will then be able to build internal AI teams that push their industries forward and create unique AI solutions. I recently released the *AI Transformation Playbook* to help organizations in all industries navigate their own AI transformations.

In order to help more people and businesses harness the potential of AI, we should consider the following three actions:

1. **Build more public–private partnerships**: When companies and universities or government organizations work together, both sides can benefit. For example, university researchers can access more data and understand relevant problems, and corporations can understand the latest breakthroughs in technology.
2. **Continue promoting the free and open sharing of AI knowledge and resources**: Companies have joined universities as leading forces for publishing free and open AI research. The arXiv repository has made a huge difference to the AI revolution, as has the hosting service GitHub because it dramatically accelerates the free dissemination of ideas. Other fields can learn this lesson and move away from paywalled journals.
3. **Promote increased understanding of AI**: Today, you can get a PhD to learn AI, but it's not the only option. Traditional degrees, jobs that allow you to learn, and at-home online

learning programs (such as MOOCs) are all good ways for people to learn and work on important problems. The more widely accessible information we have, the more flexibility people will have to learn.

Today, a significant amount of AI research and education is taking place in the United States and China. These countries are home to many of the best universities in the world, and their governments have provided funding and created thoughtful regulations that enable innovation. But the United States and China have also built incredible business ecosystems. It's very difficult for other countries, even those with great education, to compete with the business, engineering and investing talent of those two countries.

To close this gap, and work towards decentralizing the concentration of AI technology, we must invest in education. Governments should invest heavily in educating their citizens and enter public–private partnerships to adopt AI-powered systems safely.

AI will transform every facet of society. It brings tremendous promise to improve our lives and the world we live in, but it will require the creation of an AI ecosystem to ensure long-term, sustainable growth. As this report highlights, AI technology and innovation has until now been focused on a small number of regions and organizations. In building a fairer and more equitable AI-driven society, we must empower businesses, governments and citizens who may be impacted by automation to ensure that the benefits of AI are widely shared.

About the contributors

This report includes contributions from experts in AI, data, intellectual property, policy, and innovation. Their viewpoints and comments complement and add context to the information revealed in patent data, addressing issues such as existing and potential uses and impact of AI technology, legal and regulatory questions, data protection and ethical concerns.

Seth G Benzell is postdoctoral associate at the Massachusetts Institute of Technology (MIT) Initiative on the Digital Economy

Nick Bostrom is Director of the Future of Humanity Institute and author of *Superintelligence: Paths, Dangers, Strategies*

Erik Brynjolfsson is Director at the MIT Initiative on the Digital Economy

Yoon Chae is a senior associate Baker McKenzie

Frank Chen is a partner at Andreessen Horowitz

Myriam Côté is Director of AI for Humanity at Montreal Institute for Learning Algorithms (Mila)

Boi Faltings is Professor of AI and Director of the AI Lab at École polytechnique fédérale de Lausanne (EPFL)

Kay Firth-Butterfield is Head of AI and Machine Learning at the World Economic Forum (WEF)

John G. Flaim is a partner and global head of the IP group at Baker McKenzie

Dario Floreano is Director of the Laboratory of Intelligent Systems at EPFL and founding director of the Swiss National Center of Competence in Robotics

Dominique Foray is Professor of Economics at EPFL

Martin Ford is a futurist and author of *Rise of the Robots: Technology and the Threat of a Jobless Future*

Jay Iorio is a futurist

Malcolm Johnson is Deputy Secretary General of the International Telecommunications Union (ITU)

Konstantinos Karachalios is Managing Director of IEEE Standards Association and a member of IEEE's Management Council

Kai-Fu Lee is founder of Sinovation Ventures and author of *AI Superpowers: China, Silicon Valley, and the New World Order*

Ben Lorica is Chief Data Scientist at O'Reilly Media

Miguel Luengo-Oroz is Chief Data Scientist at UN Global Pulse

Kazuyuki Motohashi is Professor in the Department of Technology Management for Innovation at the University of Tokyo

Paul Nemitz is Principal Adviser to the European Commission

Eleonore Pauwels is Research Fellow on Emerging Cybertechnologies at the UN University's Center for Policy Research

Rosalind Picard is founder and Director of the Affective Computing Research Group at the Massachusetts Institute of Technology (MIT) Media Laboratory

Hefa Song is Professor of the Institute of Science and Management, Deputy Director of the Center for IPR Research and Training, and Deputy Dean of the Intellectual Property School at the Chinese Academy of Sciences (CAS)

Petr Šrámek is the founder of AI Startup Incubator and co-founder of the Platform on AI at the Confederation of Industry of the Czech Republic

Aristotelis Tsirigos is Director of the Applied Bioinformatics Laboratories at NYU School of Medicine

Haifeng Wang is Senior Vice President at Baidu

Herbert Zech is Professor of Life Sciences Law and Intellectual Property Law at the University of Basel

Acknowledgments

The report was prepared under the direction of Francis Gurry (Director General) and Yo Takagi (Assistant Director General, Global Infrastructure Sector), supervised by Alejandro Roca Campaña (Senior Director, Access to Information and Knowledge Division), under the responsibility of Irene Kitsara (IP Information Officer, Access to Information and Knowledge Division).

The report draws on commissioned background research, based on search strategy and methodology developed by the core analytics team led by Irene Kitsara (WIPO), consisting of Sophie Gojon, Adrien Migeon and Philippe Petit (CNRS Innovation) and Patrice Lopez (science-miner). The AI dimensions used for the report and the related glossary were developed by Patrice Lopez, who also provided expert advice on AI in patent literature, with inputs by the core team, the WIPO Advanced Technologies Application Center (ATAC) and team members of Mila (Simon Blackburn, Pierre Luc Carrier, Mathieu Germain, Margaux Luck, Gaétan Marceau Caron and Joao Felipe Santos).

Interviews were conducted and AI expert contributions were compiled by James Nurton, who was the editor of the report, under the responsibility of Charlotte Beauchamp (Head, Editorial and Design Section). Case studies were kindly provided by contributors, Angela Harp (IBM Research), Mohamad Ali Mahfouz (Microsoft Switzerland) and Sven Zirnite (Siemens Healthcare).

The report team benefited greatly from external reviews of the draft chapters by Boi Faltings (EPFL), Patrice Lopez (science-miner) and Alexandros Tsirigos (NYU Medical School), and by WIPO colleagues Carsten Fink (Chief Economist), Akshat Dewan and Bruno Pouliquen (from ATAC), and Marco Aleman, Allison Mages and Tomoko Miyamoto (from WIPO's Patent Law Division).

The core team was skillfully assisted by colleagues from WIPO's Access to Information and Knowledge Division, under the direction of Andrew Czajkowski. Thanks are due in particular to Alica Daly, who validated the data, prepared the visualizations and contributed together with Alex Riechel to reviewing and finalizing the report. Vipin Saroha prepared the maps. Julie Summers provided valuable administrative support. Additional data and comments for the comparison of the report findings with overall patent statistics were provided by Kyle Bergquist, Mosahid Khan, Julio Raffo and Hao Zhou, all from the Economics and Statistics Division.

Gratitude is due to the 27 leading experts in AI and contributors to the report who shared their views, provided their comments on different aspects which enriched and contextualized the report findings – their time and contribution are much appreciated. Thanks also to Andrew Ng for providing the Foreword of the report, and to Bridget Hickey for her facilitation.

The report also draws on helpful input received in the conceptualization phase from Phillippa Biggs (Senior Policy Analyst at ITU), Virginia Dignum (Assistant Professor at the Faculty of Technology, Policy and Management, Delft University of Technology), Kay Firth-Butterfield (Head, AI and Machine Learning at WEF), Jay Iorio (futurist), Konstantinos Karachalios (Managing Director at IEEE Standards Association), and the law committee members of the IEEE Global Initiative on Ethics of Autonomous and Intelligent Systems, as well as from WIPO colleagues Carsten Fink, Allison Mages, Christophe Mazenc, Bruno Pouliquen, Ning Xu; and on experience drawn from previous WIPO publications from the Economics and Statistics Division, shared by Mosahid Khan, Julio Raffo and Sacha Vincent-Wunsch.

Gratitude is also due to the WIPO Communications Division, in particular Charlotte Beauchamp for all the valuable contributions and support throughout the preparation of the publication, Edwin Hassink and Sheyda Navab for the design of the report and Ed Harris for helpful inputs; and to staff in the Printing Plant for their high-quality services. Gratitude is expressed to everyone who worked hard and constructively towards creating a new publication type and meeting challenging deadlines.

Executive summary

Artificial intelligence (AI) is increasingly driving important developments in technology and business, from autonomous vehicles to medical diagnosis to advanced manufacturing. As AI moves from the theoretical realm to the global marketplace, its growth is fueled by a profusion of digitized data and rapidly advancing computational processing power, with potentially revolutionary effect: detecting patterns among billions of seemingly unrelated data points, AI can improve weather forecasting, boost crop yields, enhance detection of cancer, predict an epidemic and improve industrial productivity.

AI is the new electricity. I can hardly imagine an industry which is not going to be transformed by AI.

Andrew Ng, Landing AI and deeplearning.ai

Technology trends can be discerned through patent analytics

Drawing on WIPO's expertise in patent data analytics, this first publication in the series WIPO Technology Trends investigates the trends in the emerging AI era: it analyzes patent, scientific publishing and other data to review past and current trends in AI, while offering insights into how innovation in this field is likely to develop in the coming years.

This publication is among the first to systematically research trends in AI technology in order to discover which fields show the largest amount of innovative AI activity, which companies and what institutions are leading AI development, and the location of future growth markets.

WIPO has devised a new framework for the understanding of developments in the field, with AI-related technologies grouped to reflect three dimensions of AI: techniques used in AI, such as machine learning; functional applications, such as speech processing and computer vision; and application fields, including telecommunications and transportation.

For each of these areas, this report provides data and analysis that identify trends, key players, geographical spread and market activity, including acquisitions and litigation. In addition, it includes contributions from AI experts from across the globe, addressing issues such as existing and potential uses and impact of AI technology, legal and regulatory questions, data protection and ethical concerns.

AI-related inventions are booming, shifting from theory to commercial application

Since artificial intelligence emerged in the 1950s, innovators and researchers have filed applications for nearly 340,000 AI-related inventions and published over 1.6 million scientific publications.

Notably, AI-related patenting is growing rapidly: over half of the identified inventions have been published since 2013.

While scientific publications on AI date back decades, the boom in scientific publications on AI only started around 2001, approximately 12 years in advance of an upsurge in patent applications. Moreover, the ratio of scientific papers to inventions has decreased from 8:1 in 2010 to 3:1 in 2016 – indicative of a shift from theoretical research to the use of AI technologies in commercial products and services.

Some areas of AI are growing more quickly than others...

Machine learning is the dominant AI technique disclosed in patents and is included in more than one-third of all identified inventions (134,777 patent documents). Filings of machine learning-related patent have grown annually on annual average by 28 percent, with 20,195 patent applications filed in 2016 (compared with 9,567 in 2013).

The machine learning techniques revolutionizing AI are deep learning and neural networks, and these are the fastest growing AI techniques in terms of patent filings: deep learning showed an impressive average annual growth rate of 175 percent from 2013 to 2016, reaching 2,399 patent filings in 2016; and neural networks grew at a rate of 46 percent over the same period, with 6,506 patent filings in 2016.

Among AI functional applications, computer vision, which includes image recognition, is the most popular. Computer vision is mentioned in 49 percent of all AI-related patents (167,038 patent documents), growing annually by an average of 24 percent (21,011 patent applications filed in 2016).

Those AI functional applications with the highest growth rates in patent filings in the period 2013 to 2016 were AI for robotics and control methods, which both grew on average by 55 percent a year.

The growth rates observed in the identified AI-related patent data are noticeably higher than the average annual growth rate for patents across all areas of technology, which was 10 percent between 2013 and 2016.

...and many AI patents include inventions that can be applied in different industries...

AI-related patents not only disclose AI techniques and applications, they often also refer to an application field or industry. Analysis shows that many sectors and industries are exploring the commercial exploitation of AI. Twenty application fields were identified in the present analysis and at least one was mentioned in 62 percent of the total identified AI patent data. These include, in order of magnitude: telecommunications (mentioned in 15 percent of all identified patent documents), transportation (15 percent), life and medical sciences (12 percent), and personal devices, computing and human–computer interaction (HCI) (11 percent). Other sectors featuring in the results include banking; entertainment; security; industry and manufacturing; agriculture; and networks (including social networks, smart cities and the Internet of things).

Many AI-related technologies can find use across different industries, as shown by the large number of patents in AI that refer to multiple industries. Transportation is prominent not only in the overall results, it also features among those fields showing the highest growth rates in AI-related patent applications, with a 33 percent annual growth between 2013 and 2016 (8,764 filings in 2016). Rapidly emerging within the transportation category are aerospace/avionics (67 percent annual growth, with 1,813 filings in 2016) and autonomous vehicles (42 percent annual growth, with 5,569 filings in 2016). The boom in transportation technologies becomes more evident when we look at trends over the period 2006–2016: representing just 20 percent of applications in 2006, by 2016 it accounted for one-third of applications (more than 8,700 filings).

While not showing the same high rate of growth as transportation, patent filings in AI-related telecommunications still grew annually by an average of 23 percent between 2013 and 2016, with 6,684 filings in 2016. Within telecommunications, the most growth was seen by computer networks/Internet (17 percent) and radio and television broadcasting (17 percent). Life and medical sciences grew by 12 percent in the same period, with 4,112 filings in 2016, including medical informatics (18 percent growth) and public health (17 percent growth). Personal devices, computing and HCI grew an average of 11 percent annually between 2013 and 2016, with 3,977 filings in 2016, and within this category notable growth occurred in the sub-field of affective computing (37 percent), which recognizes human emotion.

Other sectors and sub-categories within sectors with notable growth in patent filings include: smart cities (47 percent annual growth); agriculture (32 percent); computing in government (30 percent); and banking and finance (28 percent).

...while certain AI techniques, applications and industries appear to be closely linked.

Nearly 70 percent of inventions related to AI mention an AI technique, application or field in combination with another. The most frequent combinations in patent filings are: deep learning with computer vision; computer vision with transportation, telecommunication and security; ontology engineering with natural language processing; and machine learning with life and medical sciences. These combinations suggest areas to watch for rapid developments in AI in the near future.

Companies, in particular those from Japan, the United States of America (U.S.) and China, dominate patenting activity

Companies represent 26 out of the top 30 AI patent applicants, while only four are universities or public research organizations. This pattern applies across most AI techniques, applications and fields. Of the top 20 companies filing AI-related patents, 12 are based in Japan, three are from the U.S. and two are from China. Japanese consumer electronics companies are particularly heavily represented.

Machine learning is the dominant AI technique disclosed in patents and is included in more than one-third of all identified inventions.

IBM and Microsoft are leaders in AI patenting across different AI-related areas

IBM has the largest portfolio of AI patent applications with 8,290 inventions, followed by Microsoft with 5,930. Both companies' portfolios span a range of AI techniques, applications and fields, indicating that these companies are not limiting their activity to a specific industry or field. Rounding out the top five applicants are Toshiba (5,223), Samsung (5,102) and NEC (4,406). The State Grid Corporation of China has leaped into the top 20, increasing its patent filings by an average of 70 percent annually from 2013 to 2016, particularly in the machine learning techniques of bio-inspired approaches, which draw from observations of nature, and support vector machines, a form of supervised learning.

In certain techniques and fields, the highest numbers of patent applications originate from companies with a high degree of specialization and expertise in that field. Examples include Baidu, which ranks highly for deep learning, Toyota and Bosch, which are prominent in transportation, and Siemens, Philips and Samsung in life and medical sciences. Some well-known companies that do not feature among the top overall players in AI patents are nonetheless prominent in certain areas; these include Facebook and Tencent in networks and social networks. Industry expertise and access to specialized data may explain why certain companies lead in specific industries.

Universities contribute significantly to AI research in specific fields, with Chinese universities dominating

Despite the dominance of companies in AI, universities and public research organizations play a leading role in inventions in selected AI fields such as distributed AI, some machine learning techniques and neuroscience/neurorobotics.

Chinese organizations make up 17 of the top 20 academic players in AI patenting as well as 10 of the top 20 in AI-related scientific publications. Chinese organizations are particularly strong in the emerging technique of deep learning. The leading public research organization applicant is the Chinese Academy of Sciences (CAS), with over 2,500 patent families and over 20,000 scientific papers published on AI. Moreover, CAS has the largest deep learning portfolio (235 patent families). Chinese organizations are consolidating their lead, with patent filings having grown on average by more than 20 percent per year from 2013 to 2016, matching or beating the growth rates of organizations from most other countries.

The Republic of Korea's Electronics and Telecommunications Research Institute (ETRI) stands out as second in patent filing among universities and public research organizations and ranks among the top 30 patent applicants overall.

There are 167 universities and public research organizations ranked among the top 500 patent applicants. Of these, 110 are Chinese, 20 are from the U.S., 19 from the Republic of Korea and 4 from Japan. Four European public research organizations feature in the top 500 list; the highest-placed European institution is the German Fraunhofer Institute, which is ranked 159th, while the French Alternative Energies and Atomic Energy Commission (CEA) is in 185th position.

The U.S. and China are the main targets for AI patent filing…

The U.S. and China are the two most popular offices for filing AI patents, in line with patenting trends in other fields, followed by Japan. These three offices account for 78 percent of total patent filings. There has been an increasing use of WIPO's PCT System, which allows patent applicants to file in multiple jurisdictions by filing a single application. The PCT route ranks fourth among the top targets for AI patent filings.

…but filings are increasingly international

Many patent applications are extended to more than one jurisdiction. One-third of all AI patent applications are filed in additional jurisdictions after their first filing and 8 percent are filed in five or more jurisdictions.

Out of the top three filing offices, 40 percent of patent applications first filed in Japan and 32 percent of patent applications first filed in the U.S. are subsequently also filed elsewhere. Just 4 percent of patent applications first filed in China are subsequently filed in other jurisdictions.

Chinese companies and universities currently tend to file in China only, compared with applicants from other countries, particularly the U.S.

Acquisitions complement internal research and IP strategies

In total, 434 companies in the AI sector have been acquired since 1998, with 53 percent of acquisitions having taken place since 2016. The number of acquisitions identified in the AI sector has increased every year since 2012, reaching 103 in 2017. Although Alphabet (including Google, DeepMind, Waymo and X Development) ranks 10th in the number of inventions filed, with 3,814 in total, it ranks 1st in terms of acquisitions of AI companies. Apple and Microsoft have also been active in acquisitions.

Certain companies, such as IBM and Intel, target mature companies. The majority of acquired companies are, however, startups with small or non-existent patent portfolios.

This suggests that targets are being acquired for other assets, including talent, data, know-how and other IP.

Cooperation in AI research is limited, but so is conflict

In many cases, organizations that cooperate in research are credited as co-assignees on patent applications. However, none of the top 20 applicants shares ownership of more than 1 percent of its AI portfolio with other applicants.

Overall, the amount of litigation identified in the report is relatively low (less than 1 percent of patents being litigated), which may be due to the fact that products have not yet come to the market and infringement may be difficult to prove. There have been 1,264 AI patent families identified in litigation, with 74 percent of cases in the U.S., and 4,231 in patent opposition cases worldwide. The top three plaintiffs in litigation over AI patents are Nuance Communications, American Vehicular Sciences and Automotive Technologies International.

Technology trends can inform policymaking on the future of AI

The analysis presented in this report offers new insights into trends in AI innovation. It shows the extent to which artificial intelligence is playing an increasingly important role in a range of technological and other activities. The potential societal impact of AI has already been identified – and much more is to come. In this regard, AI must be viewed in conjunction with its expected effect on the workforce, the economy and society as a whole.

Policymakers will have to move quickly to keep up with AI-related developments and shape the direction of AI's evolution. A variety of stakeholders will have to reflect on the correct policy mix to maximize the widest possible benefits from AI, with particular focus on AI-related strategies, policies, laws and regulations addressing legal and ethical

Chinese organizations make up 17 of the top 20 academic players in AI patenting as well as 10 of the top 20 in AI-related scientific publications.

considerations; access to and ownership of digital data and its effect on IP systems; availability of an appropriately skilled workforce; and investment strategy and related funding.

This report documents how AI-powered technologies are rapidly entering global markets and brings together viewpoints from experts at the cutting edge of AI. It is a contribution that aims to provide decision-makers in the public and private sectors with an improved knowledge base for discussions on the future of AI and the policy and regulatory framework for this fast-moving area.

¹ Introduction

A few decades ago, it was only humans who could play chess or read handwriting. Having been the focus of research in artificial intelligence (AI) for several years, both are now routinely done by machines. Today, researchers are working on many more applications of AI which will revolutionize the ways in which we work, communicate, study and enjoy ourselves. Products and services incorporating such innovation will become part of people's day-to-day lives within the next few years as we embark on what some AI experts describe as the age of implementation.

Yet AI remains a challenging subject for many people. Definitions vary, have changed over time and are in some cases contentious. The technology is complex and wide-ranging, potentially affecting many different areas of human activity. And AI raises complex questions about privacy, trust and autonomy that are difficult to grapple with, and this has led to fears about humans themselves being under threat.

According to many observers, the current AI boom began about seven years ago. It followed a series of ups and downs, often referred to as "AI summers and winters."

For the purposes of this report, AI systems are viewed primarily as learning systems; that is, machines that can become better at a task typically performed by humans with limited or no human intervention. This definition encompasses a wide range of techniques and applications, as we will see in subsequent chapters, and can be broken down into many different categories of technology. The techniques and applications included in this report refer to individual tasks performed by AI systems, known as "narrow AI." This is to be distinguished from concepts such as artificial general intelligence or superintelligence; namely, AI systems able to successfully perform any intellectual task that could be undertaken by the human brain or the hypothetical ability of a machine to far surpass the human brain. Such concepts are not something that current technology permits, and they are therefore only addressed in passing in this report. More on these concepts and other approaches to AI can be found in the list of further reading in the Annex (see pages 150–154).

The AI wave

According to many observers, the current AI boom began about seven years ago. It followed a series of ups and downs, often referred to as "AI summers and winters," as interest in AI has alternately grown and diminished – as demonstrated by the data on research investment. Interviewed for this report, Andreessen Horowitz partner Frank Chen describes AI as "an offshoot of a resurgence of a very old technique ... where from observation, you can have sets of algorithms making predictions on business, health and legal matters." For example, he says, you can predict how a jury would vote based on testimony in court, or whether a patient has cancer based on analysis of a number of x-rays. "The technique is basically: give me examples and I will figure out which ones are relevant. The bigger the set of data you have, the better predictions you make."

The growth in computing power and connectedness, which enables large volumes of data to be compiled and shared, has opened

A short history of AI

1956
The term "artificial intelligence" is coined at a Dartmouth conference and AI is founded as an academic discipline.

1956–1974
The golden years of AI enjoy government funding in promising, logic-based problem-solving approaches.

1974–1980
Overly high expectations coupled with the limited capacities of AI programs leads to the first "AI winter", with reduced funding and interest in AI research.

1980–1987
The rise of knowledge-based expert systems brings new successes and a change in the focus of research and funding toward this form of AI.

1987–1993
The second "AI winter" starts with the sudden collapse of the specialized hardware industry in 1987. The AI hype brings with it negative perceptions by governments and investors, as expert systems show their limitations and prove expensive to update and maintain.

1993–2011
Optimism about AI returns and increases. New successes are marked with the help of increased computational power and AI becomes data-driven. In 1997, IBM's DeepBlue beats world champion Kasparov at chess. In 2002, Amazon uses automated systems to provide recommendations. In 2011, Apple releases Siri and IBM Watson beats two human champions at the TV quiz Jeopardy.

2012–today
Increased availability of data, connectedness and computational power allow for breakthroughs in machine learning, mainly in neural networks and deep learning, heralding a new era of increased funding and optimism about the AI potential. In 2012, Google driverless cars navigate autonomously and in 2016 Google AlphaGo beats a world champion in the complicated board game Go.

up many new opportunities for AI technologies, which are in turn reinforced by the greater availability, systematic collection of and access to data. But, as we will see in this report, this accumulation and analysis of data raises further questions for AI researchers.

The impact of AI technologies on humans is likely to be profound. Martin Ford, author of *The Rise of the Robots*, thinks many workers will have to become skilled in different areas, while employers and governments will have to address how best to deal with the loss of employment and growing inequality. "In the next 10 to 20 years," he predicts, "the jobs that will be most vulnerable to automation will be those that are routine and predictable. If what you do is encapsulated in data, at some point it's a pretty good bet that there will be an AI that can do that kind of work."

Assessing the state of AI

Now is therefore a good time to take a close look at the state of research and exploitation of AI technologies. Patents provide a valuable means of assessing trends in research as they reveal the areas of innovation that inventors are focused on. Moreover, patent application documents are publicly available once published, and include useful information, such as the name of the applicant, date of patent application and technical details of the invention.

By analyzing patent data, it is possible to track changes over time and identify which jurisdictions are seeing most patenting activity. Moreover, digging deeper into the substance of applications provides insight into the types of technologies being developed and those that are emerging, what they are applied to and which fields they cover.

Much of this report therefore focuses on analysis of patent data: a description of the methodology, categorizations and classifications used are presented in the next section of this chapter. Chapter 2 highlights the main trends across all areas, while Chapters 3 to 6 explore the data in greater detail. Chapter 3 looks at trends in patents related to AI over time, Chapter 4

discusses the most prominent companies and universities and public research organizations filing patents, Chapter 5 focuses on geographical trends and Chapter 6 looks at market trends.

Patents, however, only provide a part of the picture, as much research is never patented. This report therefore also includes analysis of scientific publications, identifying trends over time and by geography as well as by subject area. In addition, Chapter 6 provides other relevant information on acquisitions and funding as well as patent litigation and oppositions and open source investment.

The analysis of the data in this report is complemented by the viewpoints and comments given by invited AI experts, some focusing on specific issues in AI or case studies and others addressing more general concerns. Some of these contributors sent written submissions and others were interviewed during the research. A list of contributors can be found on pages 10–11.

The final two chapters in this report, Chapters 7 and 8, look at public policies and the future of AI, and draw in more detail on some of these contributions. In a field that is evolving so fast, it is hard to make predictions, but some areas merit particular attention. Data ownership is clearly a central concern, along with issues around data access, privacy and bias. Related to this is the role that businesses, governments, intergovernmental organizations and educational institutions should play in the development and regulation of AI technologies, including the related intellectual property (IP) framework.

The insights offered, combined with the data on trends presented throughout this report, should provide a valuable guide to key technological developments, issues of concern in AI and the policy responses in place.

How the research was done

This section explains the methodology used for the analysis in this report, which was conducted by CNRS Innovation, and how the data were collected, classified and categorized.

_____Methodology and data

The bulk of this report comprises analysis of data on patents and scientific publications, and it is important to distinguish how they differ and what each can tell us about research and innovation trends.

AI technologies may be described in patent applications, protected by patents, disclosed in scientific publications, shared through open source projects or collaboration platforms, or developed in-house and protected by trade secrets. As the most commonly used means of sharing research developments and protecting technical inventions, patents and scientific publications provide particularly useful ways to analyze trends in AI technologies. In addition, as they are systematically collected in a structured data format in patent and non-patent databases and can be publicly accessed, they provide an appropriate source of data to analyze and draw meaningful conclusions. Patents and scientific literature are habitually used by industry academia and economists as an established indicator to track and analyze technology trends, bearing in mind that certain technologies' advances may not be published in scientific articles or described in patent applications.

Patents are intellectual property rights. Patents are territorial, meaning that they provide protection only in the jurisdiction where an application was filed and a patent is granted. Patents are thus generally granted by national patent offices – or through regional systems, such as the European Patent Convention (EPC) administered by the European Patent Office (EPO). In many jurisdictions, the patent office examines each application to see whether it meets certain requirements, including that the invention must fall under a patentable subject matter in the jurisdictions in question (e.g., discoveries, scientific theories, mathematical methods and computer programs _per se_ are in general not patentable, whereas software is patentable in some jurisdictions), be novel (i.e., not be part of the state of the art), involve an inventive step (i.e., be "non-obvious"), have a potential industrial application, and the claimed invention be sufficiently disclosed. Where patents for the same invention are filed in

A definition of AI

**Aristotelis Tsirigos,
NYU School of Medicine**

In recent years, accelerated urbanization, globalization and the abundance of products, services and information has begun to fundamentally transform our society. As individuals, we are experiencing an increasingly complex and demanding environment. In response, mobile applications and automated services are being developed, allowing us to more effectively navigate this complex new world. All this is made possible by powerful algorithms that are slowly acquiring fundamental human-like capabilities, such as vision, speech and navigation. Collectively, these computer algorithms are called artificial intelligence (AI). Beyond emulating these ordinary human capabilities, AI is quickly moving forward to master more specialized tasks performed routinely by human experts.

numerous jurisdictions, they are described as being members of the same patent family (see the box on Data collection and preparation on page 22) and equate to a single invention.

Patents are normally published 18 months after filing. If the patent office decides that the application meets all the patentability criteria and other requirements, the patent is granted, though this may take several years. The term of protection is ordinarily 20 years from the filing date in most jurisdictions, though it may lapse before, if the applicable renewal fees are not paid, and some jurisdictions have provisions to extend the patent protection term under certain circumstances.

In many fields of technology, and across all jurisdictions, many patent applications filed do not meet one or more of the patentability criteria and are not granted or are withdrawn by the applicants for different reasons. A patent family may include members for which patents have been granted, others not granted or still under patent examination.

Once a patent is granted, a patent holder has, in general, the right to exclude others from making, using, selling, offering for sale, or importing for those purposes, the claimed invention, without

Data collection and preparation

The patent data have been prepared using the patent database Questel Orbit and were extracted on March 31, 2018. Scientific publication data have been prepared using Elsevier Scopus and were extracted between June 15, 2018 and June 29, 2018. Litigation data is based on Darts-IP and Orbit databases. The coverage of these databases is available in the background paper to this report (see *Data collection method and clustering scheme*, available at www.wipo.int/tech_trends/en/artificial_intelligence) and like any data source may not be exhaustive.

Patent data are extracted from the FamPat collection provided by Questel. The FamPat collection indexes patent applications and granted patents from more than 100 patenting authorities. These patents are grouped into patent families. A patent family includes all those patents in different offices that relate to the same or similar technical content. The earliest application in the family has what is known as the priority number, and other applications in the family share one or more pieces of priority data for the purposes of novelty and inventive step. There are different definitions of patent families; for the current report the FamPat families were used, grouping together the same invention sharing the exact priority data seeking patent protection in different jurisdictions. More information about patent families and the impact the choice of the patent family type may have on the analysis can be found in the section of further reading in the Annex (see pages 150–154).

In the graphs and analysis, each patent family is represented by one single patent document chosen from among the different filing offices in this order of preference: EPO, WIPO, USPTO, INPI (France), DMPA (Germany), UK IPO (the United Kingdom) and then other offices of first filing. This ensures that even where there are several members of a patent family it is only counted once.

For patent data in this report, the earliest priority date is used in most of the graphs and analysis that include a date. This is the date when the first patent application in a patent family was filed at a patent office (priority application). It is the closest point of reference to the time when the invention was actually made.

Some graphs in this report use the earliest publication date to present data for patents. The publication date is the date on which a patent application is first published (i.e., made available to the public) and thus becomes part of the prior art. In general, first patent publications are made 18 months after the earliest priority date. Studying data based on the publication year provides insight that is closer to the present day and also helps compare patent publications with scientific publications.

---

their consent. Generally speaking, an inventor has the right to a patent, which can be assigned to another natural or legal person. In cases where an invention is created by an employee, many jurisdictions provide a special rule for the determination of the ownership of the invention.

Many patent offices provide mechanisms for third parties to challenge patent rights through administrative mechanisms, namely opposition/ observation proceedings, invalidation or other equivalent processes such as *inter partes* review. Patents can also be challenged in court proceedings (litigation). Trends in oppositions and litigation regarding AI patents are analyzed in Chapter 6.

Among the different data sources available, patents provide several advantages for analyzing trends in AI. They are collected in accessible databases. They also include much relevant information, such as the application date, the name of the applicant (organization or individual) and inventor(s), and a thorough technical description of the invention, including previous technical solutions known as "state of the art."

Once published, the information in a patent is available for researchers to read, study and analyze for research or academic purposes and once a patent has expired or lapsed, it is part of the public domain.

However, much research is not patented but published instead in scientific journals. These publications have also been analyzed in the research for this report. In each chapter, trends in scientific publications related to AI are discussed in detail and compared with the patenting activity in the same field. Once an invention is disclosed in a scientific publication, it is no longer considered novel and therefore cannot be patented, except in those jurisdictions allowing a grace period. Scientific publications therefore complement the information available in patent databases, while the information in patent publications may be of use to researchers working on scientific publications as they can contain unique information, in particular in those cases where companies choose to file a patent application and not publish a scientific paper.

Counting and categorizing patents

Patent applications and the related patent families in AI can be identified by using patent databases. For the purposes of this report, patent families from different offices around the world have been searched, with no time limits imposed. The total numbers used in this report refer to these overall results.

Despite the availability of information in patent documents, it can however be difficult to identify exactly which patent families relate to AI because of the lack of an agreed definition and the changing concepts of what constitutes AI. The data in this report are based on the classification scheme discussed below, the classification codes used by patent offices and an extended list of specific keywords, which were selected based on a review of existing literature, well-established hierarchies and web resources. Samples of the results were manually checked and validated using a text-mining tool. Full details of the data analysis are provided in the appendix.

This process resulted in a total list of 339,828 patent families related to AI, and these patents form the basis of the analysis in the chapters that follow. The patent families related to AI represent about 0.6 percent of all patent families, based on the total collection of 59.3 million patent families at the time of the search.

How will industry adopt AI?

Kai-Fu Lee, Sinovation Ventures

I personally think it will be making all the known technologies really honed to fit actual applications – that will be the largest social contribution to humanity. If you look at the history of speech recognition or computer operating systems, or the notion of the Internet, we're at the end of the age of discovery and there's likely to be an age of implementation. They were experimental in laboratory conditions and not yet applied in industry. Which are the early adopters? Which ones are the momentum drivers? Which are mainstream usage? Fixing and tweaking technologies so that they can become applicable – that will be 100 percent the most important thing.

In the next five years, probably Internet and financial and e-commerce are the biggest industries that will be affected – those where there are immediate transactions of money. After that we will see areas such as retail, healthcare, manufacturing, transportation and automotive, and logistics, including warehousing/transportation/delivery. Eventually AI will penetrate everything.

Patent classification

Patent examiners use codes to classify patent applications and other documents according to their technical features. This facilitates searching and examination. There are several patent classification systems used by patent offices. The patent search for this report drew on the three main ones:

- International Patent Classification (IPC): maintained by the World Intellectual

Figure 1.1. AI techniques

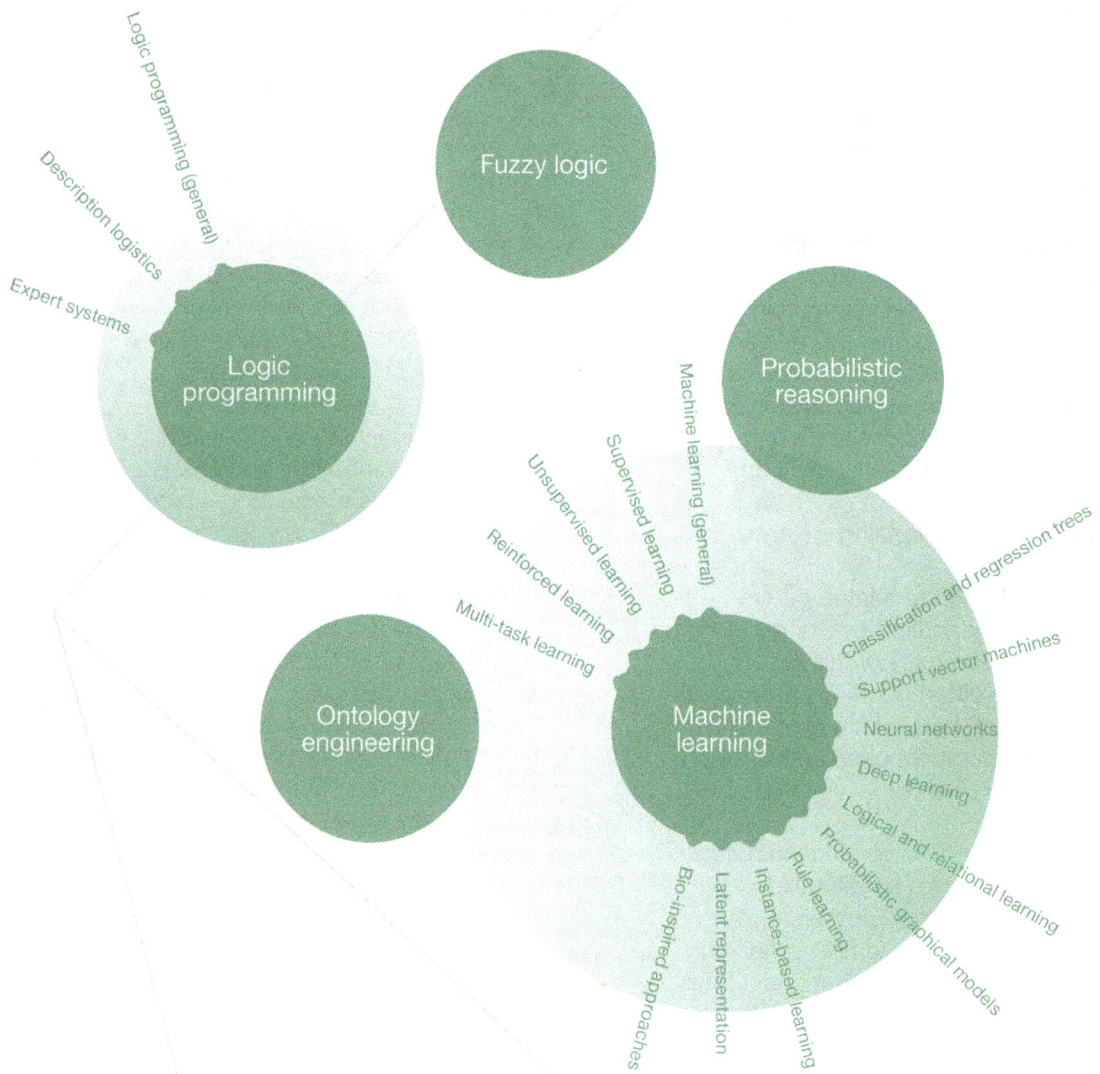

Fuzzy logic

Logic programming
- Logic programming (general)
- Description logistics
- Expert systems

Probabilistic reasoning

Ontology engineering

Machine learning
- Machine learning (general)
- Supervised learning
- Unsupervised learning
- Reinforced learning
- Multi-task learning
- Classification and regression trees
- Support vector machines
- Neural networks
- Deep learning
- Logical and relational learning
- Probabilistic graphical models
- Rule learning
- Instance-based learning
- Latent representation
- Bio-inspired approaches

Property Organization (WIPO) and used by more than 100 offices.

- Cooperative Patent Classification (CPC): jointly developed by the United States Patent and Trademark Office (USPTO) and the EPO and based on the IPC, it is also used by China's Patent Office (CNIPA).
- FI and F-term list: these classification codes are developed and used in Japan (JPO).

Each of these classification schemes contains more than 100,000 codes (so-called classes or symbols), rising to around 250,000 in the case of the CPC. This report identified several hundred classification codes relevant to AI.

_____ Categorization of AI technologies

Throughout this report, AI technologies are analyzed using the scheme illustrated in figures 1.1 to 1.3. This was chosen based on the Association for Computing Machinery (ACM) Computing Classification Scheme, which has been developed over the past 50 years. As this scheme was last updated in 2012, it has been adapted to take account of recent technological developments such as the emergence of deep learning. While AI experts may have different perspectives and use different definitions of AI technologies, this scheme has the advantage of providing a clear analytical framework for the report and the presentation of the evolution of AI technologies over time.

The scheme comprises three main categories:

- AI techniques: advanced forms of statistical and mathematical models, such as machine learning, fuzzy logic and expert systems, allowing the computation of tasks typically performed by humans; different AI techniques may be used as a means to implement different AI functions.
- AI functional applications: functions such as speech or computer vision which can be realized using one or more AI techniques.
- AI application fields: different fields, areas or disciplines where AI techniques or functional applications may find application, such as transportation, agriculture or life and medical sciences.

The deep learning revolution

Myriam Côté, Mila

Deep learning has been at the heart of Mila's research since the 1990s, with Yoshua Bengio being one of the founders of the field and the scientific director of the Institute. Seen in earlier years as a marginal research topic, recent breakthroughs in deep learning applied to speech recognition, computer vision and machine translation have been so outstanding, with AI algorithms functioning at close to human performance levels in some cases, that it soon became clear its impacts on industry, society and economy are likely to be profoundly disruptive. In a nutshell, deep learning is fueling a new industrial revolution based on AI.

This scheme is used for categorizing both patent publications (using classification code and keywords) and scientific publications (using keywords).

Figure 1.2. AI functional applications

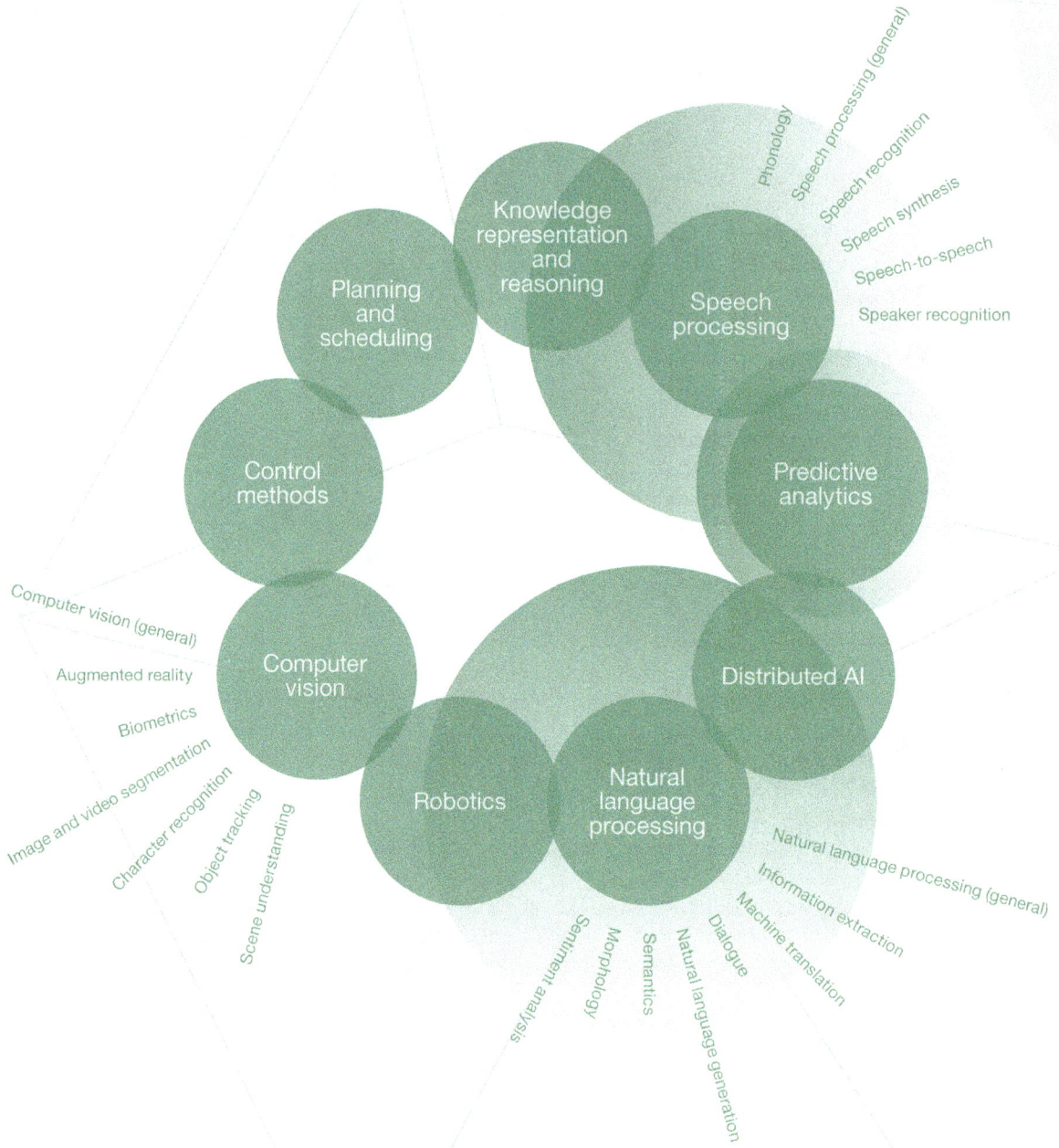

Figure 1.3. AI application fields

- Bioinformatics
- Biological engineering
- Biomechanics
- Drug discovery
- Genetics/genomics
- Medical imaging
- Medical informatics
- Neuroscience/neurorobotics
- Nutrition/food science
- Physiological parameter monitoring
- Public health

- Internet of things (IoT)
- Smart cities
- Social networks

- Customer service
- e-commerce
- Enterprise computing

- Affective computing
- Personal computers and PC applications

Networks

Business

Banking and finance

Military

Cartography

Physical sciences and engineering

Personal devices, computing and HCI

Life and medical sciences

Arts and humanities

Computing in government

Agriculture

Telecommunications

Energy management

Entertainment

Document management and publishing

Education

Industry and manufacturing

Law, social and behavioral sciences

Transportation

Security

- Industrial property
- Law, social and behavioral sciences

- Computer networks/internet
- Radio and television broadcasting
- Telephony
- Videoconferencing
- VoIP

- Aerospace/avionics
- Autonomous vehicles
- Driver/vehicle recognition
- Transportation and traffic engineering

- Anomaly detection/surveillance
- Authentication
- Cryptography
- Cybersecurity
- Privacy/anonymity

The digital twin

Digital twins mirror reality and can detect problems that would otherwise remain imperceptible, representing the next step towards the goal of providing "the right treatment for the right patient at the right time." They are part of a technology that links the real and digital worlds, using AI to turn data into actionable insights. First, millions of examples of curated data are leveraged to train deep learning neural networks. In a second step, the neural networks are used to approximate parts of a combined individualized multi-scale physiological model. This holds the potential for evaluating the effectiveness of tailored treatments, paving the way for the expansion of precision medicine.

The first organ to be precisely simulated using the digital twin method was the heart. Based on MRI and ECG measurements, the model simulates the physiological processes of a patient's most vital organ. Virtual planning can then be performed to visualize its responses to treatment on a computer before the actual intervention.

Siemens Healthineers is developing intelligent algorithms that generate digital models of organs based on vast amounts of data. Cardiologists tested the use of these algorithms in cardiac resynchronization in a research project at the University of Heidelberg. Cardiac resynchronization therapy is a treatment option for patients suffering from chronic congestive heart failure. It involves an advanced pacemaker that resynchronizes the beating heart using two electrodes, one implanted on the right ventricle, the other one on the left ventricle. The Heidelberg cardiologists created a digital twin of the patient's heart, virtually implanted the electrodes, and virtually generated electrical pulses. If the asynchronous pumping of the virtual heart was corrected, it served as an indication that resynchronization therapy could also be successful in the real patient.

This is an excellent example of using digitalization and AI to help physicians develop more precise prognoses. The simulation of different scenarios not only improves treatment but also offers the potential for major time savings. Time is a critical factor in many areas of healthcare, and every minute saved by optimizing processes can significantly improve patient experience and transform the delivery of care.

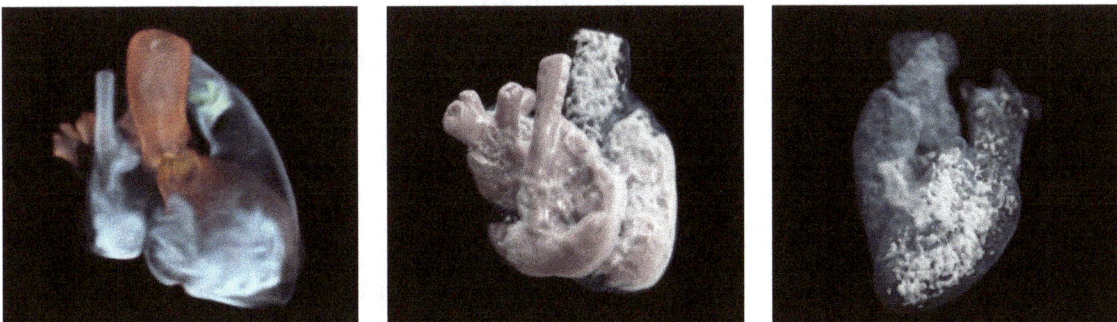

Photo © Siemens Healthineers. Note: The system is currently under development and not for sale. Its future availability cannot be guaranteed.

Case study by Siemens

2 Trends in artificial intelligence

Looking first at trends in AI techniques, machine learning predominates, representing a massive 89 percent of filings mentioning this AI technique and 40 percent of all AI-related patents.

One of the most striking characteristics of research in artificial intelligence (AI) is the rapid growth that has been seen over the past five years. The impressive numbers of patent filings in this period and the decrease in the ratio of number of scientific papers to inventions are indicative of a shift from theoretical research to the use of AI technologies in commercial products and services. This trend is also reflected in the types of patents being filed, with significant growth in specific AI applications and sector-specific fields.

In this chapter, we present the overall trends in AI, including the behavior of its key players, geographical trends, and acquisition and enforcement trends, using the three categories of 1) AI techniques, 2) AI functional applications, and 3) AI application fields, illustrated in figures 1.1 to 1.3 in Chapter 1. The growth rates reported below are based on the average annual growth rate of patent filings from 2013 to 2016. The findings are analyzed in more detail in Chapters 3, 4, 5 and 6 that follow.

Trends in AI techniques

Looking first at trends in AI techniques, machine learning predominates, representing a massive 89 percent of filings mentioning this AI technique and 40 percent of all AI-related patents. Machine learning grew by 28 percent from 2013 to 2016; in the same period, fuzzy logic has grown by 16 percent and logic programming by 19 percent.

Within machine learning, every AI technique showed an increase in annual filing numbers for the same period, but some stand out. Deep learning is the fastest growing technique in AI, with an 175 percent increase over the period. Multi-task learning, the next fastest, grew by 49 percent. Other techniques with notable increases were neural networks, latent representation and unsupervised learning.

Trends in AI functional applications

Turning to trends in AI functional applications, computer vision, which includes image recognition, is the most popular. Computer vision was mentioned in 49 percent of all AI-related patents and grew by 24 percent during 2013 to 2016. The other two top areas in functional applications are natural language processing (14 percent of all AI-related patents) and speech processing (13 percent).

While these three functional applications are the most important in terms of the total number of filings, others are emerging and growing fast. AI filings concerning both robotics and control methods have increased by 55 percent, for example, while those for planning/scheduling have grown by 37 percent.

Within computer vision – the top functional application – biometrics has seen an average annual growth rate of 31 percent and scene understanding one of 28 percent. Within natural language processing, semantics has grown by 33 percent and sentiment analysis by 28 (though it still only accounts for 1 percent of natural language processing applications). Within speech processing, speech-to-speech has grown by 15 percent, and speech

Does the data reflect reality?

Haifeng Wang, Baidu

Regarding AI techniques, machine learning, particularly deep learning for nearly the past ten years, has been well studied and significant progress has been made. And for functional applications, computer vision, speech processing and natural language processing have also shown vast industrial potential and have already been utilized in practical applications. Such developments correspond to the trends in patent filings and in scientific publications.

For industry, there is a trend to combine hardware with software to make AI technologies more practically applicable. Deep learning framework with chips for AI could be another opportunity for players aiming to dominate the future AI industry. For application systems, the need for the combination of different AI techniques with functional applications is getting more serious. AI application systems also need to be integrated with business scenarios.

recognition and speaker recognition have both grown by 12 percent.

Trends in AI application fields

Lastly, in AI application fields, the top industries are transportation (15 percent of all AI-related patents), telecommunications (15 percent), and life and medical sciences (12 percent). Growing industries are transportation, agriculture, and computing in government, with annual growth rates of at least 30 percent between 2013 and 2016.

Looking at trends over ten years, the boom in transportation technologies becomes more evident: representing just 20 percent of applications in 2006, by 2016 it accounted for one-third of applications (with more than 8,700 filings).

Telecommunications, the second most important application field, has remained at around 24 percent during this period, but the proportion of filings mentioning business,

Deep learning is the fastest growing technique in AI, with an 175 percent increase between 2013 and 2016.

document management and publishing or life and medical sciences has decreased.

Key players

Companies represent 26 of the top 30 applicants, most of them active in consumer electronics, telecommunications and/or software, as well as in sectors such as electric utility and automobile manufacture. Just four of the top 30 are a university or public research organization.

IBM is the company with the largest patent portfolio (8,290 applications), followed by Microsoft (5,930 applications). Of the top 20 companies, 12 are based in Japan, three are from the United States of America (U.S.) and two are from China.

Computer vision is the main functional application mentioned in patents by the top companies (19 out of 20), though IBM has a greater focus on natural language processing. Machine learning is by far the most represented AI technique in the top applicants' portfolios.

One notable trend concerns the leaders in deep learning, the fastest-growing area of machine learning. The Chinese Academy of Sciences possesses the largest patent portfolio explicitly dealing with deep learning techniques (235 patent families), and most of the main portfolios in this field have been filed by Chinese universities. Baidu leads among companies

owning quite large portfolios of patents related to the deep learning sub-category of machine learning, followed by Alphabet, Siemens, Xiaomi, Microsoft, Samsung, IBM and NEC.

Organizations that cooperate in research may be credited as co-assignees on patent applications. However, the data indicate that co-ownership of patents is rare for most technologies. None of the top 20 applicants co-owns more than 1 percent of its AI portfolio.

Around one-fifth of the top 500 applicants, ranked by number of patents, are from universities and public research organizations from China. The highest placed such organization is the Chinese Academy of Sciences, which has 2,652 patent families, placing it 17th in the overall list of applicants. Patenting activity from Chinese universities and public research organizations has seen significant growth (between 20 and 80 percent annually on average between 2013 and 2016), while patenting activity from top U.S. universities and public research organizations has diminished (by between 20 and 26 percent annually) from 2013 to 2016.

Among universities and public research organizations, computer vision is the main functional application mentioned in patent portfolios (as with companies), while machine learning and neural networks are the most frequently mentioned techniques.

The top universities/public organizations make the vast majority of their priority patent filings in their country of origin. Fraunhofer is the main exception, with some priority filings also made in the U.S. or via the European patent route.

Geographical trends

Looking at those offices where patents are filed, it is possible to identify trends in developments in AI research. The first patent filings in AI were made in Japan in the early 1980s, but this office was subsequently overtaken by both the U.S. and China. Since 2014, China has led the world in the number of first patent filings in AI, followed by the U.S. Together, these three offices account for 78 percent of total patent filings. China and the U.S. also lead in the number of scientific publications.

Two-thirds of AI patent families are filed at one office only, while 9 percent are filed in five or more jurisdictions and just 0.6 percent are filed at more than 10 offices. The vast majority of Chinese applications seem to be focused on the domestic market, with only 4 percent protected in another jurisdiction. This compares with 40 percent of patent applications first filed in Japan and 32 percent of those first filed in the U.S. that are then subsequently filed elsewhere.

However, there are indications that patent filings are becoming more international. The PCT System, which allows applicants to file in multiple jurisdictions by filing a single application, is extensively used, as is the European Patent Office. Popular offices for filing subsequent applications after the first one has been made include the U.S., China, Canada and Australia.

The Chinese and U.S. offices lead in all techniques and functional applications, though Japan is prominent in fuzzy logic, computer vision and speech processing, while the Republic of Korea stands out in ontology engineering.

Acquisition of AI patents

While it is too early to assess the impact of AI technologies on individuals and society, certain data can provide insight into business and economic activity. For example, acquisitions can be part of a company's strategy and complement its intellectual property (IP) protection and development efforts.

Available data on acquisitions indicates that 434 companies in the AI sector have been acquired since 1998, and that 53 percent of acquisitions have taken place since 2016. The vast majority of acquired companies in the field of AI are U.S. ones (283 acquired companies), while the United Kingdom (U.K.) ranks second with 25 acquired companies.

Science and techno- logy in AI-innovations

Kazuyuki Motohashi,
University of Tokyo

Recent progress in AI innovations has been driven by the interaction between computer science and cognitive science. As an example, the idea of a deep neural network (used for AI applications such as autonomous driving, condition-based maintenance of jet engines and new drug discovery) comes from the mechanism of how the human brain works. The sheer speed of technological change in this field demands interaction between scientific research and technological progress, blurring the distinction between academic research and private enterprise.

This co-development of science and technology can be captured by tracing the evolution of research articles (scientific findings) and patents (new technologies). My own research shows an upward trend in both scientific publications and patents, but with the volume of publications rising earlier. The crossover of people between academia and private firms contributes to this process – those who had published AI-related publications in public research organizations later became involved in patenting activities at a private company (either through a joint appointment or by moving job).

Science contributes to the development of AI technology, but the role played by the private sector increases over time as it obtains IP rights over inventions. Policymakers therefore need to be alive to the interplay between open science and proprietary technology in the AI field. Policies promoting AI should cover both public and private sectors, while at the same time recognizing the potential for tension between open science and proprietary technology. They should also be developed in line with competition policy concerning the private ownership of data and IP rights.

How big data and AI can help support sustainable development and humanitarian action

Malcolm Johnson, ITU

Advances in information and communication technologies (ICTs) are driving global changes in our society – from the way we communicate and behave with each other, to the forces shaping our economies and societies. Without doubt, AI offers opportunities to unlock the value of big data to enable more evidence-based decision-making, to measure progress toward the Sustainable Development Goals (SDGs), and to drive transformations in development.

There are many examples of how big data and AI can be used to help achieve each and every of the 17 SDGs. AI tools and techniques can be used to analyze poverty and hunger and their root causes. In health, AI can improve the working methods of doctors and help complement traditional medical tools and techniques, improving the accuracy and speed of diagnosis. In education, AI and data analysis can be used to personalize education packages for individual students. A key advantage to AI lies in its ability to analyze huge datasets and identify patterns and correlations that may pass unnoticed in smaller, or more piecemeal, data. AI can be used to monitor, plan and manage responsible production and consumption across different industrial sectors.

However, there is growing public recognition that along with the opportunities, AI creates challenges that are very complex and multifaceted. Navigating AI-related ethical, technical, and socio-economic challenges such as its disruptive impact on employment may be as difficult as delivering the solutions for social good — and both will require unprecedented collaboration. If not, there is a risk of opening up another more sophisticated form of digital divide, one with profound implications for inequality globally.

Recognizing that AI potentially impacts the work of every UN agency in their efforts in contributing to the achievement of the SDGs, the UN is working hard to consider the implications of AI. Every year, ITU hosts the "AI for Good" Summit in partnership with sister UN agencies, XPRIZE Foundation and ACM to foster global multi-stakeholder dialogue to ensure trusted, safe and inclusive development of AI technologies and equitable access to their benefits. In January 2019, the ILO's Global Commission on the Future of Work published its findings. The first countries are issuing frameworks for autonomous driving, including Germany, and UNECE is considering the implications of autonomous and self-driving cars on the Vienna Convention on Road Traffic. In these and other ways, the UN hopes to promote and advance the benefits of AI towards the three pillars of the UN: peace and security, human rights, and development.

U.S. companies also lead the way as acquirers. Six out of the top 20 companies have acquired AI companies. Ten companies have made at least five acquisitions in this field and between them have made 79 acquisitions in total. Alphabet, Apple and Microsoft have been the most active entities, with 18, 11 and nine AI-related acquisitions, respectively. The number of acquisitions identified in the AI sector has increased every year since 2012, reaching 103 in 2017.

Funding provides further insight into AI activity. As of May 2018, 2,868 companies related to AI have been identified as receiving a disclosed amount of funding (44 percent of 6,538 companies). This represents about US$46 billion in funding in total.

Enforcement of AI patents

Turning to legal disputes over AI patents, available data on litigation and opposition cases from different regions can be analyzed to identify trends over time, as well as the most active parties as plaintiffs and defendants: 1,264 AI patent families are mentioned in litigation cases and 4,231 are mentioned in opposition cases for the period 1975 to 2017 (years correspond to earliest priority years of the patents implicated in the litigation/ opposition cases). There are 492 patent families mentioned in both types of dispute.

The top three plaintiffs in litigation cases are Nuance Communications, American Vehicular Services and Automotive Technologies International, while Microsoft, Apple and Alphabet are the top defendants. The biggest filers of oppositions to AI patents are Siemens, Daimler and Giesecke+Devrient, while the main defendants in oppositions are Samsung, LG Corporation and Hyundai.

Examples of AI applications

Boi Faltings, EPFL

Distributed AI can be used to optimize resource sharing without appearing to place restrictions on people's behavior. To take one example, recent work has shown how to best place electric vehicle charging stations so that users will find them naturally and conveniently available. Another use of distributed AI is to enable intelligent infrastructure such as smart grids. These connect intelligent devices such as heating and washing machines to renewable energy supplies so that demand on the devices can be matched continuously to the available electricity supply, without noticeably affecting the comfort of their users. Such a technology is indispensable for the large-scale take up renewable energy, which is difficult to store.

Another area where AI can have a huge impact is digital medicine. For instance, utilizing recent advances in deep learning, a smartphone app can detect skin cancer at an early stage using an image taken from a cellphone camera. In the future it will be possible to detect diseases from data collected by wearable sensors, and to suggest optimal treatments to prevent these diseases from developing. This will however require a major data collection effort and possibly new advances in ensuring data privacy.

AI also has the potential to have a large, beneficial influence on the tertiary sector. Machine translation, for example, allows people to communicate and do business across language barriers, and thus creates many new opportunities, not only for profit, but also for enriching people's lives.

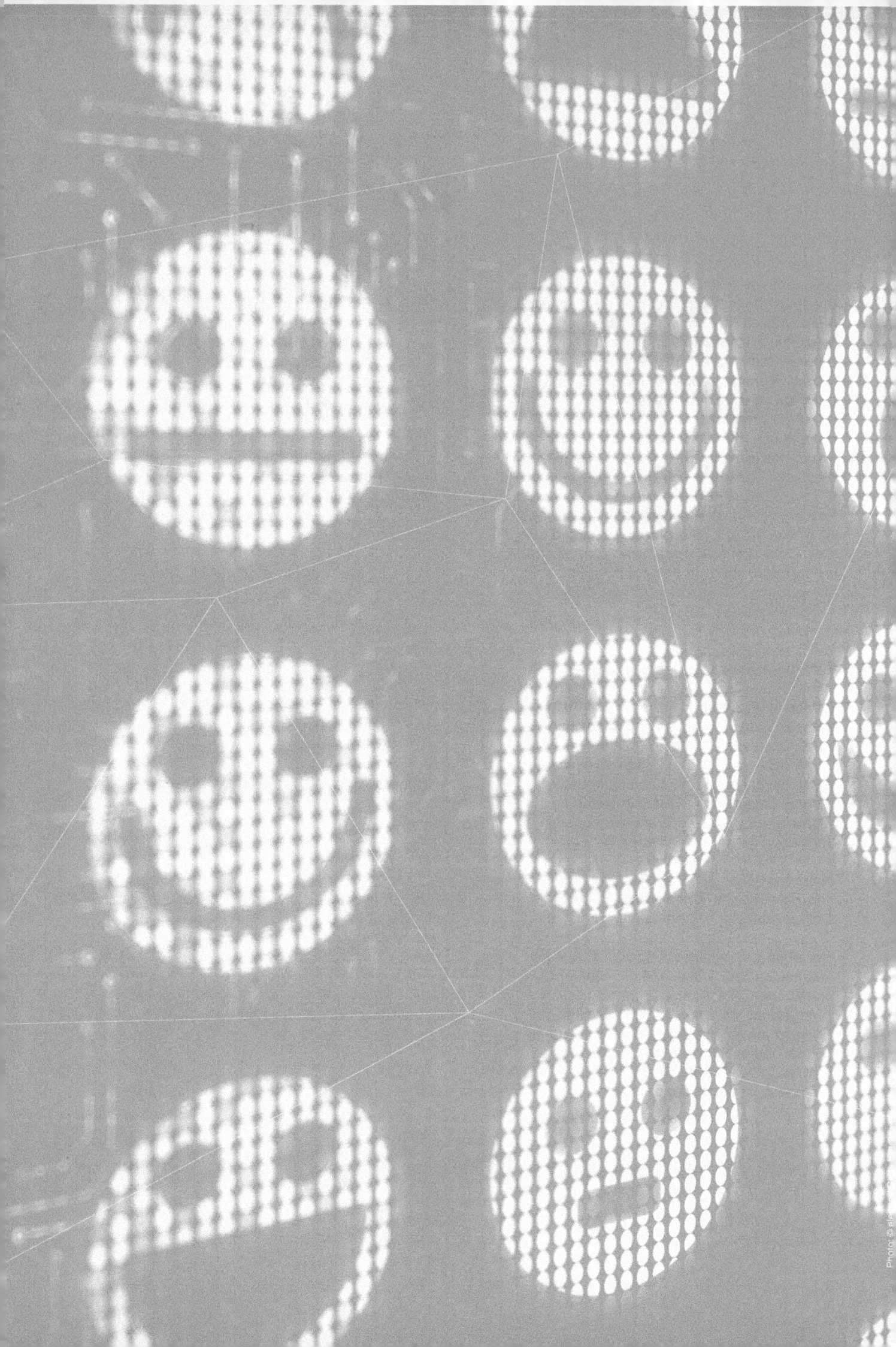

Affective computing

Imagine your family has a history of depression on one side and panic attacks on the other and your daughter is entering a highly demanding university program where she has a nearly 50 percent chance of experiencing depression. To prevent this from happening, she downloads a new AI app on her phone, and consents to have it securely track her sleep, activity, mood, times of sending/receiving texts and calls, and to communicate with her smart watch, which continuously collects data related to her sleep, stress and physical activity.

The AI app provides her privately with information that is like a weather forecast, but personalized to predict her mood, stress and health. For example, it might indicate for tomorrow "30 percent chance of feeling happy," "80 percent chance of higher stress" or "40 percent chance of becoming sick (20 percent higher than yesterday)." As she uses the AI app, its forecasts become increasingly accurate. The app also has the ability to make evidence-based personalized recommendations, such as "40 percent higher chance of happiness and 30 per cent lower stress if you go to bed an hour earlier tonight and talk with a friend today – here are some you might consider to call."

This describes an area of active research in the field of affective computing, with technology that helps an individual better understand, monitor and regulate their emotions. The most successful methods today for solving mood forecasting rely upon getting large sets of labelled data for supervised machine learning, and either using the data to train deep neural networks – deep learning – or using a hybrid approach that allows personalized variations in your data to guide the selection of the machine learning method used for your personal forecast. In one application where there were more than 345,000 days of data, the approach takes as input the answers to questions a person provides every day, and uses these in a recurrent neural network to try to learn whether the person is likely to become "severely depressed." Another approach requires only passive data sensed from smartphones and wearables, so that the user does not have to enter anything manually, and then uses this passive data to predict the scores given by a trained psychiatrist.

Another area of active research is making personalized recommendations. To solve this requires not only lots of data mining and modelling to learn which evidence-based behaviors to suggest for each person (if the recommendations are supporting improved health), but also engineering ways to make suggestions that are inspiring and successful, as opposed to being irritating, frustrating or annoying, which is what happens with most of today's technology that lacks emotional intelligence. This latter challenge is part of a much larger body of work in affective computing, where systems sense and respond to the user's affective state in ways that help the user successfully achieve their goals (e.g., increasing focus and calm, or improving their sleep regularity).

Case study by Rosalind Picard, MIT Media Laboratory

3 Evolution of AI patent applications and scientific publications

A significant growth of patents in a field is usually observed long after scientific publications. There is a 10-year delay for most techniques, with the exception of deep learning.

Key findings

- Nearly 340,000 patent families and more than 1.6 million scientific papers related to artificial intelligence were published from 1960 until early 2018.
- The number of patent applications filed annually in the AI field grew by a factor of 6.5 between 2011 and 2017.
- The boom in patent applications, oriented towards the industrial application of technical solutions, lags that in scientific publications by about 10 years. In addition, the ratio of scientific articles to patents published is reducing, suggesting a greater interest in the practical use of AI technologies.
- The AI techniques on which the patent literature focuses most extensively are machine learning, followed by logic programming (expert systems) and fuzzy logic. The most predominant AI functional applications are computer vision, natural language processing and speech processing.
- The AI application fields most commonly mentioned in patent literature include telecommunications, transportation, and life and medical sciences, but almost all fields show a growth in patenting activity in recent years.

- The most marked increases in patenting activity between 2013 and 2016 features a machine learning technique, deep learning. Deep learning had an average annual growth rate of 175 percent in this period. Robotics and control methods (both 55 percent) were the fastest growing AI functional applications, and aerospace/avionics (67 percent) and smart cities (47 percent) were the fastest growing application fields.
- There are also strong linkages between clusters. For example, deep learning often co-occurs with computer vision applications.

Historical development

_____The AI patent boom

Nearly 340,000 patent families and more than 1.6 million scientific papers related to artificial intelligence were published between 1960 and early 2018. As explained in Chapter 1, each patent family is counted once and is represented by the patent application filed earliest. For the purposes of this report the terms "patent family," "patent application," "patent filing" or "invention" may be used interchangeably, referring to the representative patent family member and the corresponding invention.

Looking back over time, the data show that interest in the field has grown constantly since the early 1980s, and accelerated in 2012. Between 2006 and 2011, patent publications grew by about 8 percent a year on average, but between 2012 and 2017, they grew by an average of 28 percent a year. The actual number of published applications per year rose from 8,515 in 2006 to 12,473 in 2011 and 55,660 in 2017. This represents a 6.5-fold increase in annual filings over a 12-year period. It also means that 53 percent of all patents in the AI field have been published since 2013 – a remarkable recent increase in patent publications.

Figure 3.1 shows the trends in AI patent applications published from 1960 to 2017, based on the earliest publication of a member of a patent family. Patent applications are typically published 18 months after the priority date. Figure 3.1 also shows trends in scientific publications from 1960 to 2017.

Scientific literature

AI is a major topic in scientific literature, with a total of 1,636,649 papers published up to mid-2018.

Figure 3.1 also compares patent filings and scientific publications since 1960. It shows that the boom in AI-related scientific papers started about 10 years before that in patents, with an average annual growth rate of 8 percent between 1996 and 2001, almost doubling to 18 percent between 2002 and 2007. Figure 3.2 shows the annual ratio of scientific papers to patent families. The ratio fell from eight papers per patent in 2010 to just three papers per patent in 2015, suggesting an increased interest in the practical uses and industrial applications of AI technologies during that period.

Categorization of AI technologies

Patents can be categorized according to their technological content. Using the scheme described in Chapter 1, we know that 44 percent of all AI patents mention at least one AI technique, while 75 percent mention a functional application and 62 percent an application field. Since patent documents can refer to one or more of these categories, Figure 3.3 shows the overlaps between the three areas as they are mentioned in patent documents.

The majority of patent families (68 percent or 232,423 inventions) fall into at least two

Figure 3.1. AI patent families and scientific publications by earliest publication year

AI patent families grew by an average of 28 percent and scientific publications by 5.6 percent annually between 2012 and 2017

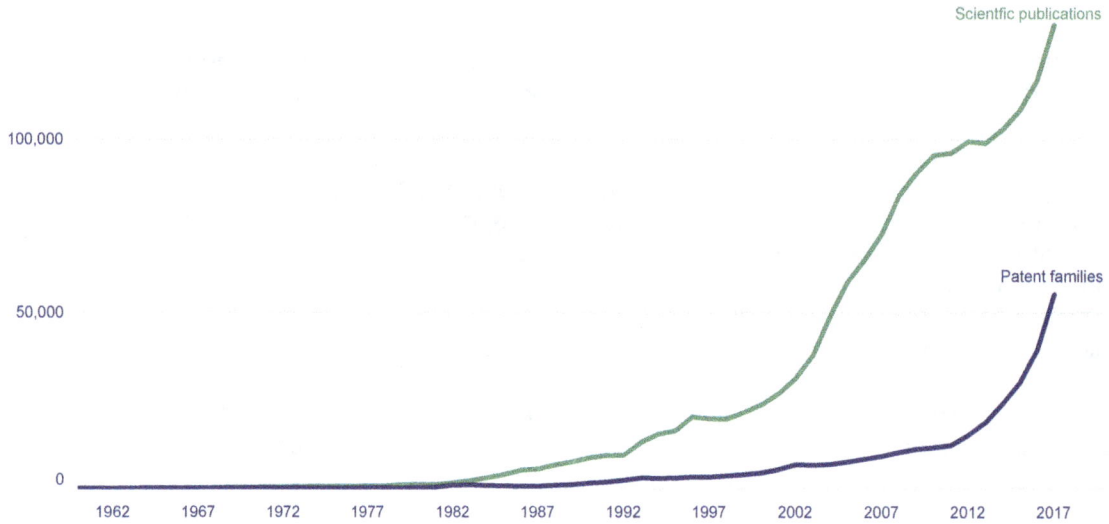

Figure 3.2. Ratio of scientific publications to patent families by earliest publication year

The ratio of scientific publications to patent families dropped from 8 to 1 in 2010 to 3 to 1 in 2016

Figure 3.3. Patent families related to AI techniques, functional applications, application fields and their overlaps

AI technologies are often combined: over 68 percent of AI-related patents fall into more than one category

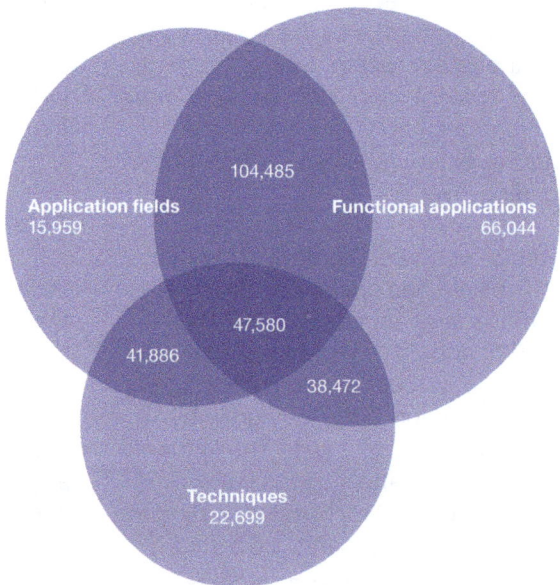

Application fields
15,959

Functional applications
66,044

104,485

47,580

41,886

38,472

Techniques
22,699

categories, and 14 percent (47,580 inventions) fall into all three categories. Among those patent families that fall into a single category alone, representing only 31 percent of all patent families (104,473 inventions), the majority (63 percent, 66,044 inventions) mention only a functional application, while 22 percent (22,699 inventions) mention only a technique and 15 percent (15,959 inventions) mention only an application field.

The statistics indicate that patent applicants tend to focus their filings on industrial applications, unlike scientific publications which are more likely to focus on AI techniques: 64 percent of scientific AI publications mention at least one specific technique, compared with 44 percent of patent families. As pointed out by Kai-Fu Lee, "we are now in the age of AI implementation". The trends in patents and scientific publications for each of the three areas are discussed in more detail below.

_____AI techniques

A total of 150,637 patent families dealing with the development or use of a specific AI technique were published up to early 2018. This number includes documents that refer only to AI techniques as well as those that also mention functional applications and/or application fields, and represents 44 percent of all AI patent families.

Figure 3.4 illustrates the patent trends for various AI techniques. Machine learning is the dominant technique, and the only one to show a significant increase in filings in recent years.

Figure 3.5 shows the breakdown of AI techniques by total number of applications. Machine learning represents 89 percent of patent families related to an AI technique, or 40 percent of all AI patent families. This reflects the progress made thanks to machine learning in landmark applications such as reliable cat image recognition in 2012 by Google Brain's team headed by Andrew Ng and Alphabet's Google DeepMind AlphaGo beating a human in the complex board game Go in 2016.

While much less common than machine learning, other AI techniques such as logic programming (with 99.5 percent of patent families related to expert systems) and fuzzy logic show a steady filing rate since the late 1980s. A recent, though moderate, increase in patent filings is evident for these two techniques, with between 1,500 and 2,000 priority filings in 2015 and 2016. However, other AI techniques, namely ontology engineering and probabilistic reasoning, represent a very low number of filings in the field (less than 1 percent of all patent families).

It is worth noting that, if we look beyond the total numbers of patent families and examine instead the average annual growth rate of filings in the different sub-categories, we can see that deep learning demonstrates by far the biggest recent growth in the field, with an impressive 175 percent average annual growth between 2013 and 2016. Other machine learning techniques show a similar very steep increase in filing growth rate in recent years, namely multi-task learning (49 percent) and neural networks (46 percent).

This recent interest in deep learning and neural networks is confirmed by data extracted from GitHub, a collaborative platform for open source software development, which evidence a constantly increasing number of repositories mentioning these techniques between 2014 and 2017, from 238 GitHub repositories mentioning neural networks and 43 mentioning deep learning in 2014, to 3,871 and 3,276 in 2017, respectively.

Turning to the scientific literature, a total of 1,050,631 scientific publications dealing with AI techniques have been published up to mid-2018, representing 64 percent of the total scientific publications collection. Machine learning is the most common field described (representing 54 percent of scientific publications), followed by logic programming and fuzzy logic (see figure 3.6).

The growth in publications relating to AI techniques is similar to that seen with patent filings. Looking at the history of AI development, it is interesting to note when certain techniques

Figure 3.4. Patent families for top AI techniques by earliest priority year

Machine learning grew by an average of 26 percent annually between 2011 and 2016

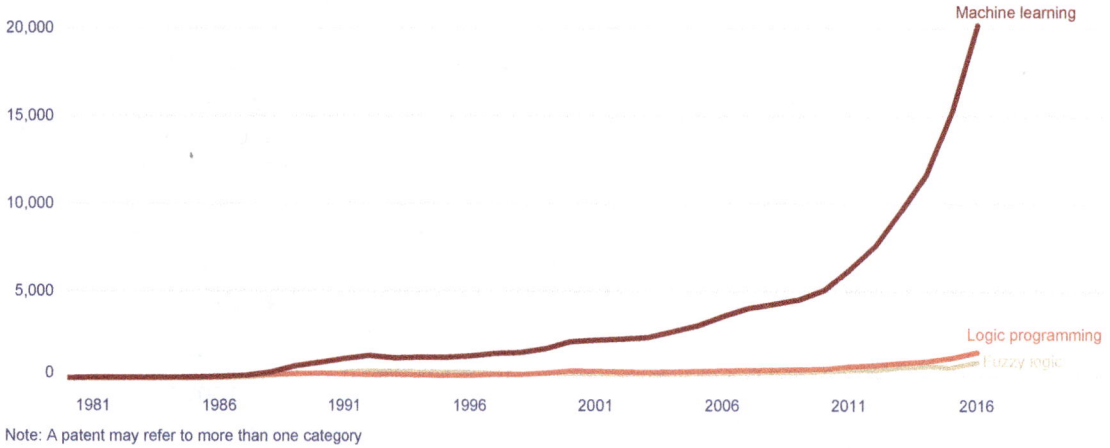

Note: A patent may refer to more than one category

Figure 3.5. Patent families for AI technique categories and sub-categories

Machine learning is the dominant AI technique, representing 89 percent of patent families related to an AI technique

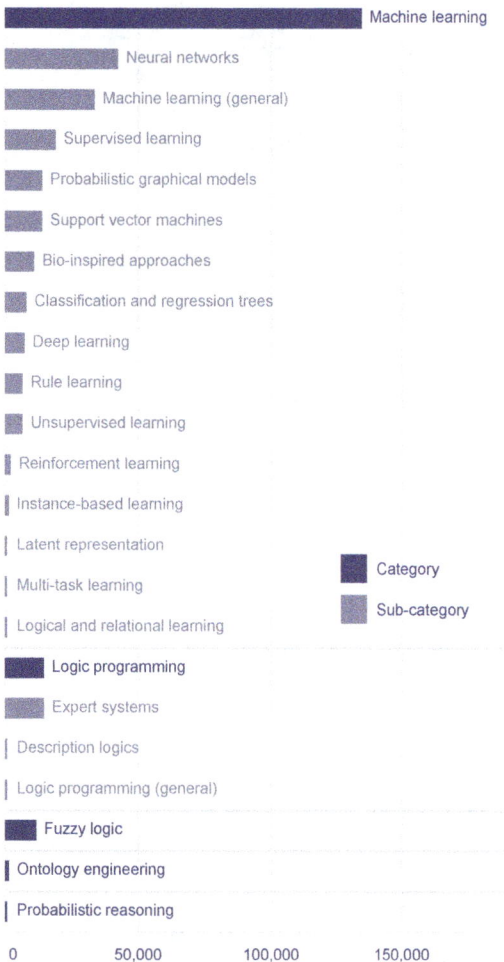

Note: A patent may refer to more than one category or sub-category

Figure 3.6. Patent families and scientific publications related to AI techniques as a share of the total for AI

The share of scientific publications is generally higher than patent families for AI techniques

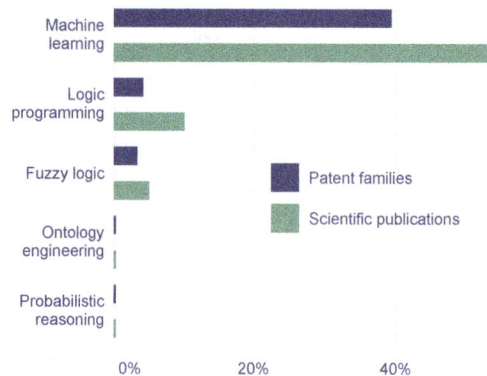

Note: A patent or scientific publication may refer to more than one category

first appeared in scientific publications, using as a benchmark the first year when there were at least 200 publications:

- 1982: logic programming is the first AI technique to be substantially addressed in the scientific literature. This technique is characterized by a very high annual growth rate from the outset (146 percent a year on average, from 208 papers in 1982 to 2,986 papers in 1985).
- 1985: machine learning techniques are substantially described from 1985 onwards. They then show moderate growth until 2002 and then an average annual growth rate of 25 percent between 2002 and 2005, before slowing down between 2008 and 2013.
- 1991: fuzzy logic appears in the scientific literature around 1991 and has shown a moderate increase since then.

Ontology engineering and probabilistic reasoning are emerging techniques, and are still under the chosen threshold of 200 publications a year (probabilistic reasoning peaked at 500 publications in 2007 but the publication rate has declined since then).

When scientific publications on various machine learning approaches are compared with patenting activity (see figure 3.7), two main trends are stand out:

- Bio-inspired approaches are significantly more common in scientific publications than in patent filings (in terms of percentage of the corresponding corpus). A similar trend is observed in neural networks, machine learning (general approaches) and multi-task learning.
- Rule learning forms an exception to the overall trend and is significantly more common in patents than in scientific publications.

A breakdown of scientific publishing in various logic programming approaches is presented in figure 3.8 and compared with patenting activity. As with patent activity, expert systems is the most common approach. Description logics and logic programming (general) are represented more in scientific literature than in patent filings.

Data and public research: the example of precision medicine

**Aristotelis Tsirigos,
NYU School of Medicine**

A growing number of academic labs, established companies and startups are shifting their focus toward the field of precision medicine, that is, the design of therapies tailored for each individual patient. Progress in this field will require the systematic collection of a vast amount of clinical data from patients in each disease type and subtype. In turn, the availability of this data will allow AI to realize its full potential and answer clinically critical questions for each patient. For example, will a patient respond better to drug A versus drug B? What is the optimal dosage? How do we minimize side-effects? What type of data do we need to monitor and to predict relapse as early as possible?

How can we deliver effective care in under-served populations? As with every new big technology that promises a big leap forward, there is a clash with existing cultural and ethical norms.

Clearly, access to data is essential for the success of AI, bringing forward many challenges related to the protection of human subjects in research, privacy concerns, ownership issues and fair access to data. Despite these challenges and occasional setbacks, our view is that it is possible to strike the right balance and protect our rights while improving patients' lives.

Each of the different types of machine learning shows a significant increase in the number of both scientific publications and patent filings over the period studied. There are, however, some interesting similarities and differences. Some examples of these illustrated in figure 3.9 are:

- Supervised learning, support vector machines, deep learning, classification and regression tree and instance based-learning all show continuous growth in the number of scientific publications.

Figure 3.7. Patent families and scientific publications related to machine learning sub-categories as a share of the total for AI

Rule learning and supervised learning are represented more highly in patent families than scientific publications

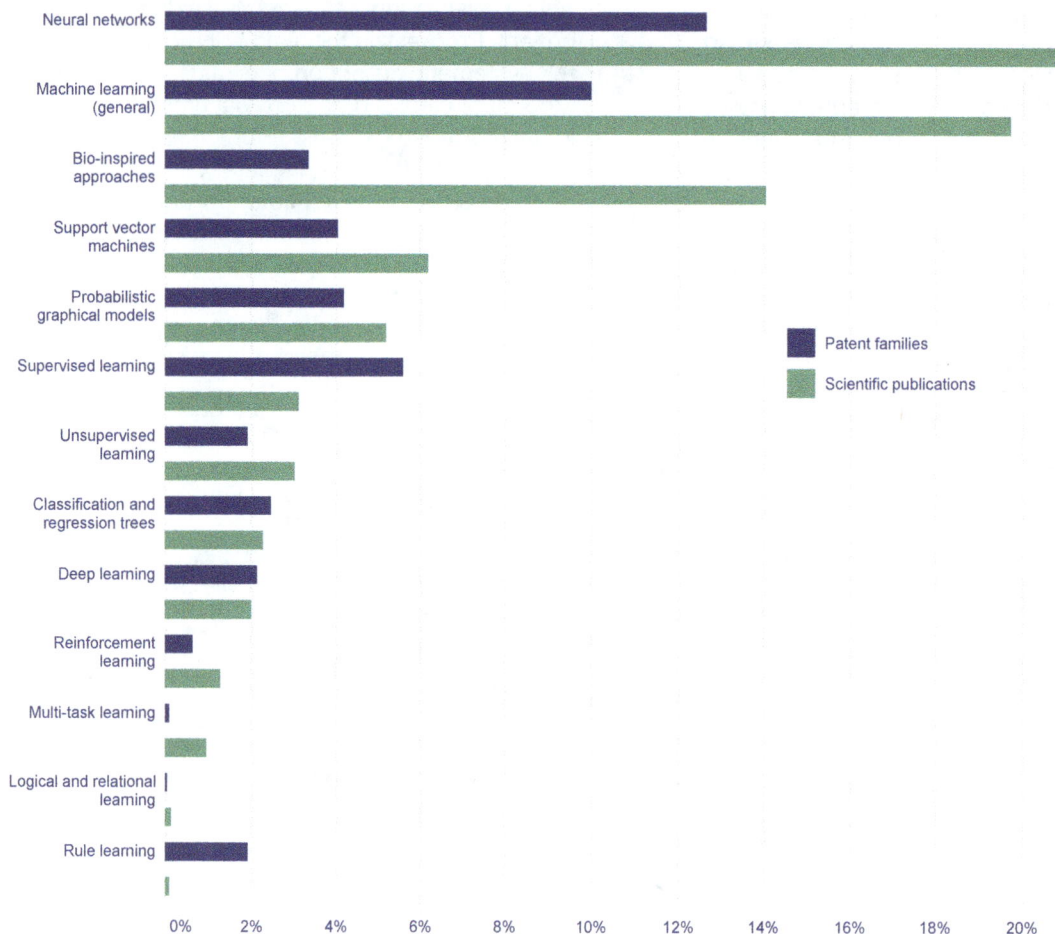

Note: A patent or scientific publication may refer to more than one sub-category

Figure 3.8. Patent families and scientific publications related to logic programming sub-categories as a share of the total for AI

Among logic programming sub-categories, description logics is represented significantly higher in scientific publications than in patent filings

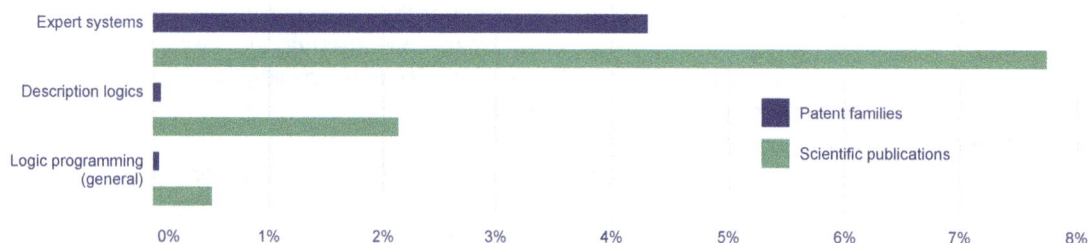

Note: A patent or scientific publication may refer to more than one category

Figure 3.9. Machine learning patent families and scientific publications, by earliest priority year and publication year, respectively

Growth in patent families usually follows scientific publications, except for rule learning which saw a burst of patent filing in 1999

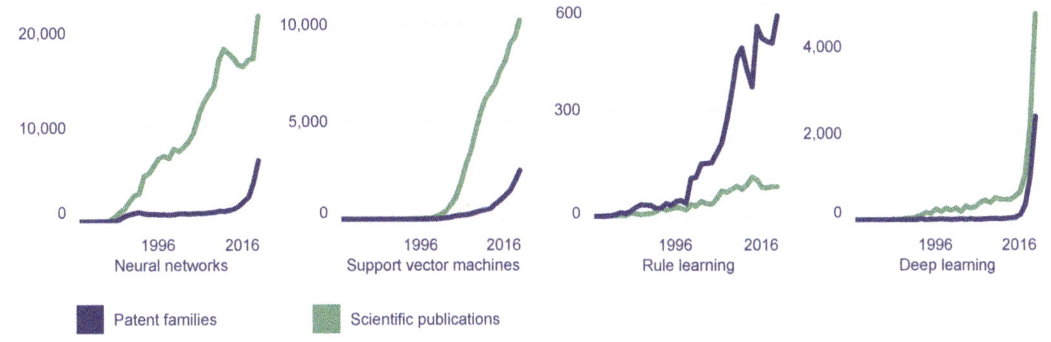

20,000
10,000
0
1996
2016
Neural networks
10,000
5,000
0
1996
2016
Support vector machines
600
300
0
1996
2016
Rule learning
4,000
2,000
0
1996
2016
Deep learning
Patent families
Scientific publications

Figure 3.10. Patent families for functional application categories and sub-categories

Computer vision represents 49 percent of patent families related to a functional application

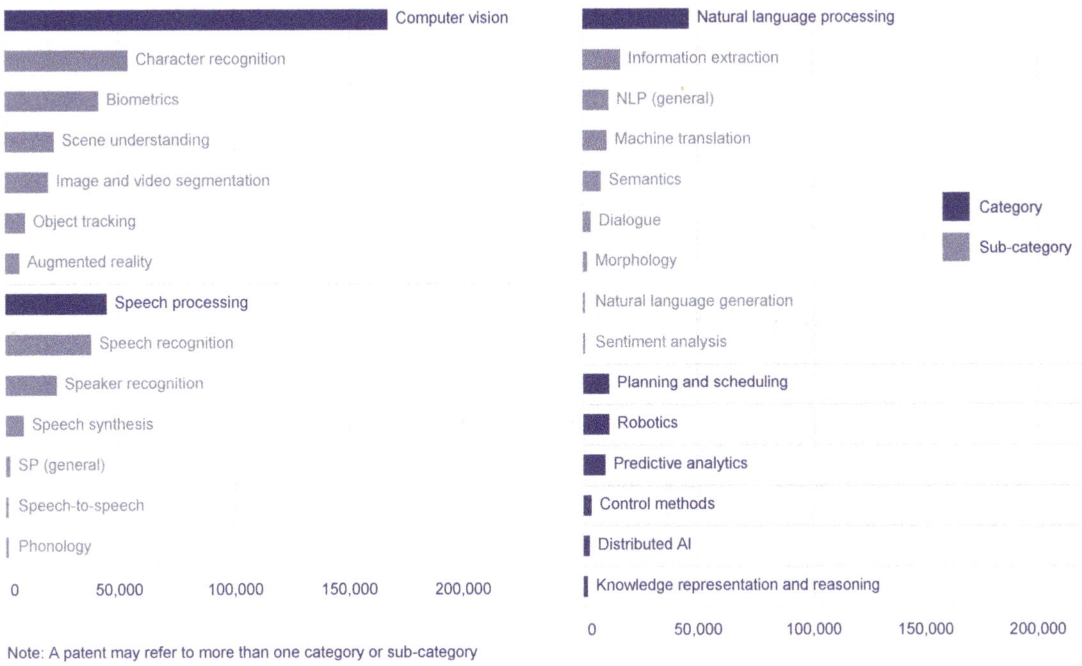

Computer vision
Character recognition
Biometrics
Scene understanding
Image and video segmentation
Object tracking
Augmented reality
Speech processing
Speech recognition
Speaker recognition
Speech synthesis
SP (general)
Speech-to-speech
Phonology
0
50,000
100,000
150,000
200,000
Natural language processing
Information extraction
NLP (general)
Machine translation
Semantics
Dialogue
Morphology
Natural language generation
Sentiment analysis
Planning and scheduling
Robotics
Predictive analytics
Control methods
Distributed AI
Knowledge representation and reasoning
0
50,000
100,000
150,000
200,000
Category
Sub-category

Note: A patent may refer to more than one category or sub-category

Figure 3.11. Patent families for top functional applications by earliest priority year

Computer vision grew by an average of 23 percent annually between 2011 and 2016

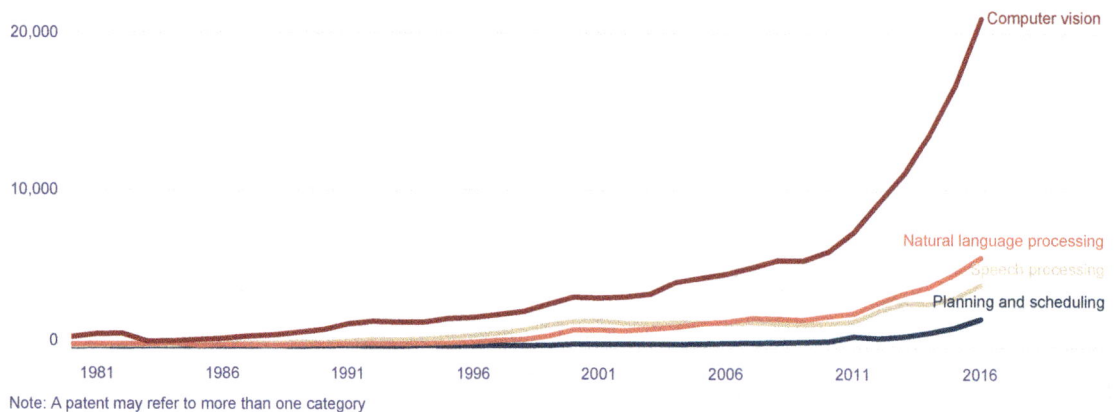

Computer vision

Natural language processing

Speech processing

Planning and scheduling

20,000

10,000

0

1981   1986   1991   1996   2001   2006   2011   2016

Note: A patent may refer to more than one category

Figure 3.12. Patent families for top computer vision sub-categories by earliest priority year

Biometrics has grown by an average of 30 percent since 2013, surpassing all other computer vision sub-categories

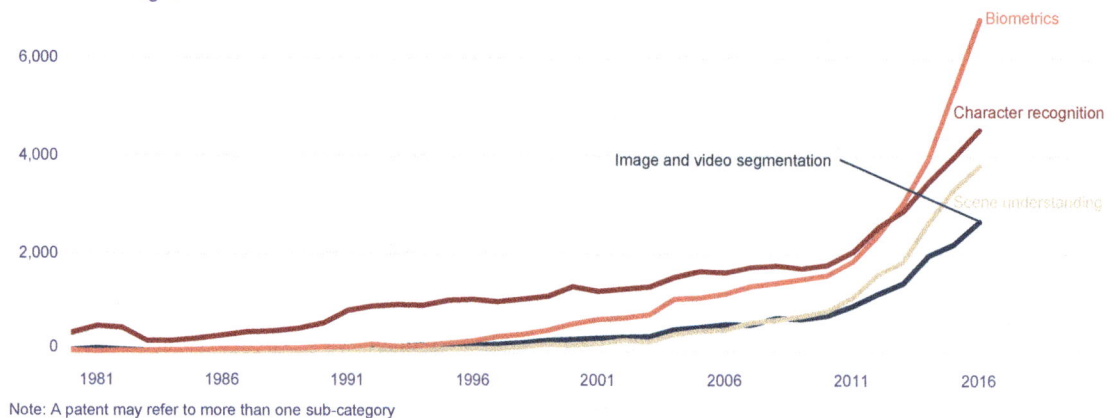

Biometrics

Character recognition

Image and video segmentation

Scene understanding

6,000

4,000

2,000

0

1981   1986   1991   1996   2001   2006   2011   2016

Note: A patent may refer to more than one sub-category

Figure 3.13. Patent families for top natural language processing sub-categories by earliest priority year

Information extraction grew by 24 percent and semantics by 33 percent between 2013 and 2016

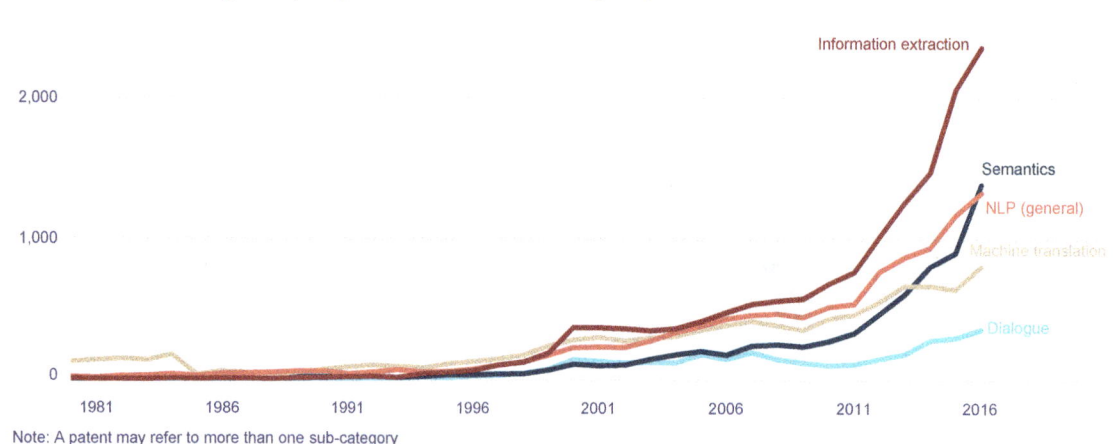

Information extraction

Semantics

NLP (general)

Machine translation

Dialogue

2,000

1,000

0

1981   1986   1991   1996   2001   2006   2011   2016

Note: A patent may refer to more than one sub-category

- Neural networks, machine learning (general), probabilistic graphical model, bio-inspired approaches, unsupervised learning and reinforcement learning show overall growth with periods of slower increase, or even temporary decrease, in scientific publications.
- Most types of machine learning show a delay between publications and patents (a significant growth of patents in a field is usually observed long after scientific publications). There is a 10-year delay for most techniques, with the exception of deep learning.
- Deep learning has an untypical profile with both scientific publications and patents showing a high growth rate from 2013 to 2016, with 96 percent and 175 percent a year on average, respectively; patents grew from a starting point of 118 in 2013, whereas scientific publications grew from 654.

_____ AI functional applications

A total of 256,456 patent families related to AI functional applications have been published up to early 2018, which represents 75 percent of all patent families related to AI. These documents may refer only to AI functional applications or include AI techniques or AI application fields.

The three AI functional applications with the highest number of patent families are computer vision, natural language processing and speech processing (figure 3.10). These represent 49 percent, 14 percent and 13 percent of all patent families related to AI, respectively. This underlines the importance of these three functional applications to the field of AI.

Figure 3.11 shows filing over time for the top four functional applications. Beyond these fields, inventions related to planning and scheduling, robotics and predictive analytics are the next most frequent in the patent literature, each of them occurring in about 10,000 patent families. Moreover, it is the areas with a relatively small number of applications that have shown the most growth recently; the average annual growth rate of robotics and control methods between 2013 and 2016 was 55 percent.

We see a lot of investment at the intersection of AI and biology – biological circuits, more efficient drug discovery – and that's red-hot right now.

Frank Chen, Andreessen Horowitz

Figure 3.12, figure 3.13 and figure 3.14 show in turn a detailed breakdown of each of the three functional applications with the highest number of patent families: computer vision, natural language processing and speech processing.

Among noteworthy findings are:

- Character recognition is the leading sub-category in computer vision, both in terms of date and the total number of patent families, with the first patent filings occurring in the 1980s.
- Biometrics has, however, overtaken character recognition in recent years, accounting for the highest numbers of patent filings since 2012.
- Scene understanding, although appearing later, is likewise showing significant growth.
- The number of patents related to augmented reality was stable between 2014 and 2016.
- Within the natural language processing category, the largest sub-categories are: information extraction (including big data), which accounts for 39 percent of the annual filings since 2010; machine translation; and semantics, which has seen a marked increase in filings since 2010.
- Within the speech processing category, speech recognition accounts for 86 percent and speaker recognition for 50 percent of patent families, as patent documents address more than one speech processing

Figure 3.14. Patent families for top speech processing sub-categories by earliest priority year

Speech recognition represents 86 percent of patent families related to speech processing

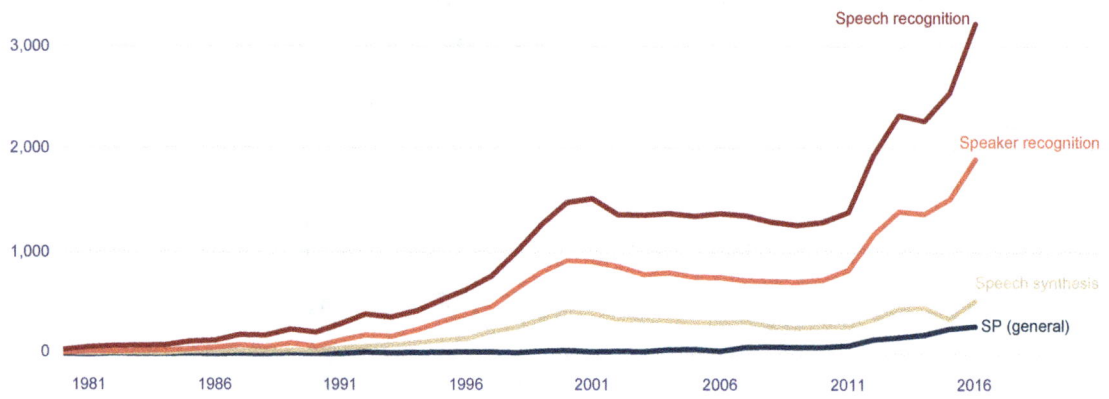

Note: A patent may refer to more than one sub-category

Figure 3.15. Patent families and scientific publications related to AI functional applications as a share of the total for AI

AI functional applications are generally more highly represented in patent families than they are in scientific publications

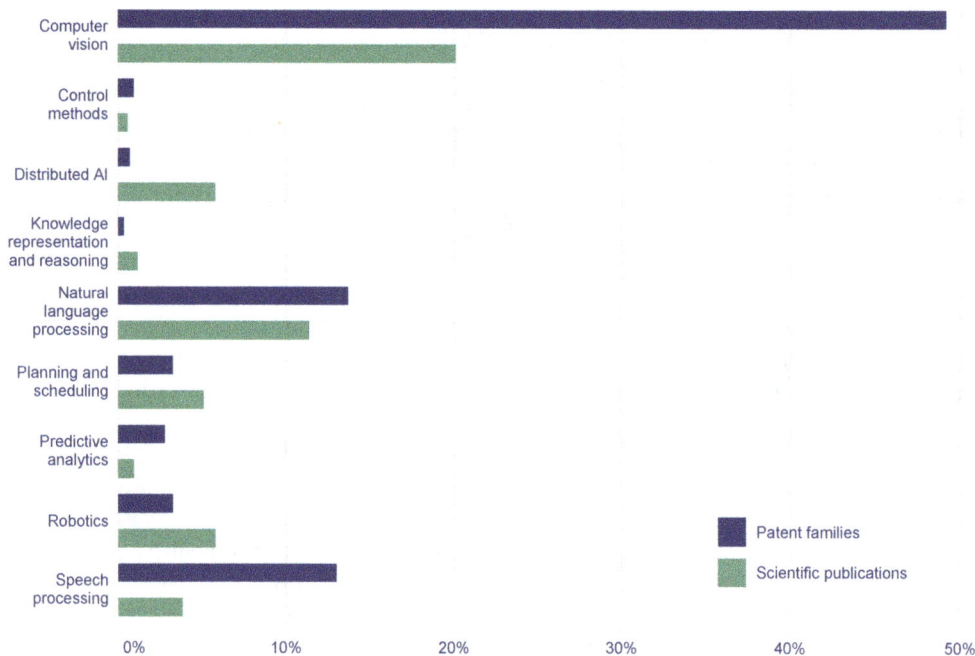

Note: A patent or scientific publication may refer to more than one category

type. Furthermore, 19,524 patent families are classified in both of these sub-categories, explaining the marked correlation in their annual filing trends.

As of mid-2018, 777,251 scientific papers relating to AI functional applications had been published, representing 47 percent of the total scientific publications collection. As with patent filings, computer vision and natural language processing are prominent in scientific publications, with 20 percent and 11 percent of all AI scientific publications, respectively (see figure 3.15). However, speech processing is less represented in scientific papers than in patents whereas distributed AI is better represented.

The order of appearance of AI functional applications in scientific publications, defined as from the first year when there were at least 200 publications, is as follows:

- 1970: computer vision
- 1982 to 1986: robotics, planning and scheduling, speech processing, and knowledge representation and reasoning
- 1992: natural language processing
- 1996: distributed AI
- 2003: predictive analytics and control methods.

In terms of trends in scientific publications, there are three distinct patterns (see figure 3.16):

- Continuous growth: natural language processing and predictive analytics
- General growth with a period of slower increase (or temporary decrease): computer vision, control methods, distributed AI, planning and scheduling
- Less regular growth: knowledge representation and reasoning, speech processing, and robotics.

Within the computer vision category, biometrics and image and video segmentation are the most represented in scientific literature, followed by character recognition. For the natural language processing category, information extraction and semantics are the most represented, while for speech processing

From the lab to the real world

Dario Floreano, EPFL

I'm not surprised to see an increase of patent applications in AI and robotics. This decade is witnessing a major ramp-up of governmental and industrial funding for research in intelligent systems, with several results being rapidly deployed from the lab to the real world.

Students and researchers with a degree in robotics and AI are in high demand and will ensure sustained innovation in the future.

it is speech recognition. These findings are similar to those obtained from patent filings.

Comparing the date of scientific publications and patenting activity, it is generally the case that little or no delay exists between the two in computer vision, predictive analytics and speech processing, whereas a significant delay (10 to 15 years) exists in natural language processing, control methods, distributed AI, knowledge representation and reasoning, planning and scheduling, and robotics. This suggests that it may have taken longer for this latter group to move from basic research, usually described in scientific literature, to practical exploitation with commercial potential.

AI application fields

In all, 209,910 AI-related patent families (62 percent of the total) refer to one or several application fields. These patent families fall into 20 different application fields identified in figure 3.17. The top two applications fields mentioned in AI patents are telecommunications and transportation, with more than 50,000 filings each, followed by life and medical sciences, and personal devices, computing and human–computer interaction (HCI). Together, these four application fields are mentioned in 42 percent of all AI patent documents.

Patent documents related to AI identifying specific application fields began emerging in the mid-1990s (see figure 3.18). While the number of patent filings specifying an application field has boomed since 2011, the proportion of these patent families in any given

Figure 3.16. Functional application patent families and scientific publications by earliest priority year and publication year, respectively

Little lag exists between growth in scientific publications and growth in patent families for computer vision and predictive analytics

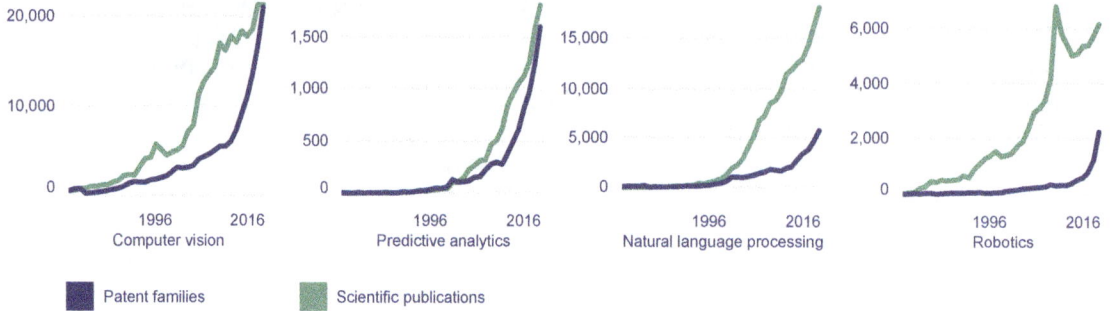

Computer vision

Predictive analytics

Natural language processing

Robotics

■ Patent families   ■ Scientific publications

Figure 3.17. Patent families for application field categories and sub-categories

Telecommunications, transportation, life and medical sciences, and personal devices, computing and HCI are the top four application fields mentioned in patent documents and represent 24, 24, 19 and 17 percent of all patent families related to AI application fields, respectively

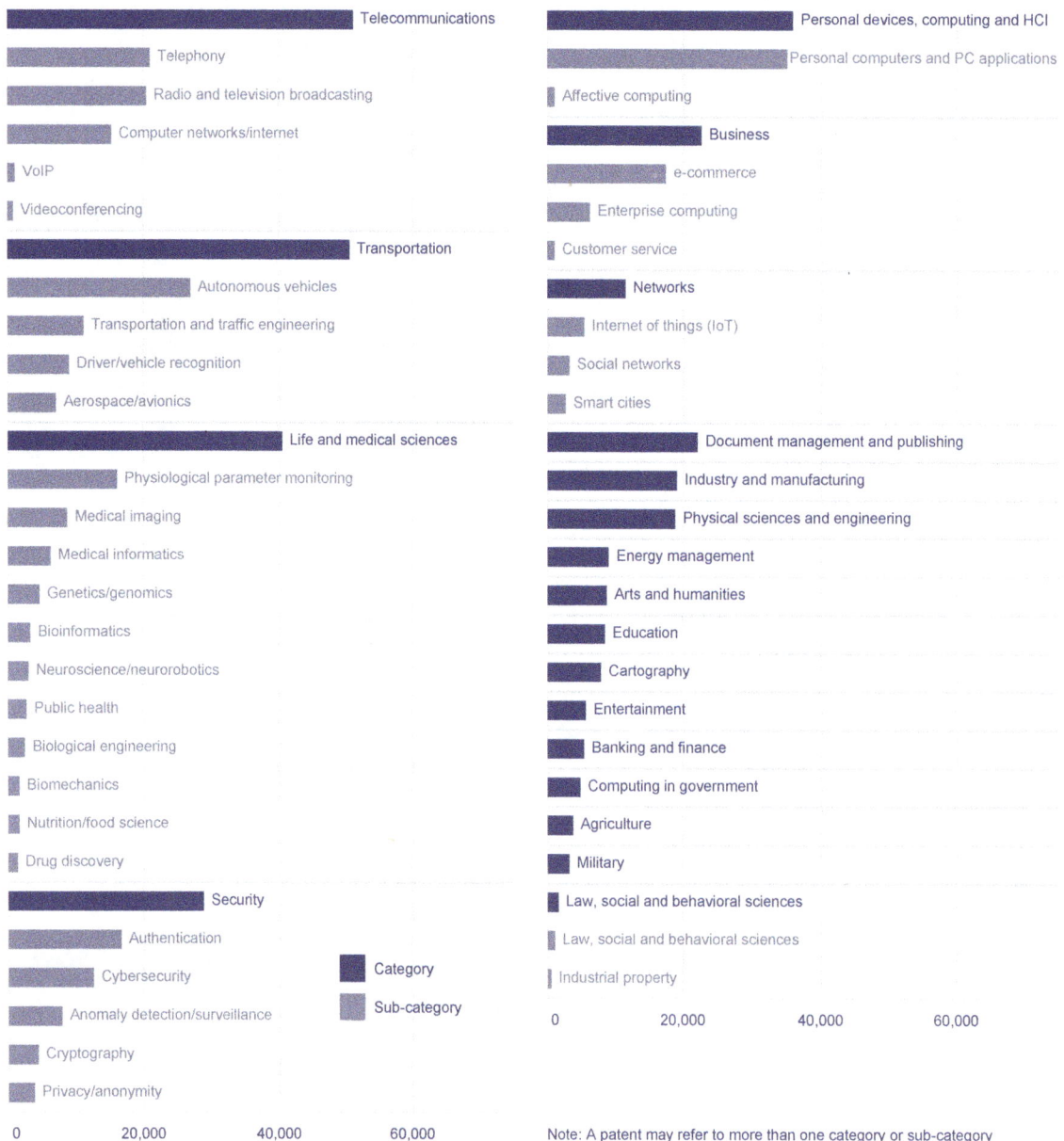

Telecommunications
Telephony
Radio and television broadcasting
Computer networks/internet
VoIP
Videoconferencing
Transportation
Autonomous vehicles
Transportation and traffic engineering
Driver/vehicle recognition
Aerospace/avionics
Life and medical sciences
Physiological parameter monitoring
Medical imaging
Medical informatics
Genetics/genomics
Bioinformatics
Neuroscience/neurorobotics
Public health
Biological engineering
Biomechanics
Nutrition/food science
Drug discovery
Security
Authentication
Cybersecurity
Anomaly detection/surveillance
Cryptography
Privacy/anonymity

Personal devices, computing and HCI
Personal computers and PC applications
Affective computing
Business
e-commerce
Enterprise computing
Customer service
Networks
Internet of things (IoT)
Social networks
Smart cities
Document management and publishing
Industry and manufacturing
Physical sciences and engineering
Energy management
Arts and humanities
Education
Cartography
Entertainment
Banking and finance
Computing in government
Agriculture
Military
Law, social and behavioral sciences
Law, social and behavioral sciences
Industrial property

■ Category
■ Sub-category

Note: A patent may refer to more than one category or sub-category

year has been almost constant since the early 2000s, corresponding to 65 percent of the total on average. AI-related inventions are often not limited to a single application field: 71 percent of these families (corresponding to 44 percent of the total) mention at least two distinct application fields.

Taking a closer look at emerging trends and the average growth rate in the period 2013 to 2016 across the different application fields and their sub-categories, the most remarkable are transportation, with an average annual growth rate of 32.9 percent, agriculture, with 32.3 percent, computing in government, with 30.3 percent, and banking and finance, with 27.7 percent.

Further interesting results can be found when looking closer at the sub-categories of application fields. Figure 3.19 shows patent filings over time in the sub-categories within transportation, the top application field identified in the patent search results. It is particularly instructive when one looks at the growth rates observed in the same period for these sub-categories: aerospace/avionics has the highest average annual growth rate of 66.7 percent, followed by autonomous vehicles, with a 42.2 percent annual growth rate.

The most remarkable growth rates observed across other application fields are smart cities (a sub-category of networks), with average growth rate of 46.9 percent; customer services (a sub-category of business), with 37.7 percent, and affective computing (a sub-category of personal devices, computing and HCl), with 37.1 percent, indicating an increasing interest within AI in the recognition and analysis of human emotions.

Cross-analysis of categories

As we have seen, there are significant crossovers between the three categories used to analyze AI patents (techniques, functional applications and application fields). We can examine these crossovers in more detail by focusing on the number of patent families tagged in different application fields.

Shift towards behavior observation

Boi Faltings, EPFL

As for all of AI, this has shifted toward increasing use of behavior observation, not only in the design, but also in the actual operation of mechanisms. For example, rewards paid for information may be determined by observations of how market participants react to different reward levels.

____Functional applications and techniques

A total of 86,052 patent families mention an AI technique and an AI functional application together. Some machine learning techniques are particularly associated with specific functional applications. These are:

- Deep learning, support vector machines and unsupervised learning for computer vision (63.2 percent, 53.2 percent and 47.9 percent, respectively).
- Bio-inspired approaches for planning and scheduling applications (13.6 percent).
- Probabilistic graphical models for speech processing (19.1 percent), natural language processing (10.3 percent) and knowledge representation (9.6 percent).
- Rule learning for knowledge representation (67.5 percent).
- Supervised learning for natural language processing (22.2 percent).

Deep learning is mainly used for computer vision (63 percent, which is the highest percentage among all machine learning techniques). Computer vision is the top functional application for this AI technique. No more than a year after the boom in deep learning had begun in 2013, interest started to increase in its usefulness for other functional applications, primarily natural language processing and speech processing.

Taking a closer look at these three functional applications – deep learning, natural language processing, and speech processing – reveals a dominant interest in:

- character recognition in computer vision,
- semantics in natural language processing, and
- speech recognition and speaker recognition in speech processing.

Figure 3.18. Patent families for top application field categories by earliest priority year

Patent families related to AI application fields emerged in the 1990s, with transportation and telecommunications overtaking all other fields

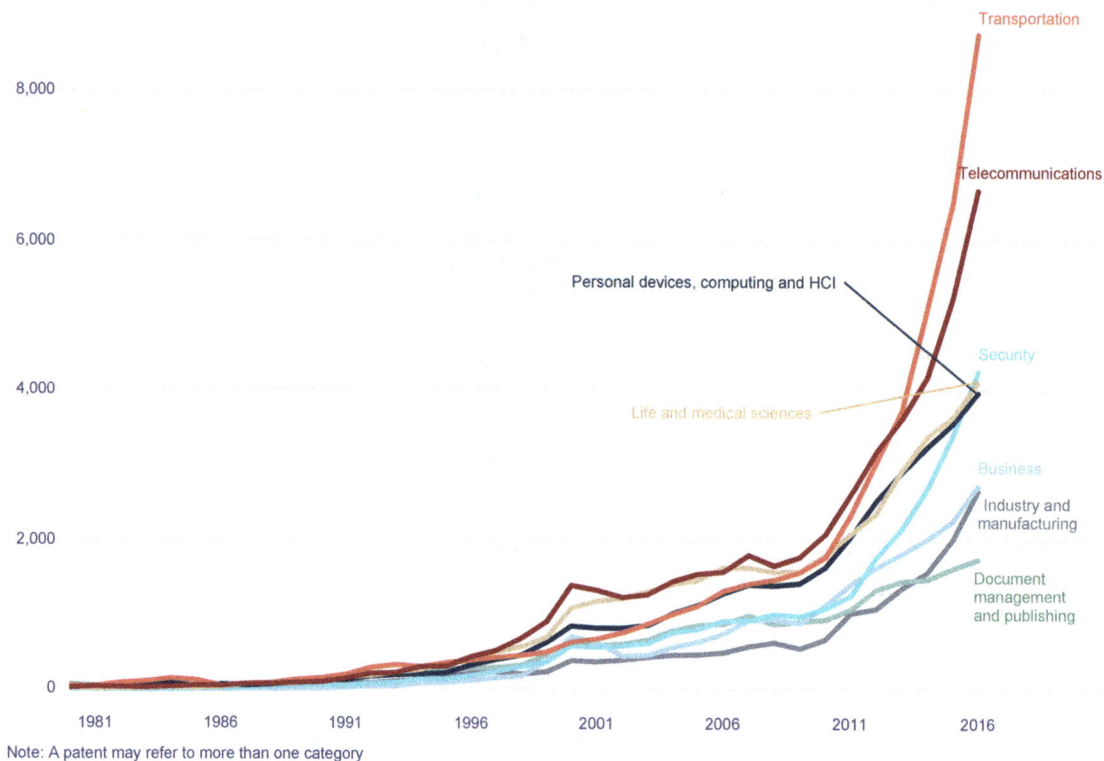

Note: A patent may refer to more than one category

Figure 3.19. Patent families for transportation sub-categories by earliest priority year

Autonomous vehicles grew an average of 35 percent annually from 2011, rising to 42 percent annually from 2013 to 2016. Over the same three years, aerospace/avionics grew even faster, at 67 percent

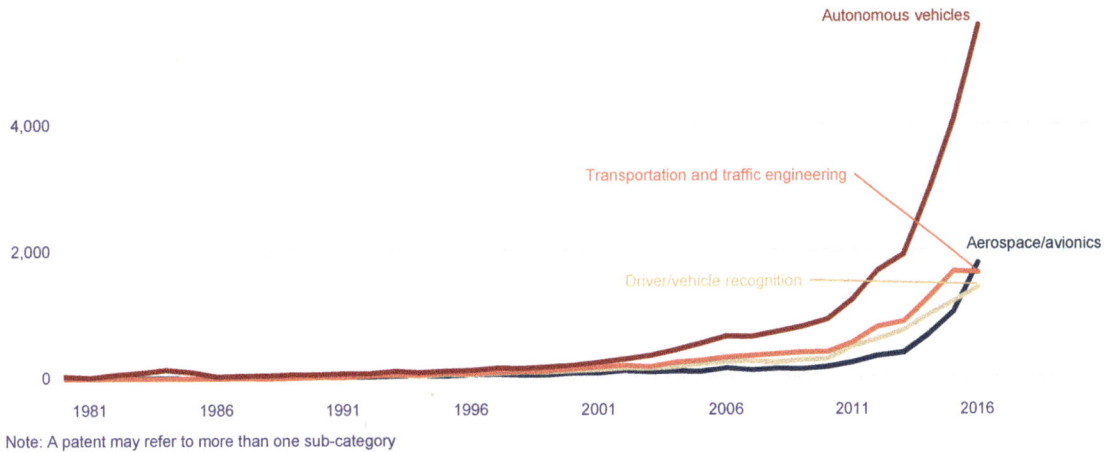

Note: A patent may refer to more than one sub-category

Figure 3.20. Patent families by co-occurrence of application fields with machine learning and functional applications

Machine learning co-occurs most frequently with the life and medical sciences and telecommunications fields; computer vision with telecommunications and transportation

	Machine learning	Computer vision	Natural language processing	Speech processing	Control methods	Planning and scheduling	Robotics	Knowledge representation and reasoning	Predictive analytics	Distributed AI
Telecommunications	16,201	22,871	7,553	12,549	3,496	2,601	2,476	1,292	1,533	516
Transportation	13,741	21,744	2,330	3,997	14,030	3,614	5,080	761	866	533
Personal devices, computing and HCI	11,585	17,164	7,920	6,678	1,625	1,663	1,416	1,838	1,069	223
Life and medical sciences	18,772	17,098	3,818	2,504	1,494	1,617	1,988	1,698	1,694	428
Security	8,813	17,235	3,033	3,075	1,162	1,401	793	795	594	243
Document management and publishing	6,841	11,530	9,526	3,291	163	517	221	880	431	83
Business	9,709	7,968	5,850	2,422	271	1,381	350	1,820	2,585	189
Industry and manufacturing	9,569	5,573	3,031	798	1,262	2,404	1,073	1,213	1,086	382
Physical sciences and engineering	8,330	5,397	1,284	1,183	1,540	721	679	444	720	171
Networks	5,296	3,659	2,350	1,498	343	789	380	630	570	183
Arts and humanities	2,489	4,852	2,669	2,615	237	273	371	203	277	44
Education	3,914	3,767	1,642	1,951	284	365	372	532	247	56
Cartography	3,276	3,334	1,610	759	697	697	257	365	425	98
Energy management	3,766	1,056	397	309	734	944	336	187	299	335
Entertainment	1,822	2,890	737	1,087	309	199	528	189	133	41
Computing in government	2,583	2,587	938	444	149	380	135	243	213	71
Banking and finance	2,368	2,047	1,055	493	87	435	99	394	449	81
Agriculture	1,430	1,196	291	126	778	282	415	82	138	48
Military	1,300	1,343	370	269	443	241	255	110	111	73
Law, social and behavioral sciences	780	404	550	121	25	153	37	123	65	23

Figure 3.21. AI patent families with a PCT or EP application, by earliest priority year

Patent families containing at least one PCT application have grown by an average 13 percent since 2009

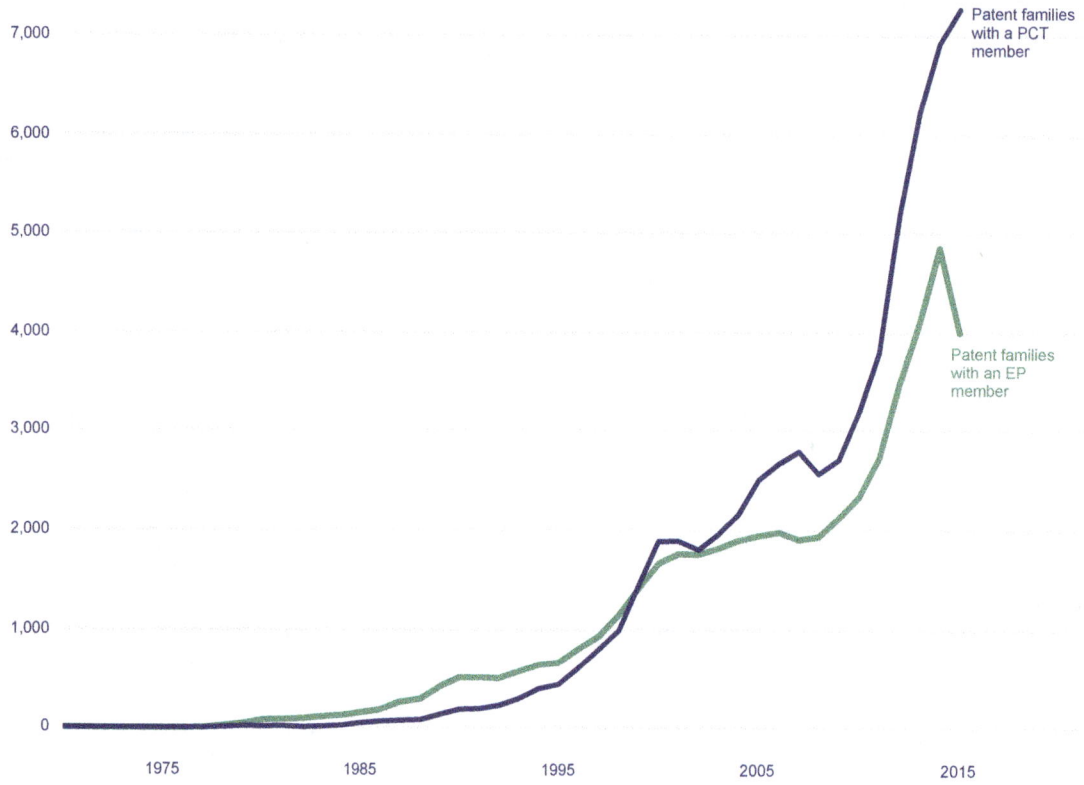

Patent families
with a PCT
member

Patent families
with an EP
member

Percentage of PCT and European applications

The Patent Cooperation Treaty (PCT) and European Patent Convention (EPC) are tools that can be used to apply for a patent in more than one jurisdiction, and therefore are indicators of the international plans of patent applicants.

69,383 (20 percent) of all AI patent families identified in this report include at least one PCT application (see figure 3.21). Based on data drawn from the WIPO Statistics Database, 25 percent of identified AI patent families had a PCT member between 2000 and 2015, compared with 12 percent of patent families across all fields of technology in the same period.

The proportion of PCT applications increased from less than 10 percent before 1995 to a steady 40 percent in the 2000s. Since 2011, this proportion has fallen slightly to an average of 28 percent from 2011 to 2017.

51,397 (15.1 percent) of all the AI patent families identified in this report include a European application (EP). Between 2000 and 2015, 18 percent of AI patent families had an EP member, according to data in the WIPO Statistics Database, compared with 10 percent of patent families across all fields of technology in the same period.

The number of PCT applications is increasing faster than the number of European ones, and since 2009 PCT applications have become more numerous than European applications. The latest ratio is about 1.5 PCT applications for every European one.

Deep learning is a technique that has proven its potential in various functional applications within a short period of only about three years. The growth in scientific publications and the subsequent boom in patent applications that followed just a year later (see figure 3.9 on page 45) suggest an expectation that deep learning will deliver added value to many such applications over the coming few years.

Application fields and techniques

A total of 89,466 patent families simultaneously mention an AI technique and an AI application field. While machine learning is used in every sector, it is cited in particular in patents dealing with life sciences (see figure 3.20, first column). The main machine learning techniques associated with life sciences are supervised learning, support vector machines, bio-inspired approaches, and classification and regression trees. Logic programming approaches are mainly used in the life sciences, telecommunications, and personal devices, computing and HCI fields.

Application fields and functional applications

A total of 152,065 patent families simultaneously mention an AI functional application and an AI application field. Computer vision is used in all application fields, but especially for telecommunications and transportation (see figure 3.20, second row). Some functional applications are particularly associated with application fields. These are:

- Control methods and robotics for transportation applications
- Speech processing and natural language processing for telecommunications and also in the field of personal devices, computing and HCI
- Predictive analytics and natural language processing for business applications
- Natural language processing in the field of document management and publishing
- Planning and scheduling for industry and manufacturing and transportation applications.

Bringing art and science together

The ability to craft a fragrance that leaves a positive impression is quite a talent – one that takes years of experience to develop. Seasoned perfumers have a knack for bringing art and science together, knowing that scent is one of the most important components a consumer considers when forming a positive or negative opinion about everyday products like laundry detergent, deodorant, air freshener and, of course, cologne and perfume. What if AI could learn from fragrance experts and augment their process of crafting new scents? What if it could assist them in identifying novel creative pathways? These were some of the questions that popped up when a group of IBM researchers and skilled perfumers at Symrise, a global producer of flavors and fragrances, got together to explore the possibilities.

Mixing artistic and scientific thought into one big pot resulted in Philyra – an AI product composition system that can learn about formulas, raw materials, historical success data and industry trends. Philyra uses new and advanced machine learning algorithms to sift through hundreds of thousands of formulas and thousands of raw materials, helping identify patterns and novel combinations. As Philyra explores the entire landscape of fragrance combinations, it can detect the whitespaces in the global fragrance market to design entirely new fragrance formulas.

Creating a fine fragrance requires precision, as even the slightest change in the amount of an ingredient can make or break a new perfume. This is why Philyra was developed with a data-driven approach, relying on a database of hundreds of thousands of fragrance-formulas, fragrance families (e.g. fruity or floral), raw fragrance materials and historical information that captures the success of previously designed fragrance formulas. With this wealth of data, Philyra uses machine learning to generate new scent combinations that fit specific design objectives, such as creating a unique fragrance for Brazilian millennials.

Of course, novelty is a major driver when is come to crafting a fragrance. So, Philyra is learning a distance model to identify fragrances that have similar scents to existing commercial fragrances. The larger the difference between the scents, the more novel the perfume is predicted to be.

Philyra demonstrates how AI can assist in domains where creativity is key. The art and science of designing a winning perfume is something humans have explored for hundreds of years. Now perfumers can have an AI apprentice by their side that can analyze thousands of formulas as well as historical data to identify patterns and predict novel combinations that have never been seen on the market before.

AI systems like Philyra can also be applied to designing flavors, cosmetics and consumer products like shampoo or laundry detergent, as well as industrial products like adhesives, lubricants or construction materials. While this is still research today, the technology has the potential to be made available as a service to help any number of businesses accelerate and scale their creative design process.

Case study by IBM Research and Symrise

4 Key players in AI patenting

Key findings

- Companies represent 26 of the top 30 patent applicants. Most of these are conglomerates active in consumer electronics, telecommunications and/or software, as well as sectors such as electric power and automobile manufacturing. Just four of the top 30 are universities or public research organizations.
- IBM has the largest portfolio of AI patents with 8,290 patent applications, followed by Microsoft with 5,930 patent applications.
- Of the top 20 companies, 12 are Japanese.
- The main functional application mentioned by the top companies in their patent applications is computer vision (19 out of 20), though IBM has a greater focus on natural language processing.
- Machine learning is by far the most represented AI technique in the top applicants' portfolios.
- Patent co-ownership is rare: no entity among the top 20 applicants co-owns more than one percent of its AI portfolio, similar to other areas of technology.
- Seven out of the top 20 companies have acquired AI companies. Among them, Alphabet has acquired the largest number (18), while at the same time reducing its patent filing activity over the last several years.

IBM has the largest portfolio of AI patents with 8,290 patent applications, followed by Microsoft with 5,930 patent applications.

China's strong position

Boi Faltings, EPFL

Since AI-related innovations are enabled by data, the organizations that generate the most AI-related patents are often the ones that own the most data. This explains many of the observations, in particular the surprisingly strong position of China – there are far fewer obstacles to collecting vast amounts of data in China than in other countries, and China has the best training data collections for speech recognition, human behavior modeling and medical data, for example. For Western nations to compete, they will have to develop better mechanisms to share and pool data.

- The leading institution among universities/ public research organizations is the Chinese Academy of Sciences (CAS) (ranked 17th in the overall results). Altogether, there are around 100 Chinese institutions in the top 500 patent holders, while 17 out of the top 20 academic players are in China.
- Patenting activity by Chinese universities/ research organizations has seen significant growth (between 20 and 60 percent annually), matching or beating the growth rates of organizations from most other countries.
- As with companies, computer vision is the main functional application mentioned in the patent portfolios of the top universities/ public research organizations. Machine learning and neural networks are the most frequently mentioned AI techniques.
- The top universities/public research organizations make the vast majority of their priority patent filings in their country of origin (Fraunhofer being the main exception, with some priority filings also in the U.S. or via the European Patent route).
- Key players in an area that has seen significant recent growth, namely deep learning, are the Chinese Academy of Sciences (CAS), which is the leader in the deep learning sub-category of machine learning, and Baidu, followed by Alphabet, Siemens, Xiaomi, Microsoft, Samsung, IBM and NEC.

In Chapter 3, we examined some of the broad trends in artificial intelligence (AI) research as revealed by patenting activity and scientific publications. Because patent documents contain details of the patent applicant or patentee (also known as the assignee), it is also possible to identify which companies and organizations are filing the most patents, as well as track trends over time and by geography and category.

This chapter looks in more detail at the activity of the top applicants named in the AI patent families discussed in Chapter 3. These comprise both companies and universities and public research organizations. For the purposes of this research, where relevant, subsidiaries have been grouped under their parent company or institution, based on available public information. Further analysis is provided based on the three areas set out in Chapter 1: AI techniques, AI functional applications and AI application fields.

The top applicants

Figure 4.1 lists the top applicants in the AI field, based on the number of AI-related patent families identified in their portfolio. Companies dominate the list, accounting for 26 of the top 30 applicants, whereas universities and public research organizations account for just four.

Figure 4.1. Top 30 patent applicants by number of patent families

Companies represent 26 of the top 30 AI patent applicants worldwide

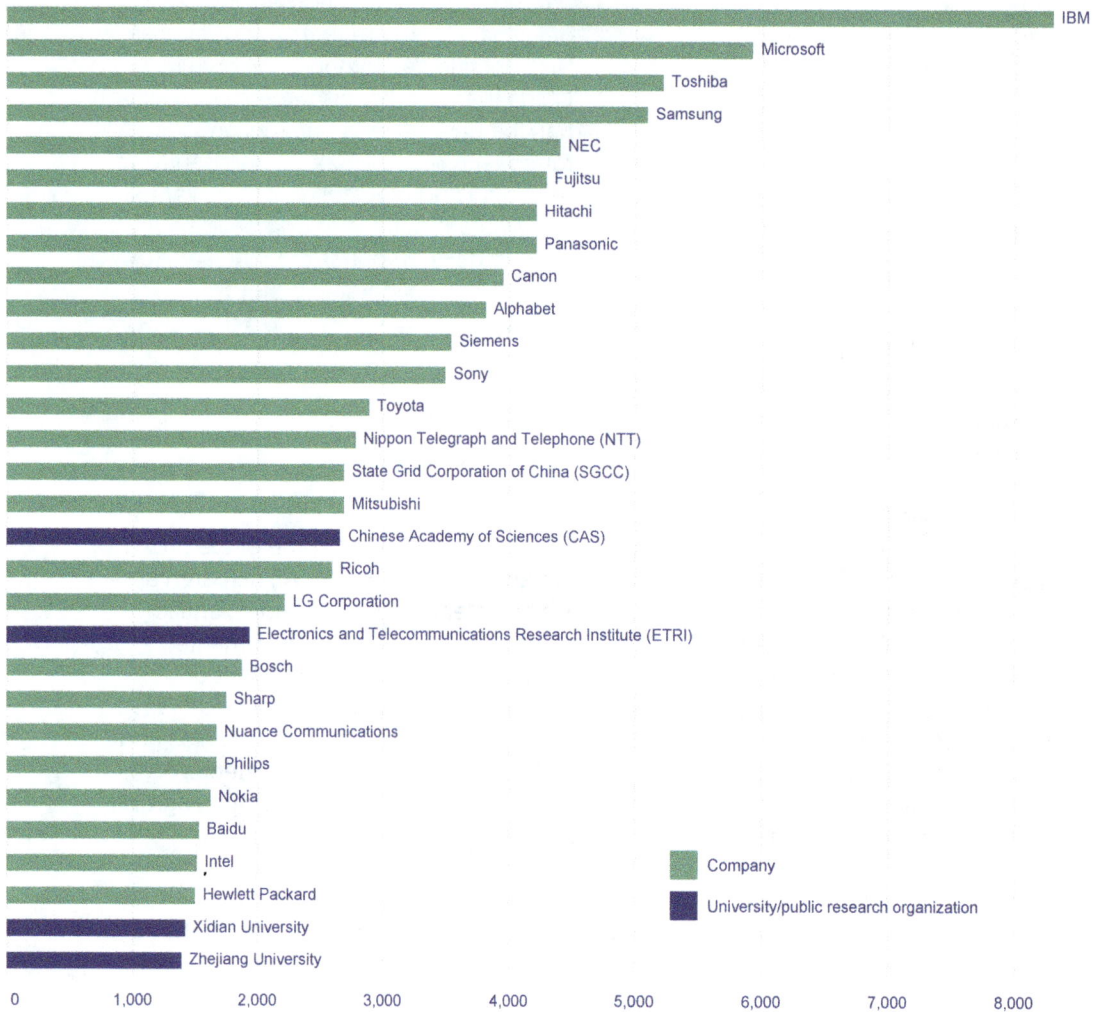

IBM	
Microsoft	
Toshiba	
Samsung	
NEC	
Fujitsu	
Hitachi	
Panasonic	
Canon	
Alphabet	
Siemens	
Sony	
Toyota	
Nippon Telegraph and Telephone (NTT)	
State Grid Corporation of China (SGCC)	
Mitsubishi	
Chinese Academy of Sciences (CAS)	
Ricoh	
LG Corporation	
Electronics and Telecommunications Research Institute (ETRI)	
Bosch	
Sharp	
Nuance Communications	
Philips	
Nokia	
Baidu	
Intel	
Hewlett Packard	
Xidian University	
Zhejiang University	

Legend:
- Company
- University/public research organization

X-axis: 0, 1,000, 2,000, 3,000, 4,000, 5,000, 6,000, 7,000, 8,000

Note: Fujitsu includes PFU; Panasonic includes Sanyo; Alphabet includes Google, Deepmind Technologies, Waymo and X Development; Toyota includes Denso; and Nokia includes Alcatel

Top 20 companies

Most of the companies listed among the top 30 applicants in figure 4.1 are conglomerates active in the consumer electronics, telecommunications and/or software sectors, though there is also one electric utility company (SGCC) and one auto manufacturer (Toyota) included.

Of the top 20 companies, 12 are Japanese conglomerates; however, the two biggest AI portfolios belong to U.S. companies (IBM, with 8,920 patent families, and Microsoft, with 5,930 patent families). The top 20 also includes two companies from the Republic of Korea (Samsung and LG Corporation) and two from Germany (Siemens and Bosch). The portfolios of the top patent applicant companies are examined in more detail below.

Top 20 universities and public research organizations

Out of the top 20 universities and public research organizations in the AI field, the vast majority (17) are in China and the remaining three in the Republic of Korea. The two largest portfolios belong to the Chinese Academy of Sciences (CAS), which ranks 17th in the overall top 30 applicants, and Korean Electronics and Telecommunications Research Institute (ETRI).

Outside of China and the Republic of Korea, there are no universities or public research organizations with more than 500 patent families. Figure 4.2 shows the highest ranked universities and public research organizations in China, the Republic of Korea, the United States of America (U.S.), Japan and Europe. The highest ranked U.S. public organization is the University of California (400 patent families) followed by the U.S. Navy (389), while the National Institute of Advanced Industrial Science and Technology (AIST) is the highest ranked organization in Japan (244) and Fraunhofer (244) the highest ranked in Europe.

China's dominance is further evident if we consider the list of the top 500 applicants:

Five steps to success at the Chinese Academy of Sciences (CAS)

Hefa Song, CAS

1. Clarification of the objectives of intellectual property (IP) creation and application through the formulation and implementation of an intellectual property strategy. In 2007, the Chinese Academy of Sciences (CAS) issued "Several Opinions on Further Strengthening the Work of Intellectual Property Rights," the first in a series of policies and regulations.

2. Building an IP work system. The Intellectual Property Management Office was established in the Science and Technology Promotion and Development Bureau, and in 2016 the number of patent applications reached 14,881.

3. Vigorously carrying out IP training and information. Since 2008, 16,000 people have been trained and at the end of 2016, CAS had 1,891 people engaged in IP management, transfer and service.

4. Strengthening AI technology innovation through IP rights. CAS has established a number of AI research institutions, resulting in the following patent applications from 2008 to 2018: machine learning 715, computer vision 417, natural language processing 246, and speech processing 203.

5. Strengthening the transformation of scientific and technological achievements. From 2008 to 2016, CAS transferred and transformed 7,000 IP assets (transfer, license, self-implementation, price-for-share, technology development and technical services) with a contract value of more than RMB12 billion.

China is represented by more than 100 institutions; the U.S. and the Republic of Korea each have around 20, while Japan and Europe have four each (see figure 4.3).

Figure 4.2. Top patent applicants among universities and public research organizations in selected locations, by number of patent families

CAS (China) and ETRI (Republic of Korea) rank first and second in patent filings among universities and public research organizations

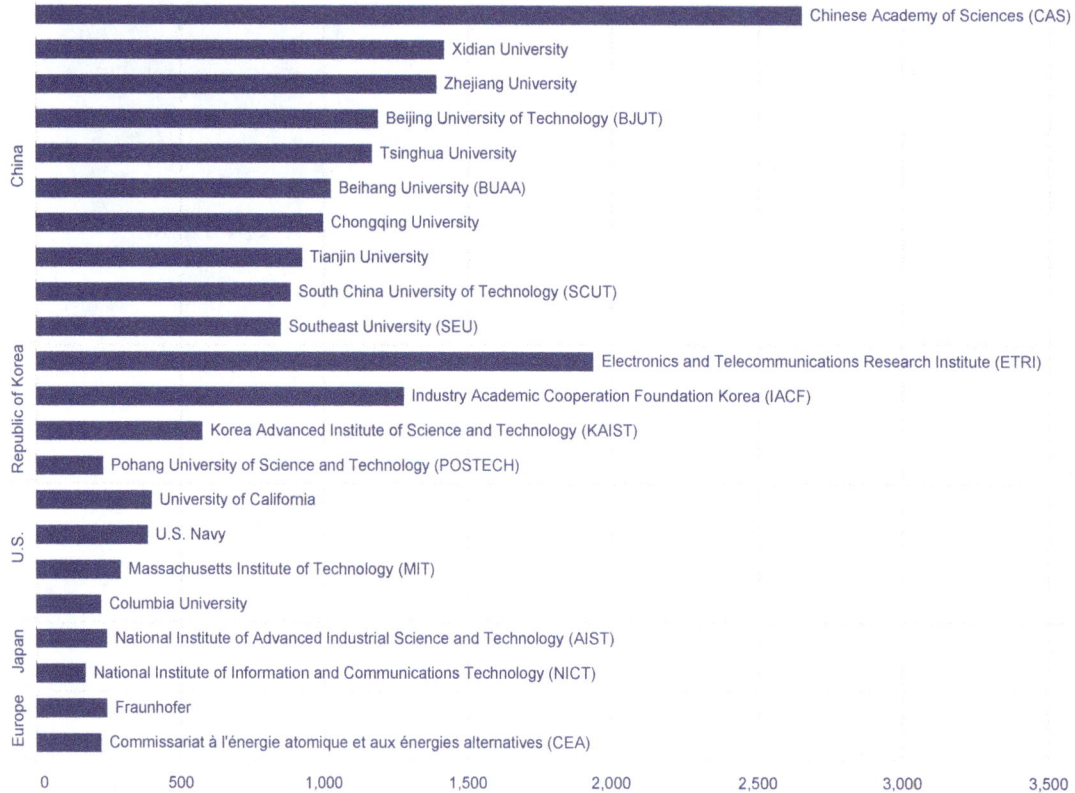

Figure 4.3. Geographical origin of universities and public research organizations in the top 500 patent applicants, by number of organizations

Chinese universities and public research organizations account for more than one-fifth of the top 500 patent applicants

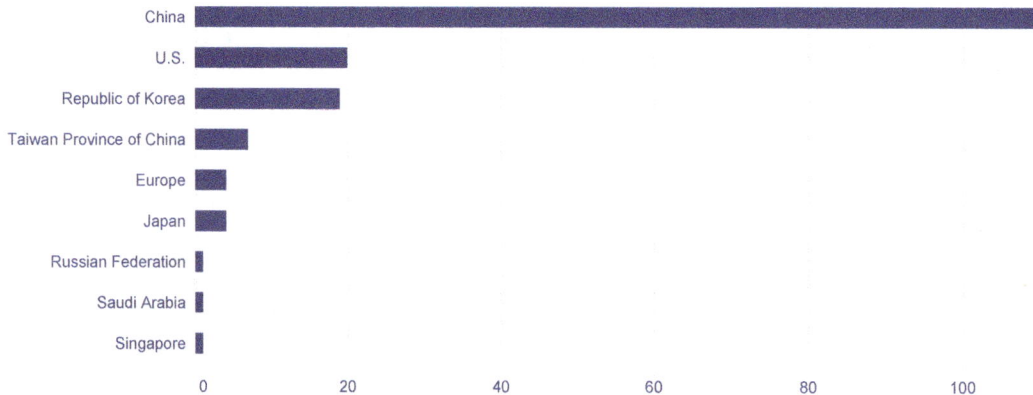

Scientific publications – top 20

The large number of scientific publications attributed to universities and public research organizations in the top 20 is in contrast to the small number of universities and public research organizations among the top patent applicants (see figure 4.4). China again dominates the list, with 10 out of the top 20 public research institutions being Chinese and the Chinese Academy of Science (CAS) ranking first. Among the remaining top 20 public research organizations, one is Japanese and two Singaporean; unlike the respective top patent applicants list, there are six U.S. public research organizations and one French one featuring among the top 20 organizations. This shows that U.S. and French public research organizations have greater scientific publication activity than patenting activity.

Top applicants by category

The top players in the AI patent collection can be further analyzed using the scheme set out in Chapter 1, providing insight into the leading companies and universities and public research organizations in each category. For access to data on the top 20 players across all categories and sub-categories, see www.wipo.int/tech_trends/en/artificial_intelligence.

_____AI techniques

AI techniques includes 25 categories and sub-categories. IBM leads in 10 of these, and, in general, companies rank top in most categories. In rule learning, all of the top 20 entities are companies. Nonetheless, universities and public research organizations dominate certain AI techniques, in particular support-vector machines, bio-inspired approaches, unsupervised learning and instance-based learning.

Figure 4.5 shows the top two applicants in each AI technique category and sub-category. The largest portfolios mentioning any kind of machine learning techniques belong to IBM (3,566) and Microsoft (3,079): each of these companies account for almost twice as many patent families as the next applicant in this field (CAS with 1860 patent families). Based on the background data, other major portfolios dealing with any kind of machine learning are owned by conglomerates active in information technology or consumer electronics (e.g., NEC, NTT, Hitachi and Samsung) and by Chinese universities (e.g., CAS and Xidian University).

The topic of neural networks is central to the field of machine learning, and the largest portfolios explicitly naming this technology belong to Siemens and SGCC (with 677 and 650 patent families, respectively). However, no clear leader emerges and most of the top AI players listed in Figure 4.1 possess more than 300 patent families in this field. Microsoft (with 1,039 patent families), Alphabet and IBM (both with 731) own the largest patent portfolios mentioning supervised learning techniques. Microsoft and IBM (with 492 and 431 patent families, respectively) are the top two applicants in probabilistic graphical models. Support vector machines, unsupervised learning and bio-inspired approaches

Figure 4.4. Top 20 universities and public research organizations producing AI scientific publications, by number of articles

10 of the top 20 organizations in AI scientific publications are in China, six in the U.S., two in Singapore and one each in Japan and France

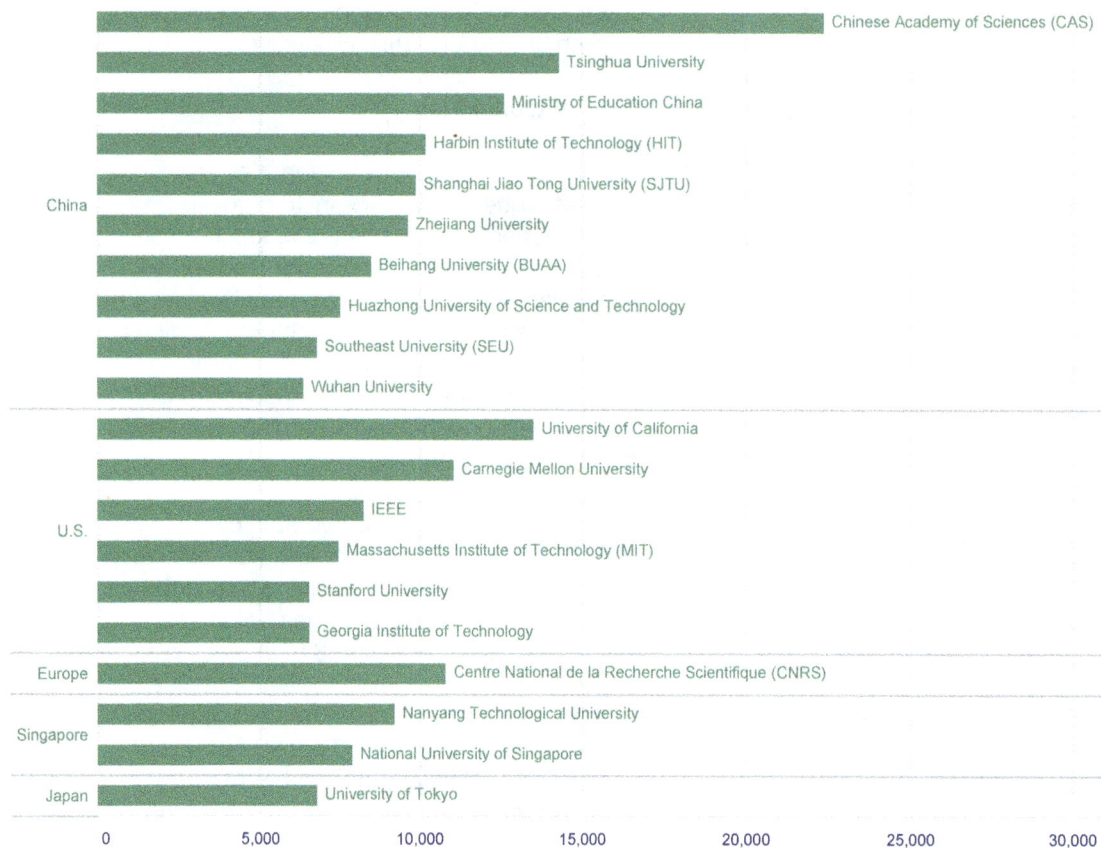

Figure 4.5. Top two patent applicants for each AI technique category and sub-category by number of patent families

IBM and Microsoft rank first and second in most AI techniques

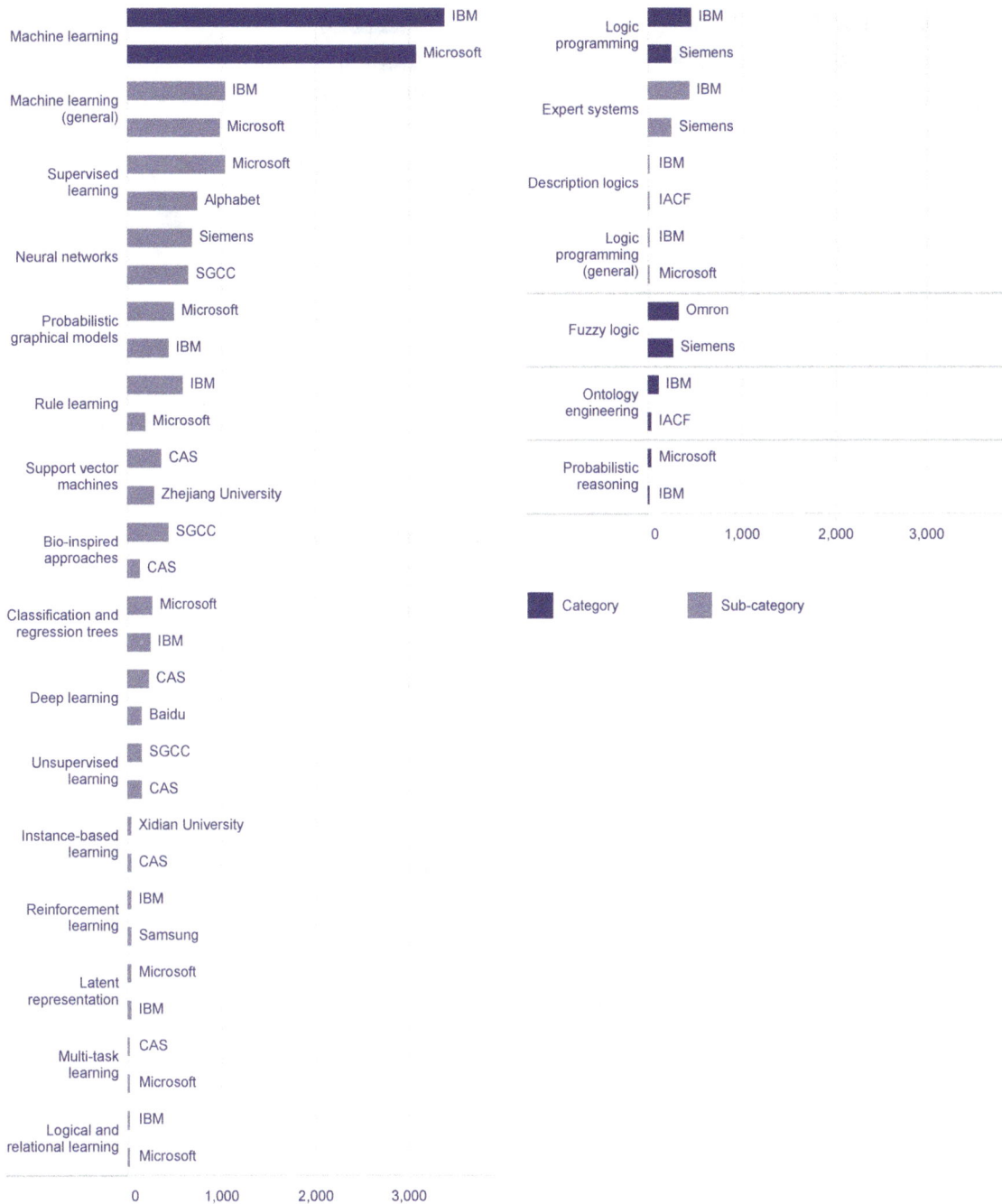

Note: A patent may refer to more than one category or sub-category

Figure 4.6. Top two patent applicants for each AI functional application category and sub-category by number of patent families

Different companies feature as top patent applicants across AI functional application categories and sub-categories

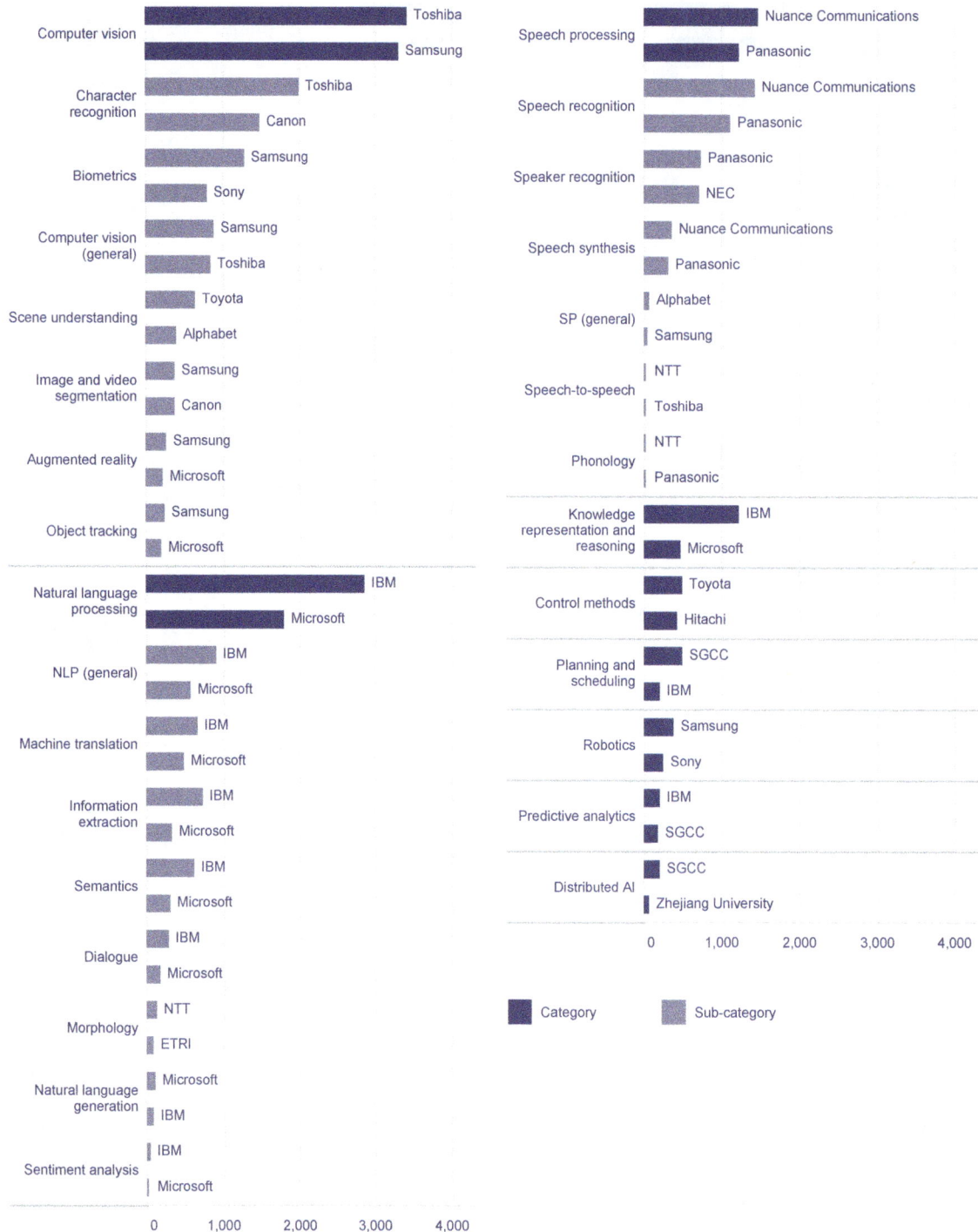

Category | Sub-category

Note: A patent may refer to more than one category or sub-category

are topics mainly mentioned in Chinese universities' portfolios.

The CAS possesses the largest patent portfolio explicitly dealing with deep learning techniques (with 235 patent families), and most of the significant portfolios in this field are held by Chinese universities (e.g., Zhejiang University, Xidian University and South China University of Technology). Some companies own quite large portfolios in the field, namely Baidu, ranking second in the deep learning category, followed by Alphabet, Siemens, Xiaomi, Microsoft, Samsung, IBM and NEC. Omron owns the largest portfolio involving fuzzy logic techniques (with 330 patent families), while logic programming (expert systems) and rule learning technologies are led by IBM (with 440 and 581 patent families, respectively).

AI functional applications

Figure 4.6 shows the top two applicants in each of the 31 AI functional applications categories and sub-categories. In general, there is a greater diversity among the leading players compared with AI techniques, though IBM is once again dominant, leading in nine of the categories and sub-categories. Companies lead in most areas, and account for all of the top 20 players in control methods and knowledge representation and reasoning. Universities and public research organizations lead in distributed AI.

Based on the background analysis conducted for this report, Japanese and Korean companies active in consumer electronics, imaging, telephony and software (i.e., Toshiba, Samsung, Canon, Fujitsu and NEC) dominate the largest functional application, computer vision. Two research institutes, CAS and ETRI, one Chinese, the other Korean, also possess portfolios of more than 1,000 patent families mentioning computer vision. Samsung leads four out of six computer vision sub-categories (namely biometrics, image and video segmentation, augmented reality and object tracking). Toyota leads in scene understanding (with 640 patent families), while Toshiba is top for character recognition (with 1,988 patent families).

IBM and Microsoft possess by far the largest portfolios involving natural language processing. Alphabet comes third, followed by Toshiba and Fujitsu. IBM is also the leading company for knowledge representation and reasoning (with more than 1,200 patent families).

In control methods, the largest patent portfolios belong to companies, including a number active in the transportation field (e.g., Toyota, Bosch, Honda, Ford and General Motors). Nuance Communications owns the largest patent portfolio dealing with speech processing applications (with 1,776 patent families). The other major players possessing more than 800 patent families in the field, are Panasonic, Microsoft, NEC, Toshiba, NTT, Sony, Samsung, IBM and Alphabet.

The landscape looks very different in patent filings related to distributed AI, predictive analytics and planning and scheduling, which are mainly owned by Chinese universities and public research organizations.

AI application fields

A similarly diverse range of organizations characterizes the top 20 players for AI

Figure 4.7. Top two patent applicants for each AI application field by number of patent families

Specialized companies dominate in their business sector

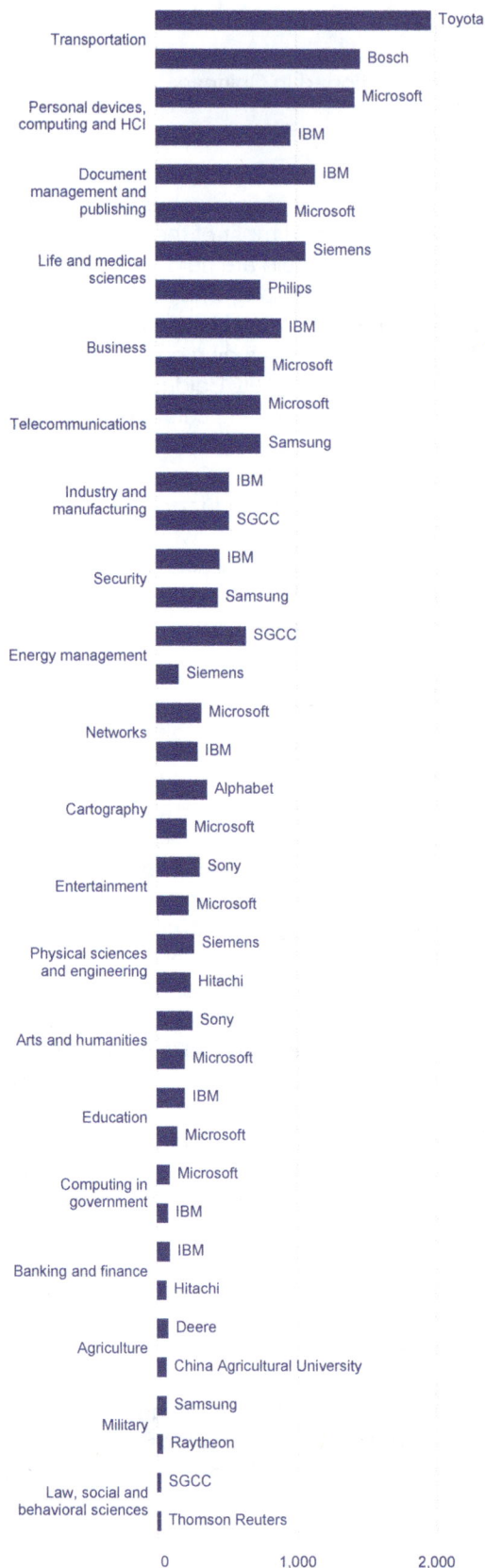

Note: A patent may refer to more than one category

application fields, which we can examine by industry sector. Companies outnumber universities and public research organizations in every application field identified. In many categories there are no universities and public research organizations identified among the top 20 patentees. The categories in which universities and public research organizations feature most prominently are neuroscience/neurorobotics (10 of the top 20) and smart cities (eight of the top 20). Figure 4.7 shows the top two applicants in each AI application field.

The field of telecommunications is dominated by companies. Microsoft leads in the telephony and computer networks/internet sub-categories (with 457 and 315 patent families, respectively), as well as VoIP and videoconferencing (with 32 patent families each). Samsung, however, leads in radio and television broadcasting (with 428 patent families). Other prominent players in telecoms are Nokia, LG and Sony.

In transportation, the largest portfolios belong to auto manufacturers or suppliers from Asia or Europe (including Toyota, Bosch and Hyundai). Alphabet and IBM also possess large portfolios mentioning transportation-related applications. Toyota leads in the sub-categories of autonomous vehicles (with 1,387 patent families), transportation or traffic engineering (with 1,013 patent families) and driver or vehicle recognition (with 677 patent families). Boeing is the main patenting player with 236 patent families in aerospace/avionics, the transportation sub-category with the highest average growth rate in the period 2013–2016, as identified in Chapter 3.

The largest portfolios dealing with life and medical sciences belong to multinational companies also active in medical technology (Siemens, Philips and Samsung), while universities and public research organizations (such as CAS, University of California and Zhejiang University) are also represented among the top 20 players. University and public research organizations are particularly active in neurosciences and neurorobotics, accounting for 10 of the top 20 players. Tianjin University is ranked first in this field with 45 patent families.

Universities lead in neurorobotics

Dario Floreano, EPFL

The current dominance of patent applications in neurorobotics from universities indicates the birth of a new field that will most likely translate in products in the near future as governmental agencies regulate the public adoption of these promising technologies.

Microsoft, IBM and Samsung have filed the largest number of patent families for personal devices, computing and human–computer interaction (HCI). Affective computing is a recent trend, and no clear leader has yet emerged. Young companies specialized in this field, such as Affectiva, possess patent portfolios comparable in size to those of larger companies such as Samsung and Microsoft.

Looking at security applications, IBM leads in three sectors (with 266 patent families in cybersecurity, 120 in anomaly detection and surveillance and 107 in privacy/anonymity). However, Samsung is top for authentication (with 385 patent families) and Microsoft leads in cryptography (with 91 patent families), followed by BBK Electronics (which ranks 46th on the overall patent corpus).

Business applications are dominated by IBM and Microsoft. Alphabet and Verizon also show a strong patenting activity in this field, along with Toshiba and Alibaba (all of the patents being mainly for e-commerce purposes).

Familiar industry names are at the top of many of the other categories. IBM and Microsoft lead document management and publishing, with 1,145 and 933 patent families, respectively. Other players are mainly active in the field of consumer electronics. Patents related to industry and manufacturing applications are mainly owned by IBM (with 528 patent families) and SGCC (with 518 patent families), and to a lesser extent Siemens.

Networks applications (including social networks, Internet of things (IoT) and smart cities applications) is led by Microsoft (with 328 patent families), followed by IBM and Alphabet.

Figure 4.8. Average annual growth rate in patent families filed by top companies for the period 2013–2016

The number of patent families filed by SGCC grew on average by 70 percent annually, while other big companies had a decreasing patent filing rate

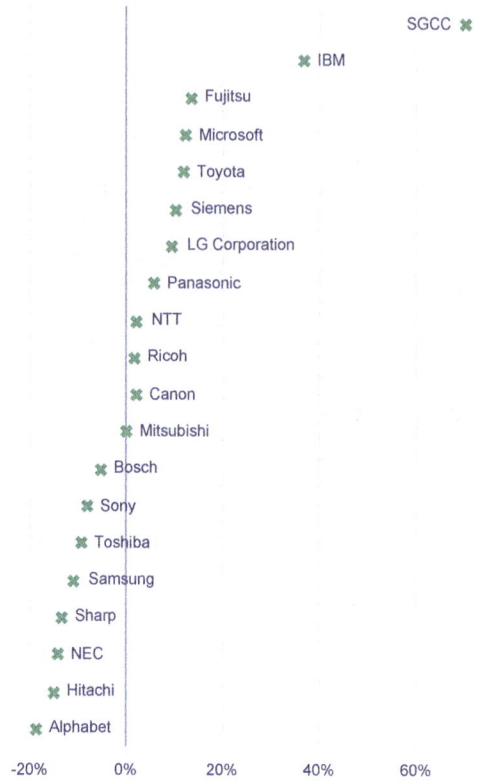

SGCC ✖
✖ IBM
✖ Fujitsu
✖ Microsoft
✖ Toyota
✖ Siemens
✖ LG Corporation
✖ Panasonic
✖ NTT
✖ Ricoh
✖ Canon
✖ Mitsubishi
✖ Bosch
✖ Sony
✖ Toshiba
✖ Samsung
✖ Sharp
✖ NEC
✖ Hitachi
✖ Alphabet

-20%   0%   20%   40%   60%

Figure 4.9. Top patent applicants by AI application field

Companies established in specific industries hold top positions in many AI application fields

	Transportation	Personal devices, computing and HCI	Telecommunications	Document management and publishing	Life and medical sciences	Security	Business	Industry and manufacturing	Physical sciences and engineering	Energy management	Arts and humanities	Networks	Education	Cartography	Entertainment	Computing in government
Alphabet	333	709	593	521	119	206	463	61	53	18	163	241	67	361	55	38
Bosch	1,469	137	185	17	129	184	14	58	230	155	9	13	25	21	10	3
Canon	56	293	195	496	380	118	56	50	33	15	89	28	31	11	11	18
Fujitsu	299	200	253	326	401	351	173	110	55	25	73	54	66	8	22	34
Hitachi	735	306	338	270	447	297	168	199	256	141	98	61	90	23	13	37
IBM	424	1,050	759	1,223	553	486	935	546	112	43	150	308	215	184	82	81
LG Corporation	451	409	524	71	113	212	94	49	57	93	84	43	15	9	13	10
Microsoft	278	1,438	754	944	319	377	780	192	155	22	209	332	151	218	236	96
Mitsubishi	501	130	179	119	171	121	50	88	148	94	42	45	49	17	17	14
NEC	190	203	438	351	368	317	197	105	69	51	97	58	63	21	17	47
NTT	42	72	273	177	129	107	61	27	23	21	55	57	36	14	11	22
Panasonic	487	323	494	251	322	261	115	96	101	97	145	53	80	21	45	31
Ricoh	163	176	134	367	55	72	95	81	22	6	62	44	24	10	7	24
Samsung	538	922	755	265	595	446	183	131	165	140	176	135	73	42	62	44
SGCC	184	160	374	43	158	322	194	518	36	646	6	148	14	114	1	55
Sharp	88	153	142	203	92	54	21	28	33	7	74	14	35	7	8	16
Siemens	415	268	458	170	1,127	293	60	266	323	164	51	58	58	39	11	31
Sony	209	495	538	196	372	299	194	46	85	34	267	88	106	67	314	32
Toshiba	286	336	274	439	390	161	232	132	108	142	158	73	37	12	12	50
Toyota	1,987	169	198	14	188	92	26	36	267	173	40	30	80	31	15	19

Note: A patent may refer to more than one category. Highlighted text refers to the top category for each applicant.

Social network patents are also owned by Facebook, Verizon and Tencent. In the other two technological categories (Internet of things (IoT) and smart cities), no player has filed more than 100 patents so far.

The State Grid Corporation of China is the clear leader in energy, with 647 patent families, and some Chinese universities also appear in the top 20 for energy. Cartography (containing localization and positioning technologies) is led by Alphabet, Microsoft and IBM.

Companies active in electronic entertainment (such as Sony, Microsoft, Konami, Nintendo and Disney) possess fairly large AI-related patent portfolios in the entertainment category, along with other players active in the consumer electronics sector.

Chinese universities are most active in computing applications for governmental matters, while specialized companies dominate agriculture and military: Deere, Husqvarna, China Agricultural University and CNH for agriculture, and Raytheon, Lockheed Martin and BAE Systems for military. None of these companies has more than 100 patent families, however.

Top applicants' portfolios analyzed

This section focuses on the patent portfolios of the top applicants, analyzing filing trends, the content of portfolios, co-ownership and acquisition and geographical coverage.

_____ Top company patent applicants: filing trends

Although IBM and Microsoft are the two applicants with the biggest portfolios, the Chinese state-owned electric utility company SGCC enjoyed the greatest growth from 2013 to 2016 with a remarkable 70 percent growth rate (see figure 4.8). While in general most companies show significant increases in filing activity since 2012, a few are stable or even decreasing. This might, however, simply indicate the impact of different business strategies: for example, filings by Alphabet itself declined in

that period, but Alphabet has acquired 18 other AI companies since 2009 (see below).

We can also look at where particular companies are active, based on keywords or classification symbols. The application fields most often mentioned in the top applicants' portfolios are document management and publishing, personal devices, computing and HCI, telecommunications, transportation, life and medical sciences and security.

Because most of the top applicants are major companies active in numerous industrial sectors, they possess patent portfolios spanning a wide area of applications (see figure 4.9). Patent filing in different sectors is linked to the companies' intellectual property (IP) strategy which may or may not lead to disclosure of a technology and/or the nature of the technology involved. However, some applicants have more specialized patent portfolios (as can be seen from figure 4.9 and also based on the top players patent portfolio analysis conducted as a background for this report, data for which is available at www.wipo.int/tech_trends/en/artificial_intelligence), such as:

- Microsoft (personal devices, computing and human-computer interaction (HCI), 24 percent of the company's AI portfolio)
- SGCC (energy management, 23 percent)
- Siemens (life and medical sciences, 32 percent)
- Mitsubishi (transportation, 19 percent)
- LG (telecommunications, 24 percent)
- Bosch (transportation, 78 percent)
- Toyota (transportation, 69 percent).

Less common application fields are mentioned by some of the top applicants. These include:

- Cartography (which includes geolocation-related technologies) and networks (which includes smart-city and social network applications) by Alphabet
- Arts and humanities (which includes applications related to music) by Sony
- Industry and manufacturing by SGCC.

Within telecommunications, all the major players (Microsoft, Samsung, IBM, LG,

Figure 4.10. Top patent applicants by AI functional application

IBM has a strong focus on natural language processing, contrary to other top patent applicants who focus principally on computer vision

	Computer vision	Speech processing	Natural language processing	Control methods	Knowledge representation and reasoning	Robotics	Planning and scheduling	Predictive analytics	Distributed AI
Alphabet	1,568	839	924	176	200	77	40	108	2
Bosch	687	92	51	285	20	46	30	11	0
Canon	3,282	587	420	17	35	36	15	8	2
Fujitsu	2,727	608	640	105	176	56	46	35	10
Hitachi	2,310	526	373	449	202	88	137	53	4
IBM	2,683	1,133	2,962	151	1,213	48	209	214	8
LG Corporation	1,362	549	177	224	2	195	13	10	4
Microsoft	2,428	1,076	1,809	33	461	46	130	171	9
Mitsubishi	1,441	589	207	225	96	64	49	36	3
NEC	2,778	1,094	569	79	255	45	48	78	9
NTT	1,336	962	472	38	131	25	23	40	8
Panasonic	2,726	1,316	406	218	75	76	32	27	3
Ricoh	1,993	341	318	42	32	24	16	9	0
Samsung	3,365	935	509	351	84	370	65	55	5
SGCC	567	39	358	5	8	51	480	186	160
Sharp	1,086	332	396	61	15	29	11	8	4
Siemens	1,792	374	207	292	125	148	139	52	14
Sony	2,477	977	436	96	112	236	37	48	5
Toshiba	3,417	1,013	641	300	177	62	82	75	10
Toyota	1,394	507	84	493	47	105	44	23	5

Note: A patent may refer to more than one category
Highlighted text refers to the top category for each applicant

Figure 4.11. Top patent applicants by AI technique

Machine learning represents over 92 percent of all top applicants' patent families

	Machine learning	Logic programming	Fuzzy logic	Ontology engineering	Probabilistic reasoning
Alphabet	1,801	70	53	19	7
Bosch	298	28	81	1	0
Canon	584	46	48	2	2
Fujitsu	1,070	85	78	17	3
Hitachi	1,302	213	246	7	2
IBM	3,566	444	172	114	27
LG Corporation	271	17	30	1	0
Microsoft	3,079	214	106	31	30
Mitsubishi	917	100	161	1	2
NEC	1,314	157	72	7	1
NTT	1,294	55	15	1	1
Panasonic	1,057	82	151	1	3
Ricoh	502	37	41	0	4
Samsung	1,257	101	88	15	2
SGCC	1,770	246	126	3	0
Sharp	329	25	19	1	1
Siemens	1,689	277	305	19	9
Sony	923	27	21	4	1
Toshiba	1,229	207	141	6	0
Toyota	582	8	48	0	1

Note: A patent may refer to more than one category
Highlighted text refers to the top category for each applicant

Alphabet, Panasonic, Sony, etc.) have filed numerous patents related to telephony. In transportation, Toyota has filed a large number of patents related to autonomous vehicles as well as transportation and traffic engineering and driver or vehicle recognition. Siemens is the major player in life and medical sciences among the top 20 and clearly leads in medical imaging and monitoring of physiological parameters.

The main functional application present in all the top applicants' portfolios is computer vision (see figure 4.10). It is the main functional application in 19 of the 20 largest AI portfolios, with the notable exception of IBM, which focuses more on natural language processing (36 percent of its AI portfolio, compared with 32 percent for computer vision).

Some portfolios have a strong focus on other functional applications:

- Speech processing: Toshiba, Panasonic, LG
- Natural language processing: IBM, Sharp
- Control methods: Bosch, Siemens, Mitsubishi, LG, Toyota
- Planning and scheduling: SGCC
- Robotics: Sony
- Knowledge representation and reasoning: NEC
- Information extraction: IBM, Fujitsu, SGCC.

Machine learning is the main AI technique, and it is by far the most represented AI technique in the top applicants' portfolios (see figure 4.11). Neural networks, the main framework for machine learning, is also frequently mentioned in the top applicants' portfolios. Some specific machine learning techniques are explicitly cited in a large proportion of several of the top applicant's portfolios:

- Supervised learning: IBM, Microsoft, Alphabet
- Probabilistic graphical models: Microsoft, Panasonic, Siemens
- Rule learning: IBM
- Bio-inspired approaches: SGCC
- Support vector machines: SGCC
- Expert systems represent a large proportion of the portfolios of: IBM, SGCC and Siemens.

What is the most critical thing to bring AI from research to the market?

Boi Faltings, EPFL

Data is owned by large corporations and cannot be accessed for research and the new services that result. Innovation could be dramatically accelerated if these corporations were forced to share access to this data on fair terms.

_____ Co-ownership and acquisitions

The co-ownership of patents can be obtained from patent data, if patent applications have more than one assignee.

From this, the data suggests that co-ownership of patent families is rare in the top applicants' portfolios: no entity among the top 20 applicants co-owns more than one percent of its AI portfolios. Co-ownership occurs most frequently between companies from the same country, while co-ownership with universities or public institutions is marginal; Samsung, SGCC, Sony and NTT are the only companies that share ownership with such organizations to any significant extent.

Seven of the top 20 companies have acquired AI companies: Alphabet, Canon, IBM, Microsoft, Panasonic, Samsung and Siemens. Of these, Alphabet has acquired the most, with 18 acquisitions since 2009, including six since 2016, spanning sectors from computer vision to task management. Other companies to have made a number of acquisitions include Microsoft (nine), IBM (five) and Samsung (four). Acquisitions are explored further in Chapter 6.

_____ University and public research organization filing trends

This section focuses on the patent portfolios of the top university and public research organization applicants, analyzing filing trends, the content of portfolios, co-ownership and geographical coverage. To give a broad geographical scope, the universities and public research organizations considered are the top 10 Chinese public organizations, plus the top four from the Republic of Korea and the U.S., and the top two from Japan and Europe.

Figure 4.12. Patent applications for top corporate patent applicants by office of filing

Most of the top applicants file patents across the top patent offices

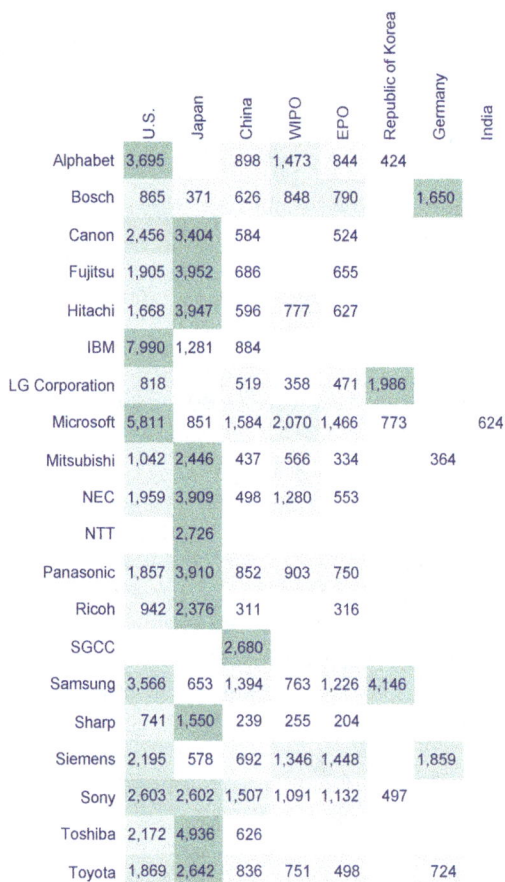

	U.S.	Japan	China	WIPO	EPO	Republic of Korea	Germany	India
Alphabet	3,695		898	1,473	844	424		
Bosch	865	371	626	848	790		1,650	
Canon	2,456	3,404	584		524			
Fujitsu	1,905	3,952	686		655			
Hitachi	1,668	3,947	596	777	627			
IBM	7,990	1,281	884					
LG Corporation	818		519	358	471	1,986		
Microsoft	5,811	851	1,584	2,070	1,466	773		624
Mitsubishi	1,042	2,446	437	566	334		364	
NEC	1,959	3,909	498	1,280	553			
NTT		2,726						
Panasonic	1,857	3,910	852	903	750			
Ricoh	942	2,376	311		316			
SGCC			2,680					
Samsung	3,566	653	1,394	763	1,226	4,146		
Sharp	741	1,550	239	255	204			
Siemens	2,195	578	692	1,346	1,448		1,859	
Sony	2,603	2,602	1,507	1,091	1,132	497		
Toshiba	2,172	4,936	626					
Toyota	1,869	2,642	836	751	498			724

Note: EPO is the European Patent Ofiice. WIPO represents PCT applications.

Figure 4.13. Average annual growth rate in patent families filed by top universities and public research organizations, 2013–2016

Chinese universities and public research organizations all have growth of more than 20 percent

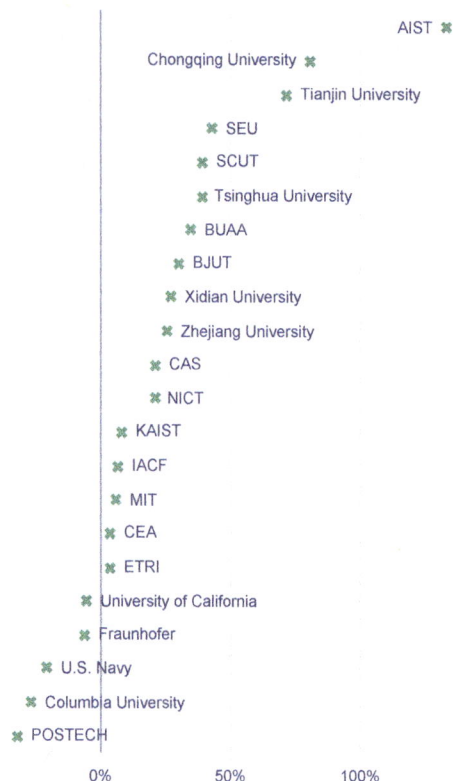

AIST ✳
Chongqing University ✳
✳ Tianjin University
✳ SEU
✳ SCUT
✳ Tsinghua University
✳ BUAA
✳ BJUT
✳ Xidian University
✳ Zhejiang University
✳ CAS
✳ NICT
✳ KAIST
✳ IACF
✳ MIT
✳ CEA
✳ ETRI
✳ University of California
✳ Fraunhofer
✳ U.S. Navy
✳ Columbia University
✳ POSTECH

0%   50%   100%

Geographical distribution of filing by top patent applicants

Figure 4.12 shows the geographical distribution of patent filings by top patent applicants for selected patent offices. The data suggests that these applicants file principally in the country in which they are domiciled. Nonetheless, most exhibit significant international patent filing activity, with the U.S. the most popular target for patent filing by foreign applicants. Microsoft uses as many as seven major offices of filing including India, while over 50 percent of patent families filed by Bosch, Canon, Samsung, Siemens, Sony and Toyota have more than one member, indicating that the majority of their patent applications have been filed at more than one office. In contrast, the two top patent applicants, namely NTT and SGCC, file almost exclusively in their home countries, with over 98 percent of their patent activity being located in Japan and China, respectively.

The total number of filings of the top Chinese and Korean universities and public research organizations is high compared with the U.S., Japanese and European institutions (see figure 4.2). AIST (Japan) had the highest average annual growth rate, however it only filed five patents in 2016. The filing activity of Chinese organizations continues to grow, with each organization having an average annual growth rate of more than 20 percent from 2013 to 2016 (see figure 4.13).

Other organizations with a positive growth rate include KAIST (Republic of Korea, up 9 percent) and the National Institute of Information and Communications Technology (NICT) (Japan, up 21 percent). The filing rates of the other organizations listed are either stable or declining.

Machine learning and neural networks are the most frequently mentioned AI techniques, as they are in the top companies' portfolios (see figure 4.14). Supervised learning and support-vector techniques are also frequently mentioned in the university and public research organizations' portfolios. Deep learning is explicitly mentioned in more than 5 percent of portfolios only for Chinese entities such as CAS, Xidian University, Tsinghua University, Chongqing University, Tianjin University and South China University of Technology. Bio-inspired approaches and probabilistic graphical models are also strongly cited in the top portfolios.

Turning to AI functional applications, computer vision is dominant for all the organizations listed, except for NICT in Japan, where natural language processing predominates (see figure 4.15). Computer vision is almost the only functional application cited in the portfolio of Xidian University and predominant for Beijing University of Technology (BJUT). Natural language processing is the second ranked functional application in the vast majority of the top universities and public research organizations.

Some organizations included in figure 4.15 have a particular specialization in certain functional applications:

Universities and industry in China

Haifeng Wang, Baidu

Research in AI technologies in Chinese universities is now catching up with their top-class peers worldwide. For some AI techniques, the gap between Chinese universities and research institutions and other AI giants is becoming smaller and smaller; and for some functional applications, we have made great progress and may be a few steps ahead of other key players. Behind these results is a continuous growth of the AI talent pool in China thanks to the efforts of AI-related enterprises such as Baidu working with Chinese universities to accelerate technological innovation and talent cultivation. Chinese universities, research institutions and companies are working closely together to conduct AI-related research and make the resulting technology transfer smooth, by for example implementing AI talent training programs and setting up cooperative laboratories.

- Information extraction (CAS, Tsinghua University, Southeast University (SEU), Industry Academic Cooperation Foundation of Korea (IACF), KAIST, POSTECH, NICT)
- Control methods (Beihang University (BUAA), U.S. Navy, CEA)
- Knowledge representation and reasoning (U.S. Navy, Columbia University, AIST)
- Planning and scheduling (Zhejiang University, Tsinghua University, Beihang University (BUAA), Southeast University (SEU))
- Predictive analytics (Zhejiang University, Chongqing University, Southeast University (SEU)
- Robotics (South China University of Technology (SCUT))

The two main application fields mentioned in the top university and public research organization portfolios are transportation and life and medical sciences (see figure 4.16). Exceptions to this rule include Zhejiang University (with 176 patent families in industry and manufacturing), Xidian University (with 107 in telecommunications), and NICT (with 41 in document management and publishing).

Figure 4.14. Top patent applicants among universities and public research organizations by AI technique

CAS ranks first in patenting across most AI techniques, except for ontology engineering (IACF) and probabilistic reasoning (AIST and Zhejiang University)

	Machine learning	Logic programming	Fuzzy logic	Ontology engineering	Probabilistic reasoning
CAS	1,860	128	62	14	3
Xidian University	1,066	8	54	0	2
Zhejiang University	1,129	60	48	8	4
BJUT	897	47	53	7	1
Tsinghua University	866	43	35	6	2
BUAA	750	53	54	6	2
Chongqing University	761	41	56	10	0
Tianjin University	740	22	41	1	1
SCUT	661	32	39	1	1
SEU	641	28	57	2	0
ETRI	599	82	13	28	2
IACF	516	32	31	35	1
KAIST	245	28	12	26	1
POSTECH	99	11	0	9	0
University of California	234	5	33	0	0
U.S. Navy	171	17	21	1	0
MIT	165	12	6	1	0
Columbia University	135	14	2	0	1
AIST	135	6	1	1	4
NICT	117	4	0	0	0
Fraunhofer	104	5	12	1	0
CEA	75	6	8	0	0

Note: A patent may refer to more than one category
Highlighted text refers to the top category for each applicant

Figure 4.15. Top patent applicants among universities and public research organizations by AI functional application

NICT has a strong focus on natural language processing, contrary to other top universities and public research organizations, which instead focus on computer vision

	Computer vision	Natural language processing	Speech processing	Planning and scheduling	Predictive analytics	Control methods	Robotics	Distributed AI
CAS	1,364	399	206	94	117	62	67	33
Xidian University	1,036	59	11	29	36	13	16	53
Zhejiang University	533	166	36	84	111	69	46	72
BJUT	529	152	35	87	50	71	68	37
Tsinghua University	466	160	79	70	57	34	23	23
BUAA	418	108	18	62	42	77	31	36
Chongqing University	402	92	32	53	58	21	30	41
Tianjin University	430	57	17	47	38	31	6	24
SCUT	443	71	67	63	40	25	74	30
SEU	254	64	34	96	53	28	33	38
ETRI	1,108	487	468	35	27	78	105	12
IACF	619	204	95	29	40	67	56	2
KAIST	293	114	61	10	11	15	35	2
POSTECH	120	62	61	5	5	8	10	1
University of California	175	25	25	6	12	7	12	2
U.S. Navy	215	11	20	10	2	40	12	6
MIT	134	9	26	6	7	21	13	0
Columbia University	98	33	16	11	5	4	3	0
AIST	88	20	57	1	2	5	6	0
NICT	55	98	61	1	0	2	5	0
Fraunhofer	148	8	39	2	5	14	16	2
CEA	129	6	1	6	4	18	12	1

Note: A patent may refer to more than one category
Highlighted text refers to the top category for each applicant

Figure 4.16. Top patent applicants among universities and public research organizations by AI application field

Life and medical sciences and transportation are the two predominant AI application fields for many top universities and public research organizations

	Life and medical sciences	Transportation	Telecommunications	Security	Industry and manufacturing	Personal devices, computing and HCI	Document management and publishing	Physical sciences and engineering	Energy management	Networks	Computing in government	Business	Cartography	Arts and humanities	Education
CAS	308	208	222	170	88	93	124	60	36	82	66	35	93	38	38
Xidian University	94	89	107	81	36	22	22	3	5	32	36	10	13	11	7
Zhejiang University	164	124	103	34	176	65	59	44	33	36	26	24	19	18	13
BJUT	123	208	99	72	70	59	63	29	22	23	36	16	25	15	13
Tsinghua University	111	122	102	63	100	52	49	34	55	25	21	14	23	13	9
BUAA	79	256	81	58	51	35	39	30	10	26	24	6	20	7	13
Chongqing University	96	154	139	67	57	34	18	40	61	44	43	32	20	11	5
Tianjin University	113	54	61	46	50	35	26	24	42	22	18	14	11	10	7
SCUT	94	99	88	48	75	70	20	20	43	24	34	25	13	16	19
SEU	67	174	98	36	59	26	17	15	88	27	26	22	23	5	5
ETRI	120	188	175	119	30	135	109	22	8	29	19	50	28	47	36
IACF	204	183	122	60	45	53	60	60	16	42	23	49	12	19	28
KAIST	74	45	59	51	10	36	50	22	7	24	8	21	7	11	19
POSTECH	9	22	8	5	1	14	10	6	2	0	3	5	1	4	18
University of California	197	31	68	33	9	48	12	85	5	9	9	14	5	5	8
U.S. Navy	28	65	19	13	12	28	6	22	3	6	4	1	9	7	2
MIT	102	30	35	16	14	25	8	46	7	3	3	7	6	8	7
Columbia University	72	25	16	22	14	23	28	22	8	6	2	9	2	3	1
AIST	55	14	25	4	14	11	17	21	0	3	1	8	1	14	8
NICT	11	2	17	3	1	2	41	2	0	7	1	0	1	26	4
Fraunhofer	47	34	30	14	17	15	5	25	9	3	2	4	2	6	5
CEA	65	29	19	12	8	6	8	18	30	1	1	0	4	3	2

Note: A patent may refer to more than one category. Highlighted text refers to the top category for each applicant.

Figure 4.17. Patent applications for top patent applicants among universities and public research organizations by office of filing

Universities and public research organizations from Europe, the U.S. and Japan file applications across many jurisdictions

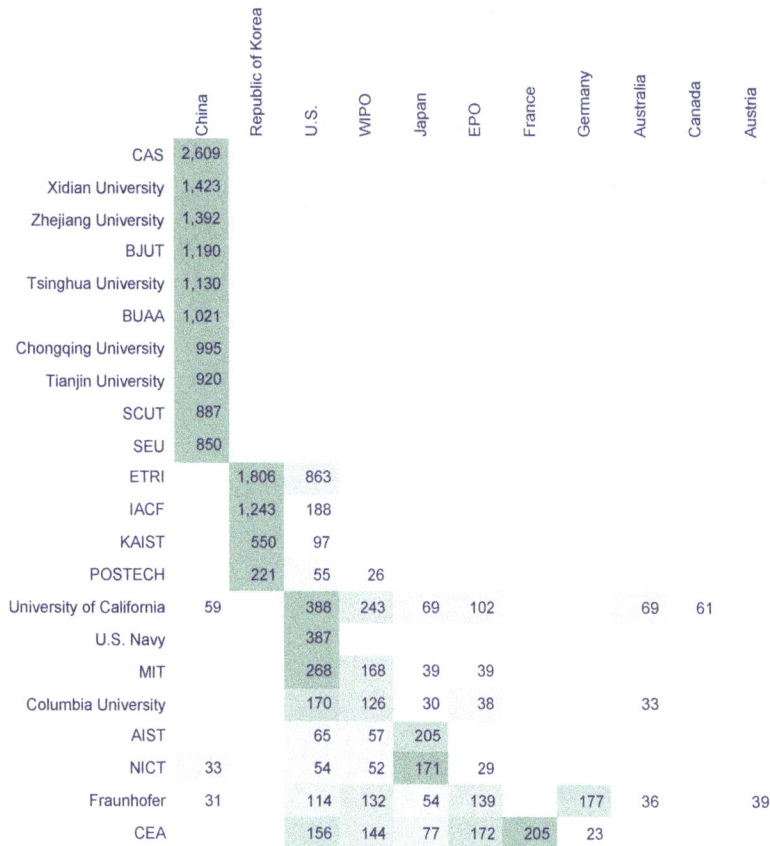

	China	Republic of Korea	U.S.	WIPO	Japan	EPO	France	Germany	Australia	Canada	Austria
CAS	2,609										
Xidian University	1,423										
Zhejiang University	1,392										
BJUT	1,190										
Tsinghua University	1,130										
BUAA	1,021										
Chongqing University	995										
Tianjin University	920										
SCUT	887										
SEU	850										
ETRI		1,806	863								
IACF		1,243	188								
KAIST		550	97								
POSTECH		221	55	26							
University of California	59		388	243	69	102			69	61	
U.S. Navy			387								
MIT			268	168	39	39					
Columbia University			170	126	30	38			33		
AIST			65	57	205						
NICT	33		54	52	171	29					
Fraunhofer	31		114	132	54	139		177	36		39
CEA			156	144	77	172	205	23			

Note: EPO is the European Patent Office. WIPO represents PCT applications.

Geographical distribution of filing by top universities and public research organizations

Figure 4.17 shows the geographical distribution of patent filings by top universities and public research organizations for selected patent offices. Similar to other top patent applicants, universities and public research organizations tend to make the majority of their patent filings in their country of origin. In contrast though, universities and public research organizations have generally lower international patent filing activity, in particular those located in China and the U.S. Navy, which file nearly exclusively in their home country. Notable exceptions to this rule include the Fraunhofer Institute, which has significant filing activity at eight major offices, and the French Alternative Energies and Atomic Energy Commission (CEA), with over 90 percent of its patent families having more than one member, indicating that the vast majority of its patent applications have been filed at more than one office.

The top universities and public research organizations make the vast majority of their priority patent filings in their country of origin.

Transportation is the main application field mentioned in six of the top 10 Chinese universities and public research organizations' portfolios and in two of the top four in the Republic of Korea. The top U.S. universities and public research organizations (University of California, MIT and Columbia University) focus mainly on life and medical sciences, though they also file numerous patent applications in the physical sciences and engineering. The top two Japanese organizations (AIST and NICT) have strong portfolios in life sciences and telecommunications, but also in arts and humanities, a pattern that is unique among the top universities and public research organizations. In Europe, the top two organizations are strong in life and medical sciences and transportation, with a specialization in industry and manufacturing for Fraunhofer (with 17 patent families), and energy management for CEA (with 30 patent families).

_____ Co-ownership

As in the portfolios of those companies most prolific in filing AI patents, co-ownership of patent families is relatively rare among the universities and public research organizations most active in this field. Where there are co-owners, they are mostly industrial companies originating from the same country as the university or public research organization. SGCC co-owns patent families with most of the top Chinese universities and public research organizations, while Samsung co-owns patent families with several organizations in the Republic of Korea, as well as with the University of California. Co-ownership of patents among U.S. universities and public research organizations is typically shared with healthcare institutions (such as Massachusetts General Hospital and National Institutes of Health).

Improving agriculture with AI and IoT

When most people think of groundbreaking digital technology, they don't picture soil sensors. But a farmer who knows the temperature, pH, and moisture level of their soil can make all sorts of informed decisions that save money and boost yield. Microsoft's FarmBeats project aims to provide an end-to-end approach to enable data-driven farming and help farmers make better decisions.

Data, coupled with the farmer's knowledge and intuition about their farm, can help increase farm productivity, and also help reduce costs. The data generated by FarmBeats is a game changer. A farmer can use up to 30 percent less water for irrigation and 44 percent less lime to control soil pH. Information on soil temperature and moisture levels can help better time the planting of seeds, so the farmer gets a more productive harvest. Because a farm is often located next to a river, flooding is a problem. FarmBeats' aerial imaging capabilities precisely document flooding patterns, so a farmer is able to better plan what they plant where.

However, getting data from a farm can be extremely difficult since there is often no power in the field, or Internet in the farms; in the United States, 20 percent of people living in rural areas don't have access to even the slowest broadband speeds. A key innovation of FarmBeats is in how sensors transmit data. Most farm data systems require expensive transmitters to connect, but FarmBeats relies on a clever workaround: it uses TV white space. White spaces are unused TV broadcast spectrum. If you've ever watched an old TV, you've seen white spaces before. They're the "snow" you'll sometimes see while flipping through channels. These gaps in spectrum are plentiful in the remote areas where most farms are located, so data can be sent over them the same way that data gets transmitted via broadband.

The whole FarmBeats system is powered by solar panels. You place a small number of sensors – one every couple hundred meters, instead of 10 meters – in the ground. You then attach your smart phone with the camera facing down to either a drone (if you have money to spare) or a helium balloon (if you don't). You walk around the fields with the camera, creating an aerial map of the farm. Data from both the sensors and the phone are transmitted via TV white space to your computer, where an edge device uses machine learning algorithms to stitch images and sensor values together into a data map. The machine learning pipeline can then use the resulting maps to make predications on soil temperature and moisture levels for the entire farm.

Microsoft's goal is thus to enable data-driven farming. The FarmBeats team believes that the AI-enabled technology will give farmers around the world the tools they need to significantly increase global food production in a context of limited arable land and water.

Case study by Microsoft

5 Geography of patent filings

For Western nations to compete, they will have to develop better mechanisms to share and pool data.

Boi Faltings, EPFL

Key findings

- The first patents related to AI were filed with the Japanese patent office at the beginning of the 1980s. In following years, the number of filings in Japan stagnated, while filings in the U.S. and, later, in China increased.
- China and the U.S. are now leading research in the field of AI in applied as well as more fundamental research, based on analysis of both patent filing data and scientific publications.
- In 2014, the number of first filings in China surpassed that of the U.S. However, only four percent of patents first filed in China are subsequently filed in another jurisdiction.
- Other major patent offices receiving patent filings in the AI field are France, Germany, the Republic of Korea and the U.K., while India is emerging as a new target for patent filing.
- The European Patent route is mainly used by European applicants to seek protection in several countries directly from first patent filing, but also by U.S. patent applicants, whereas the PCT route is used mainly by applicants in the U.S., Japan and China.
- One-third of applications are filed with two or more offices. The main office of second filing is the International Bureau of the World Intellectual Property Organization (WIPO), followed by the United States Patent and Trademark Office (USPTO) and the European Patent Office (EPO).
- China and the U.S. lead in patent filings in all AI techniques and functional applications, though their predominance is challenged by Japan, in the categories of fuzzy logic, computer vision and speech processing, and the Republic of Korea, in ontology engineering.
- China and the U.S. also lead in patent filings in all AI application fields, challenged only by Japan (arts and humanities, document management and publishing) and the Republic of Korea (military applications).

Geographical distribution of patent filings

One way to evaluate trends in AI is to look at those jurisdictions where most patenting activity is taking place. Patents are governed by laws providing protection in given territory. Each jurisdiction has a patent office responsible for examining and granting patents. There are also some regional systems, such as the route established by the European Patent Convention (EPC), administered by the European Patent Office (EPO), which grant patents covering more than one country. By comparing trends in national/regional offices, we can identify where most AI patents are being filed, and also look more closely at the trends in AI techniques, functional applications and application fields, track changes over time and see whether these filings come from resident or non-resident applicants. Similarly, we can look at scientific publications and, based on their authors' affiliations, where they came from.

Patents granted by a patent office are only valid in that jurisdiction. Often, but not always, a patent applicant will file first in their home jurisdiction. In many cases, particularly where the invention is expected to have a broad application or considerable value, the patent applicant may choose to file further applications for the same invention in other jurisdictions (also known as subsequent patent filings). The route under the Patent Cooperation Treaty (PCT), administered by WIPO, is a mechanism that facilitates extension to multiple jurisdictions. Where filings in different jurisdictions relate to the same invention, they are referred to as members of a patent family. The office of first filing refers to the office where the application is first filed, and the office(s) of second filing refers to any patent office where protection may subsequently be sought.

This chapter looks at data on where AI patent filing is taking place, including both office of

AI in Europe

Paul Nemitz,
European Commission

Europe has world-class researchers, laboratories and startups in the field of AI. The EU is also strong in robotics and has world-leading transport, healthcare and manufacturing sectors that need to develop and adopt AI applications to remain competitive. However, fierce international competition requires coordinated action for the EU to be at the forefront of AI development and use. For this purpose, the European Commission has presented a Strategy for AI in Europe, which it pursues in coordination with Member States.

first filing and the offices of subsequent filings (offices of second filing), before then looking closer into the patterns in office filings. This information can provide valuable insight into which countries and regions are perceived as an already important or potential market. For a number of applicants, foremost from the public sector, the office of first filing may coincide with the patent office located where research takes place or where the applicants see a market, mainly when there is one single patent application filed, not to be followed by subsequent ones; moreover, this jurisdiction may coincide with the headquarters of a company or the area where the patent attorney team is based; or it could even be linked to the patent grant process and practice of a certain patent office that the applicant may wish to explore first. In addition, information is included on the distribution of patent filings among resident or non-resident applicants at these patent offices.

In summary, the International Bureau of WIPO and the EPO are mainly used as extension offices and have shown considerable growth in the last several years. The China patent office shifted in about 2007 from being an office of second filing for inventors overseas, to an office of first filing for Chinese inventors, and is growing fast. The Republic of Korea has followed a similar trend to China since about 2003. The U.S. office has followed a more established path, with a parallel increase in its use as an office of first and second filing, with first filings generally ahead due to

Figure 5.1. Number of patent applications by patent office (top) and number of scientific publications by geographical affiliation (bottom)

AI research and patent protection for AI-related inventions occurs around the world

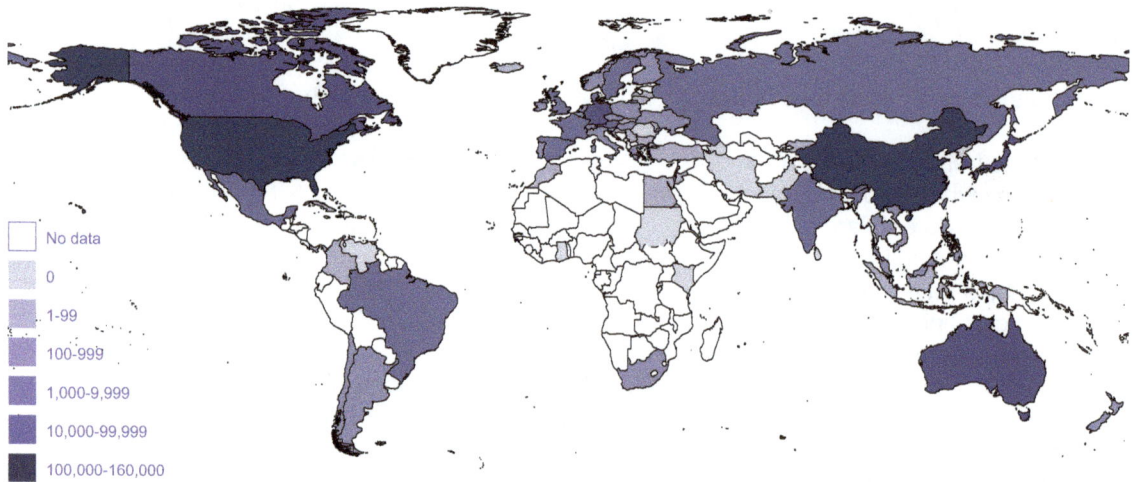

Legend (top map):
- No data
- 0
- 1-99
- 100-999
- 1,000-9,999
- 10,000-99,999
- 100,000-160,000

Note: The color is based on the number of patent applications filed at patent offices

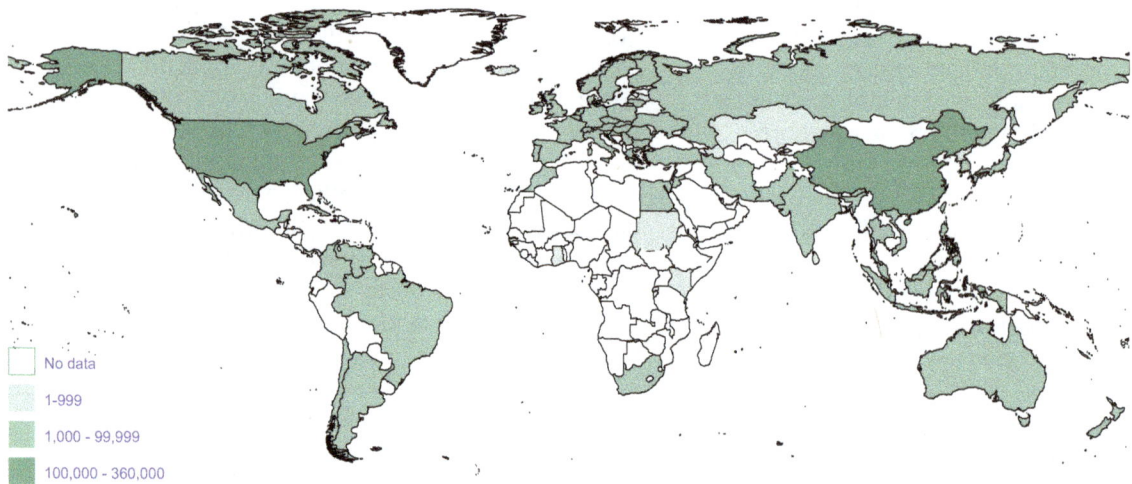

Legend (bottom map):
- No data
- 1-999
- 1,000 - 99,999
- 100,000 - 360,000

Note: The color is based on the number of scientific publications by location of entities authors are affiliated with

The role of IP policy in the knowledge economy

Seth G. Benzell and Erik Brynjolfsson, MIT Initiative on the Digital Economy

Technology has allowed us to overcome the biological limits on the concentration of power inherent in the limits of the human eyes, ears and brains. But given the economics of digital information and processing power, it may be up to IP law to create new limits on centralization. In today's economy knowledge is power, and IP policymakers are important power brokers.

the large community of AI inventors in that country. Japan is perhaps the most interesting example as it has followed an almost opposite path to China, and appears to be used more as an office of second filing than an office of first filing.

_____Top offices of filing

Most filings are made at the United States of America (U.S.) and China patent offices (see figure 5.1 (top) and figure 5.2). Both combine a high number of innovations in AI and potential as a market for AI-related inventions. PCT filings represent 20 percent of the total results. By comparison, figure 5.1 (bottom) shows the geographical distribution of AI-related scientific publications. Over 300,000 publications have been published by organizations in China (341,833 scientific publications) and the U.S. (327,880). Both these countries have more than three times the number of scientific publications than the U.K., which with 96,359 scientific publications is ranked third.

_____Office trends compared

The patent offices of China and the U.S. show the most dynamic trends in filings but for different reasons: the majority of filings in China are made by Chinese patentees (whose applications have been increasing exponentially in recent years), while U.S. filings are either a first filing or a second filing (i.e., considered as an improtant market by organizations in other juridsdictions).

The results from AI-related filings in China correspond to the overall patent filing trends observed in China, as shown in different WIPO statistics and patent analysis reports, and analyzed in a related paper by Fink (2013).

Some other jurisdictions show a less dynamic but nonetheless still growing number of filings, in particular Japan and the EPO, where the growth in patent filings has notably increased in recent years (see figure 5.3). Germany is the only office to show a decrease between 2000 and 2010, but filings have increased again since 2010.

The low numbers of filings for Germany may be due to the fact that applicants prefer to use the EPO to secure protection in Germany.

Offices of first filing: geographical distribution

_____Top offices of first filing

Looking at first filings, the top 10 main offices account for 97 percent of all AI patent filings (with 328,935 patent families) and the top four offices (China, Japan, Republic of Korea and the U.S.) together account for 86 percent of the total of first filings for all patent families (see figure 5.4).

Further analysis can be made by looking at the data relating to granted, cited or extended patent families (see figure 5.5). If at least one patent in a family has been granted, it could be seen as a validation by independent patent

Figure 5.2. Overall number of patent applications by patent office

The greatest number of patent applications are filed in the patent offices of U.S. and China, followed by Japan, while WIPO and the EPO are also often used

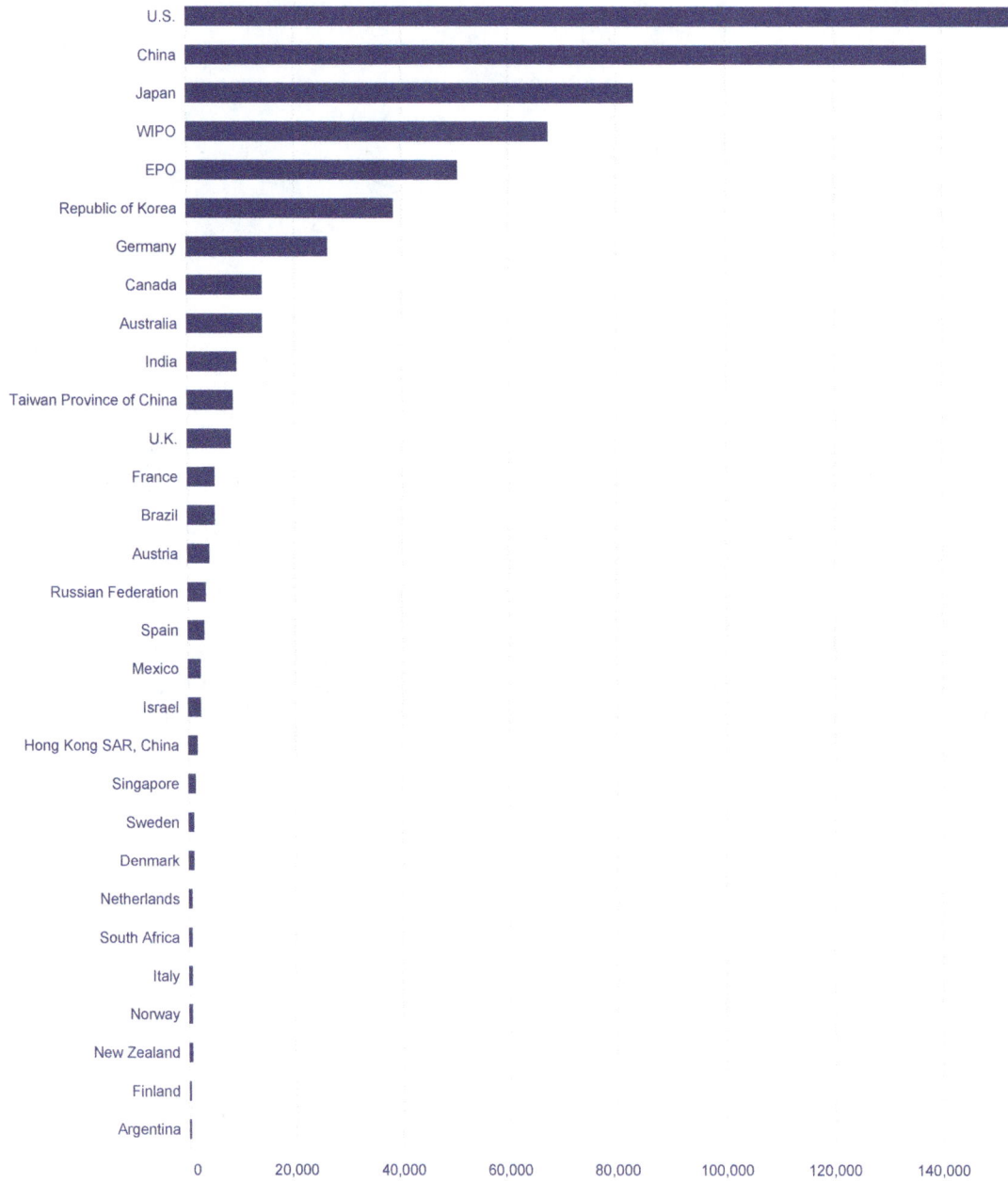

U.S.	
China	
Japan	
WIPO	
EPO	
Republic of Korea	
Germany	
Canada	
Australia	
India	
Taiwan Province of China	
U.K.	
France	
Brazil	
Austria	
Russian Federation	
Spain	
Mexico	
Israel	
Hong Kong SAR, China	
Singapore	
Sweden	
Denmark	
Netherlands	
South Africa	
Italy	
Norway	
New Zealand	
Finland	
Argentina	

0   20,000   40,000   60,000   80,000   100,000   120,000   140,000

Note: EPO is the European Patent Office. WIPO refers to PCT applications.

Figure 5.3. Number of patent applications for different offices by earliest priority date

The number of patent applications filed in China grew by an average of 25 percent since 2009

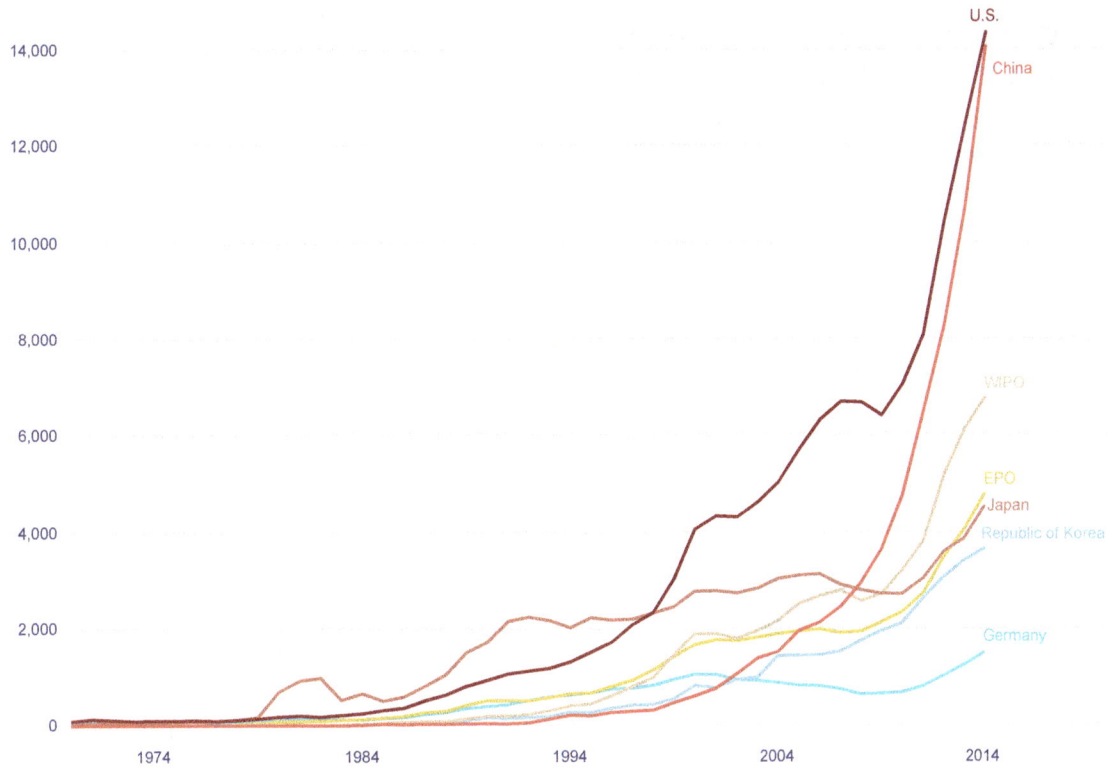

Note: EPO is the European Patent Office. WIPO refers to PCT applications.

Figure 5.4. Number of first filings by patent office

China and the U.S. are the patent offices which are most frequently chosen as offices of first filing, followed by the patent offices of Japan and the Republic of Korea

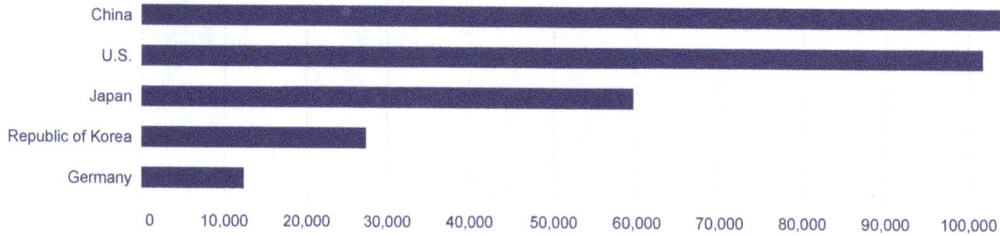

Figure 5.5. Number of families with at least one granted member and highly cited families by patent office and extension share for top patent offices of first filing

The highest number of patent families with at least one grant and highly cited patent families are filed at the patent offices of the U.S. and Japan

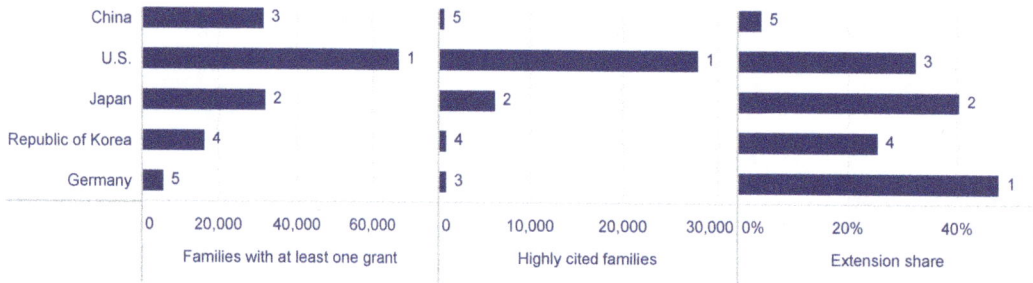

AI in Japan

**Rosalind Picard,
MIT Media Laboratory**

I'm not surprised by Japan's leadership
in AI – it has long been a leader in
AI, especially dominant in humanoid
robotics, which require AI for all
their social–emotional interactions.
Japan has been strong for decades
in speech, vision, HCI and other core
AI technologies.

China's data advantage

Frank Chen, Andreessen Horowitz

Right now, your money goes further in
China than in the U.S. For instance, let's
say you invested $10 million into a small
AI company. In the U.S., the company
would spend $2 million of that money
on labeling data, whereas in China, that
effort might take a quarter or a tenth of
the cost. You get much more through-
put for your $10 million investment. Over
the next 10 years we will have parallel
ecosystems in AI: one in Silicon Valley
and in one China. It will be interesting to
see which one pulls ahead.

examiners of the novelty and inventiveness
of the invention for which patent protection
is being sought. Citation of patent families
(in this case, where the patent is mentioned
at least 20 times in later published patents)
indicates the impact of the invention on
later inventions. Citations are often used as
a means of finding key patents in a certain
field, although one has to bear in mind that
older patents tend to have more citations than
recent ones, and that there are different types
of citations, including the self-citations of
patent applicants which do not have the same
importance and should not be considered
when estimating the impact of a patent.
Extension of patents (i.e., extension share) to
several patent offices provides an indication
of both the desire of the patent applicant
to commercialize the invention in multiple
markets and the market size.

Considering these three criteria, the ranking
of offices of first filing changes dramatically.
Whereas China ranks first in number of patent
families, its ranking falls markedly when only
granted/highly cited/extended patent families
are considered: just 4 percent of patents first
filed in China are subsequently filed in other
jurisdictions, compared with from 25 to 63
percent in all other offices; and when the data
in figure 5.5 are considered as a percentage
of filings, China ranks last among these five
offices with regards to families with at least

one granted patent, and last based on the
number of citations.

Although there are many factors that could go
toward explaining these figures, one reason for
the high percentage of applications filed only
in China could be that Chinese applicants are
more interested in the domestic rather than
overseas market. However, the low rate of
citations and grants could also be explained by
the fact that many Chinese patents related to
AI have been filed more recently than those in
other jurisdictions.

The strengths of other geographical areas can
also be identified:

- The U.S. ranks first in highly cited patent families.
  This indicates that inventions made in this country
  have a great impact. It may also reflect a general
  tendency toward a high number of citations in
  U.S. patents, which increases the chances of
  U.S. applicants being cited in other U.S. patents
  (including self-citations).
- Around 60 percent of patent applications
  first filed in the patent offices of the United
  Kingdom (U.K.) and France are subsequently
  filed in other jurisdictions (i.e., have more
  than one patent family member).
- The U.S. patent office has the largest
  number of patent families including at least
  one granted member, with double that of
  China and Japan combined.

Figure 5.6. Number of first filings for selected patent offices by earliest priority year

China is the top office of first filing, overtaking the U.S., with an average annual growth rate of 29 percent since 2006

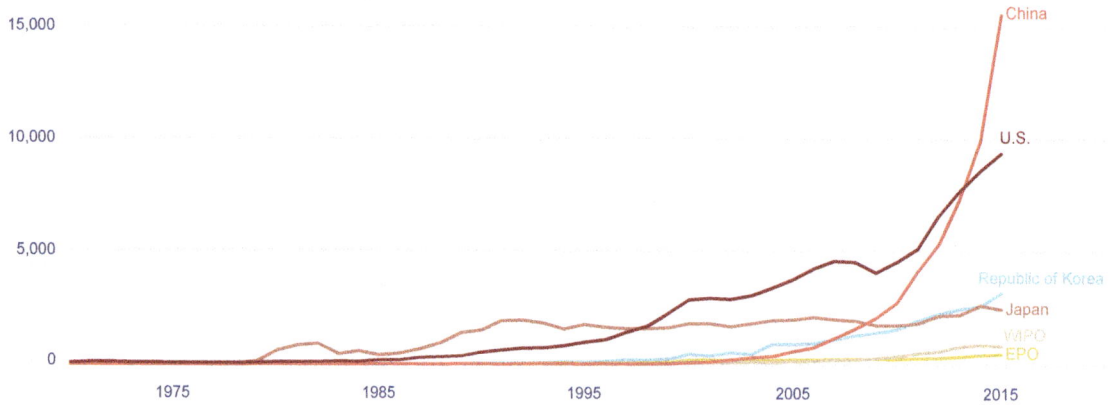

Note: EPO is the European Patent Office. WIPO refers to PCT applications.

Figure 5.7. Scientific publications for top geographical locations of entities authors are affiliated with, compared to patent families filed in that location

The U.S., China and Japan account for a larger share of patent families than scientific publications, in contrast to most other geographical territories

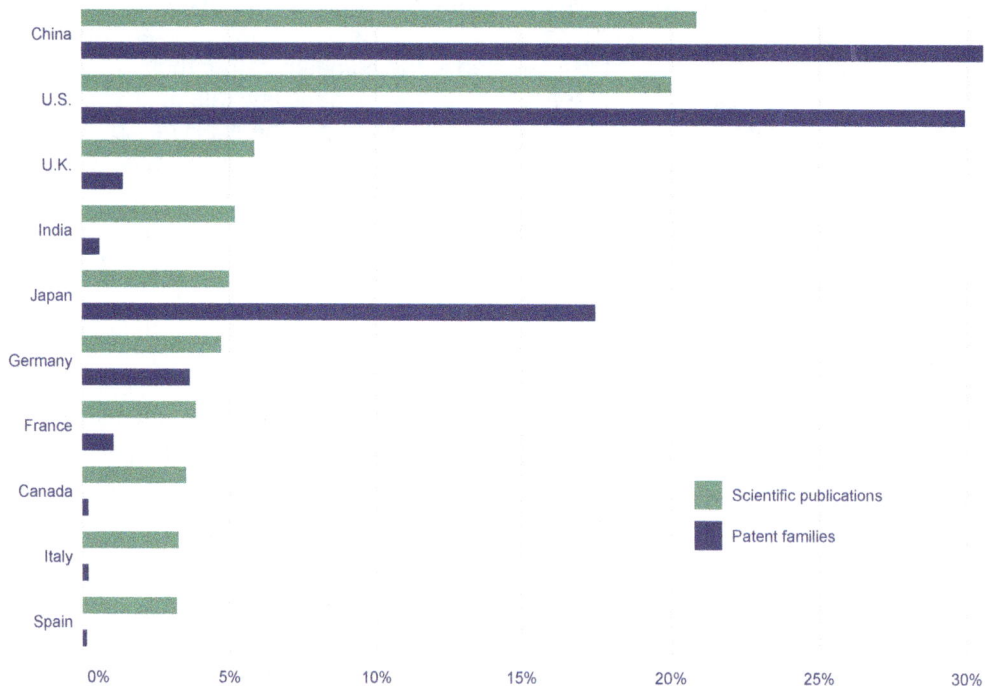

Legend:
- Scientific publications
- Patent families

Resident and non-resident filings

Most applicants choose the office of their own country as the primary area of protection. For example, almost all first filings made at the German patent office are by German-based companies (95 percent of the 12,415 patent families first filed in Germany) and German applicants chose their own office over the EPO (with 1,529 first filings) or any other office. There are, however, some exceptions to this rule:

- Israeli and Canadian applicants choose to file first in the U.S. patent office more frequently than they do the office of their own country (1,982 compared with 408 first filings for Israeli applicants, and 2,779 compared with 535 first filings for Canadian applicants).
- Dutch and Swiss applicants choose the U.S. patent office over the EPO and their own office (1,237 compared with respectively 900 and 182 first filings for Dutch applicants, and 746 compared with respectively 330 and 150 first filings for Swiss applicants).

It is noteworthy that the U.S. patent office is chosen above any other office by foreign applicants, above for example the Canadian (2.7 percent), the Japanese (2.6 percent), the Israeli (1.9 percent) and the Netherlands (1.2 percent) offices.

Among regional and international filing routes, the European patent route is used most frequently by German applicants (with 28 percent of applications), followed by Dutch and French applicants (with 16 percent and 14 percent, respectively). Non-European applicants account for a smaller proportion of European patent filings, led by U.S. applicants (12 percent), followed by Canadian and Japanese applicants (both 3 percent). The PCT route is most widely used by applicants from the U.S. (27 percent), Japan (26 percent) and China (20 percent).

Offices of first filing: change over time

Figure 5.6 shows the trend in the top six offices of first filing by earliest priority year.

Which countries are emerging?

Kai-Fu Lee, Sinovation Ventures

In terms of research, I think Canada has extraordinary talent and there are several other strong countries. However, in terms of implementation, none of these places yet has an ecosystem to turn their expertise into economic advantage.

One of the notable differences between each office is the year in which each office first reached the threshold of 200 patent filings as an office of first filing. Japan and the U.S. reached this threshold in the 1979 and 1986, respectively, while China reached it in 2002. However, today, China has the highest annual growth rate among all the offices. Looking at the top offices in more detail:

- Japan: although the country was among the first to innovate in the AI field (as early as the beginning of the 1980s), the number of patent families decreased from 1982 to 1986, then increased again between 1986 and 1991 and has been stable at around 2,000 patent applications per year since the beginning of the 1990s.
- U.S.: filings at the U.S. patent office began early (in the mid-1980s) and have grown continuously ever since (with around 10,000 patent applications in 2015), except for the two periods from 2000 to 2002 and from 2008 to 2012, when there was an economic downturn.
- Republic of Korea: filings with the Korean patent office began more recently (mid-2000s) and have seen stable growth over the past 10 years.
- France, Germany, the U.K. and the EPO: first filings have seen stable and moderate increases.
- China: filings with the China patent office began relatively late (2002) but have grown exponentially in the past 10 years (with 33,000 patent families in 2016). China was ranked second for first filings in 2009 and first in 2014. First filings in China have since overtaken first filings in the U.S. thanks to an impressive average annual growth rate of 43 percent since 2013.
- PCT: international patent applications have grown strongly, especially after 2010.

Figure 5.8. Percentage of patent families by number of family members

Two thirds of patent families have only one member, while only 5 percent have more than six members

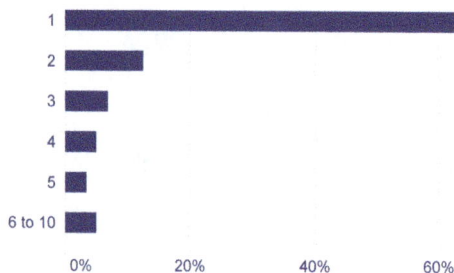

Figure 5.9. Number of first filings and number of subsequent filings for top offices of subsequent filing

China, the U.S. and Japan receive more first filings than subsequent filings, whereas the opposite is true for other offices

Note: EPO is the European Patent Office. WIPO refers to PCT applications.

Growth levelled off in the most recent year for which data is available. It remains to be seen whether this represents a trend or is a one-off event.

Two other countries are worth mentioning. Although not appearing in the top historical total, India was ranked eighth for first filings in 2015 and has enjoyed a high rate of annual growth during recent years (with an average of 33 percent in the 3 years up to 2015). First filings in Russia have also shown significant annual growth, although the number of patent families remains small (around just 100 per year).

_____ Comparison with scientific publications

The location of those organizations with which authors of scientific publications are affiliated can provide an indication as to the geographical positioning of the research described in such publications, where such information has been obtained from Scopus for the purpose of this report. Most of the countries that feature prominently in the list of top offices of first filing are also highly ranked for scientific publications (see figure 5.1 (bottom) and figure 5.7). These include China, Japan and the U.S. However, there are some differences: notably, in the case of the Republic of Korea there is less activity in terms of scientific publications than there is for first filing, whereas some other countries record higher activity in publications compared with patent filings. These latter include India, which ranks fourth in scientific publications (ahead of Japan), Italy, which ranks ninth, and Spain, which is 10th. The U.K. is ranked third.

Figure 5.7 indicates that European researchers are much more active in publishing the results of their research than in patenting. This may be due to the IP strategy universities and public research organizations in Europe may be following, the national or institutional policies to which they are required to adhere, cultural attitudes within the university or organization toward IP protection, a lack of awareness about the patent system, or laws governing the patentability of AI-related subject matter. The lack of a grace period in Europe – as opposed to the U.S., for example – that allows

patent applicants to file a patent application within a certain period after the publication of a scientific article could also partly explain these results.

Offices of second filing

_____ Top offices

A substantial majority of patent applications are not extended to additional jurisdictions after the first filing: 67 percent (227,627) of AI patent families are filed with only one office (see figure 5.8). This pattern is particularly pronounced among patent applications filed in China, where 43 percent of patent applications are not extended to other jurisdictions. The corresponding proportions for the U.S., Japan

Figure 5.10. Top patent offices by number of patent applications for different AI techniques

The most machine learning patents are filed in China, followed by the U.S. The number of filings in logic programming is close to parity in these two offices, while there are slightly more filings in fuzzy logic in the U.S. than in China

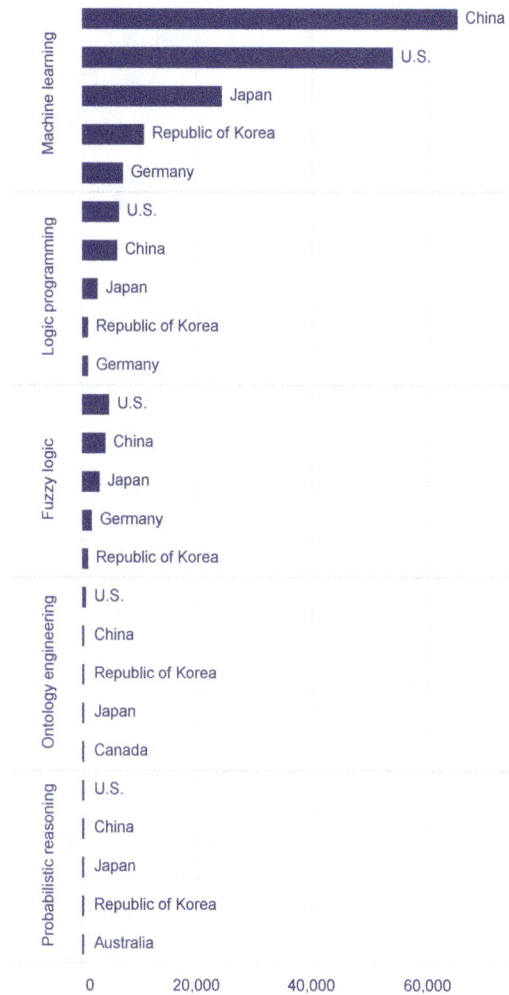

Machine learning
- China
- U.S.
- Japan
- Republic of Korea
- Germany

Logic programming
- U.S.
- China
- Japan
- Republic of Korea
- Germany

Fuzzy logic
- U.S.
- China
- Japan
- Germany
- Republic of Korea

Ontology engineering
- U.S.
- China
- Republic of Korea
- Japan
- Canada

Probabilistic reasoning
- U.S.
- China
- Japan
- Republic of Korea
- Australia

0   20,000   40,000   60,000

Note: A patent may refer to more than one category

Figure 5.11. Top geographical affiliation by number of scientific publications for different AI techniques

While it does not appear among the top offices for patent filing, India ranks third in fuzzy logic and fourth in machine learning scientific publications

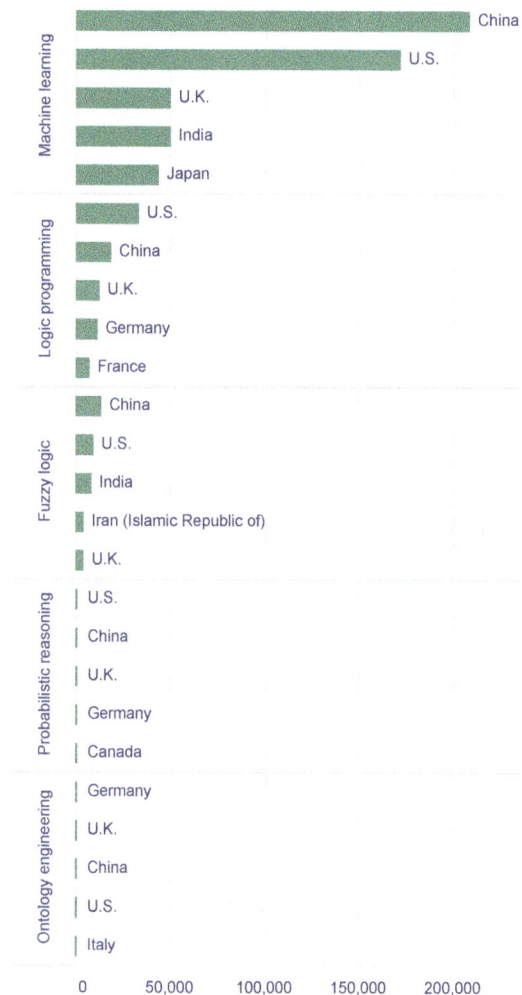

Machine learning
- China
- U.S.
- U.K.
- India
- Japan

Logic programming
- U.S.
- China
- U.K.
- Germany
- France

Fuzzy logic
- China
- U.S.
- India
- Iran (Islamic Republic of)
- U.K.

Probabilistic reasoning
- U.S.
- China
- U.K.
- Germany
- Canada

Ontology engineering
- Germany
- U.K.
- China
- U.S.
- Italy

0   50,000   100,000   150,000   200,000

Note: A scientific publication may refer to more than one category

and the Republic of Korea are 26 percent,15 percent and 9 percent, respectively. Of the 33 percent of patent families (112,201) filed at more than one office, only 1.9 percent (2,100 patent families) are filed with more than 10 offices.

The main office of second filing is the International Bureau of WIPO (18 percent of all patent families), followed by the U.S. patent office and EPO, as shown in figure 5.9. China ranks fourth with around 10 percent of all patent families being extended there. Two other offices that appear in the top 10 list are Canada and Australia.

Looking at the top offices of first filing, the chosen offices of subsequent filing can be summarized as follows:

- China: these patent filings are seldom extended to other jurisdictions (less than 5 percent of first filings with this office). When they are, the two favored patent offices are the U.S. and WIPO.
- U.S.: numerous extensions are observed, in a wide variety of market areas: mostly Europe but also Asia, Canada and Australia. The main chosen office of second filing is WIPO (31.5 percent of patent families with an earliest priority at the U.S. patent office).
- Japan: unusually, WIPO is not used very often (12.8 percent). The U.S. is the preferred choice of second office (39.3 percent), ahead of China (14.1 percent) and the EPO (13.0 percent).
- Republic of Korea: similarly to Japan, there is not much use of PCT applications (9.4 percent) and patents are most commonly extended to the U.S. (25.0 percent).
- Germany: these patents have a high ratio of extensions in general. The preferred offices of second filing are the EPO (34.9 percent), closely followed by the U.S. patent office (31.4 percent) and WIPO (30.6 percent).
- PCT: the main office chosen during the national phase is the U.S. patent office (60.7 percent), ahead of the Chinese, European and Japanese offices (from 30.8 to 36.8 percent).
- EPO: the main office of second filing is the U.S. (62.0 percent) followed by WIPO (44.5 percent).

China and developing markets

Kai-Fu Lee, Andreessen Horowitz

China has a good opportunity to get into those developing countries with similar demographics – south-east Asia, the Middle East, Africa, and probably India and potentially South America. I think Chinese AI and mobile technologies will make some inroads internationally but probably not in developed countries. The Chinese perhaps account for two-thirds of the world's population, but only a tiny percentage of its GDP – so, short-term, not worth a lot, but long-term, a lot.

- France and the U.K.: the main offices of second filing are the EPO, the U.S. patent office and WIPO (from 40.0 to 55.6 percent). The U.S. patent office is the main office of second filing when the U.K. is the office of first filing, while the EPO is the main office of second filing when France is the office of first filing.

Breakdown by techniques, functional applications and application fields

The remainder of this chapter looks at the geographical trends in applications for the three categories of AI technologies identified in Chapter 1: AI techniques, AI functional applications and AI application fields.

_____AI techniques

China and the U.S. are the top two offices for all AI techniques (see figure 5.10). China leads on machine learning patent filings, while the U.S. leads in the remaining AI technique categories, although the volumes in these categories are lower. Other countries with notable strengths in AI techniques are Japan (fuzzy logic), the Republic of Korea (ontology engineering) and Germany (fuzzy logic). Australia (probabilistic reasoning) and Canada (ontology engineering) seem to be target markets as well, based on the number of subsequent filings in these countries, although they are not countries where many patents for AI techniques are filed.

Subject-matter eligibility in the United States, Europe, Japan, China and Korea

John G. Flaim and Yoon Chae, Baker McKenzie

In the U.S., the biggest legal hurdle to obtaining a patent on an AI invention is arguably 35 United States Code (U.S.C.) § 101, which limits patent-eligible subject matter to a "process, machine, manufacture, or composition of matter," and is interpreted by the courts as excluding abstract ideas, laws of nature and natural phenomena. The standard on this patent subject-matter eligibility requirement became more stringent for software and "computer-implemented" inventions with the U.S. Supreme Court's 2014 decision in *Alice Corporation v. CLS Bank International*, which employed a heightened two-step test: (1) determining whether the invention is directed to a patent-ineligible concept, such as an abstract idea; and if so, (2) determining whether the claimed elements provide any "inventive concept" that would transform the abstract idea into a "patent-eligible application." The *Alice* Court held that the patent claims on "intermediated settlement" are directed to an abstract idea without any inventive concept because each of their elements is a "well-understood, routine, conventional" activity, failing to do more than "require a generic computer to perform generic computer functions." Lower court decisions, such as *DDR Holdings, LLC v. Hotels.com, LP, Enfish, LLC v. Microsoft Corp., BASCOM Global Internet Services, Inc. v. AT&T Mobility LLC*, and *Berkheimer v. HP Inc.*, among others, provide meaningful insights on the application of Alice's two-step test, and the United States Patent and Trademark Office (USPTO)'s guidelines, particularly the "2019 Revised Patent Subject Matter Eligibility Guidance," can bring further clarity on subject-matter eligibility.

Other jurisdictions have different standards on subject-matter eligibility, as discussed in the USPTO's "Patent Eligible Subject Matter: Report on Views and Recommendations from the Public," issued in July 2017:

- In Europe, although "Article 52(2) and 52(3) of the European Patent Convention (EPC) explicitly exclude programs for computer 'as such' from patent eligible subject matter", this exclusion can be avoided if the "claimed invention causes a further technical effect beyond those effects which occur inevitably when any program is run." In addition, the EPO also recently published Guidelines for Examination of "Artificial intelligence and machine learning" (G-II 3.3.1), providing guidance on the assessment of whether an invention on AI and machine learning has the requisite "technical character" to be patentable.
- In Japan, a software invention is patentable if its information processing aspects are required to be "specifically implemented by using hardware resources." Many view software inventions being patent-eligible, so long as their claimed inventive steps are expressly tied to hardware.
- In China, according to the examination guidelines revised in April 2017, a "computer program-related invention" that has "technical characteristics will not be excluded from patentability." This revision is viewed by many as a broadening of the scope of patent-eligible subject matter.
- The Korean Intellectual Property Office (KIPO)'s guidelines state that computer programs per se are not patent-eligible, but they also "indicate that if computer software is claimed in conjunction with hardware, then the combination, the operating method of the combination, and a computer-readable medium containing the software that implicates the combination is patent eligible." The Republic of Korea recently introduced accelerated examination for patent applications pertaining to AI and other specified emerging technology fields.

Generally speaking, software inventions can be patented in these non-U.S. offices if they are implemented with or sufficiently tied to hardware. Thus, some believe that the patent subject-matter eligibility standard outside the U.S. may be less stringent than the Alice framework, although others believe that the recent developments indicate a convergence of the *Alice* framework, particularly with respect to its second prong, and the European practice.

The trend is similar when scientific publications are considered (see figure 5.11). The U.S. and China rank first or second for each AI technique (with the exception of ontology engineering, where Germany ranks first with 148 scientific publications and the overall volume of publications is very low). The U.K. ranks third in machine learning, compared with 10th for patent filings. India ranks third in fuzzy logic and fourth in machine learning, whereas it is eighth or lower in patenting activity. This suggests that India has strengths in AI research that might become even more evident within the next few years in terms of patenting activity.

Two offices not among the main offices for patent filing in AI are the Islamic Republic of Iran and Turkey; they do, however, rank fourth and ninth, respectively, for publications in fuzzy logic. Conversely, the Republic of Korea is much less visible in scientific publications than it is for patents for AI techniques.

_____AI functional applications

As in the other areas, China and the U.S. dominate patents for AI functional applications, taking the two top spots in all categories except for speech processing, where Japan is the second ranking country behind the U.S. (see figure 5.12). Looking in more detail, the U.S. Patent Office has the most control method patent filings, while China leads in distributed AI, planning and scheduling, predictive analytics and robotics. Typically, those offices that are top overall are also the top offices in each functional application category, except for Australia, which is fifth in natural language processing, India (fifth in distributed AI) and Canada (fifth in knowledge representation and reasoning and predictive analytics).

The United States and China lead in scientific publications for all the different functional applications, similar to the case with patent filings (see figure 5.13). However, unlike in patents, India is highly ranked for scientific publications in almost all functional applications. The Republic of Korea seems to be more visible in scientific publications related to AI functional applications, compared with AI

The U.S. Patent Office has the most control method patent filings, while China leads in patent applications in distributed AI, planning and scheduling, predictive analytics and robotics.

techniques: it ranks sixth in robotics and 10th in computer vision and speech processing.

_____AI application fields

China and the U.S. feature among the top two offices of first filing for almost all application fields (see figure 5.14). Other offices to feature include the Republic of Korea, ranked second for military; Japan, which is in third place for document management and publishing; and Germany, which features in transportation and energy management. Australia and Canada seem to be target market areas as well.

Figure 5.12. Top patent offices by number of patent applications for different AI functional applications

Although China and the U.S. rank first in patent filing for all functional applications and second in most, Japan holds second position in speech processing, while Australia, Germany, Canada and India are among the top filing offices in specific applications

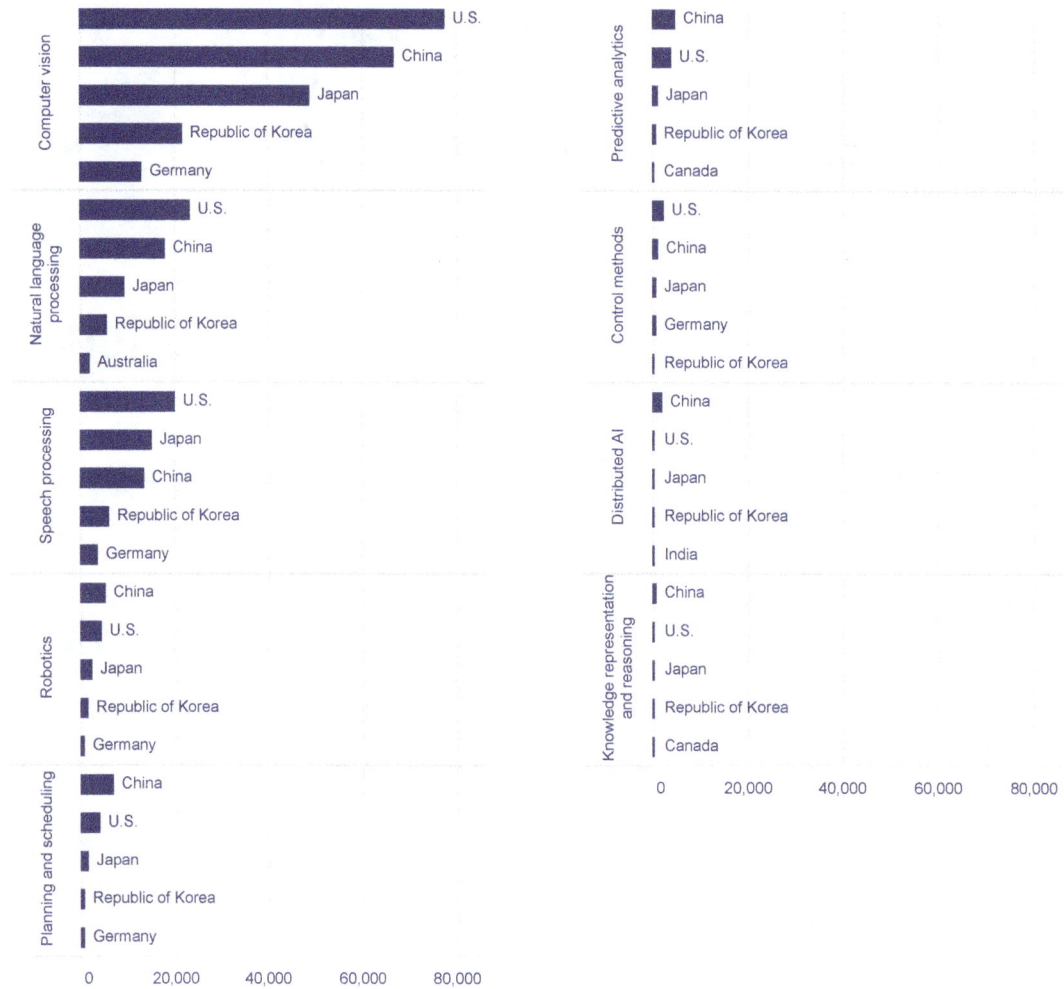

Note: A patent may refer to more than one category

Figure 5.13. Top geographical affiliations by number of scientific publications for different AI functional applications

Australia, Canada, Germany, India and the U.K. hold prominent positions in publications in specific categories

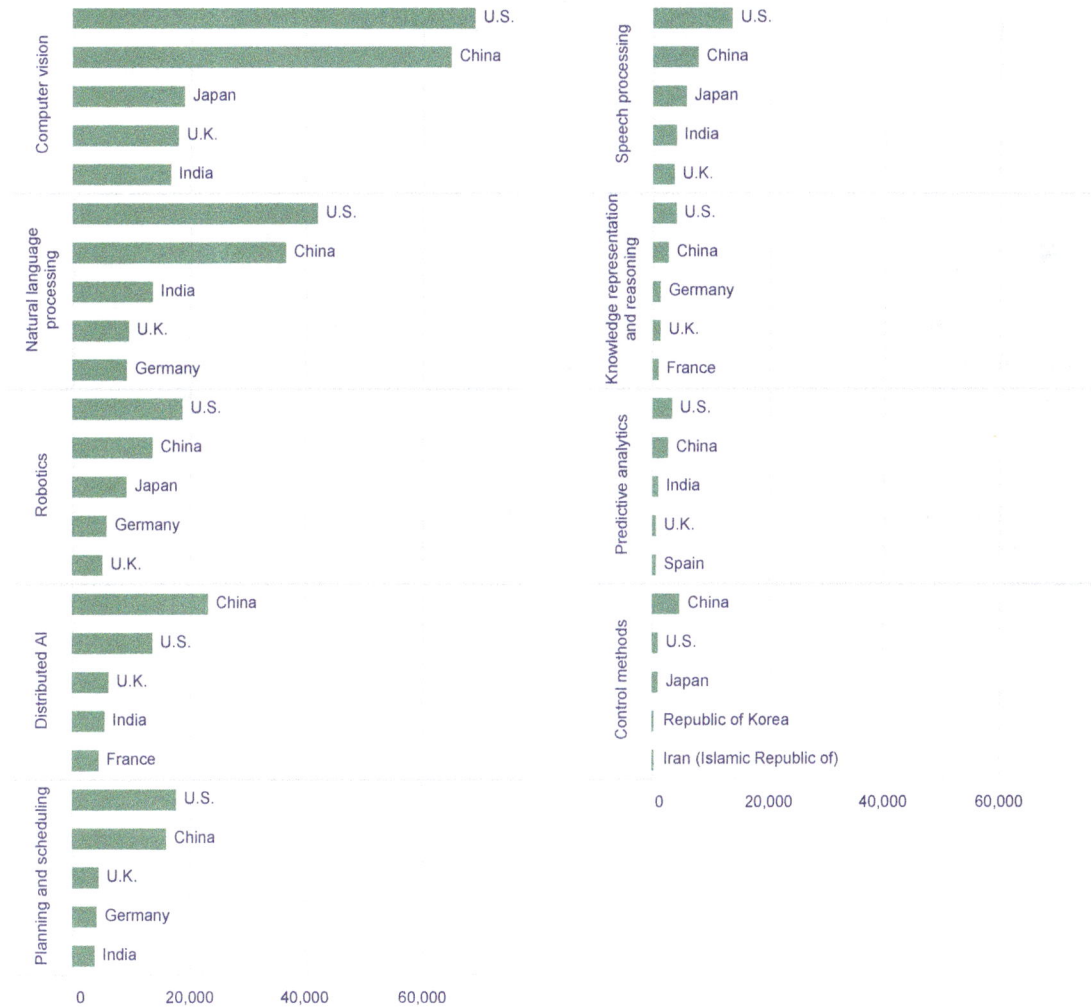

Note: A scientific publication may refer to more than one category

Figure 5.14. Number of patent families by patent office for 20 identified AI application fields

The patent offices of China and the U.S. rank first and second in all AI application fields

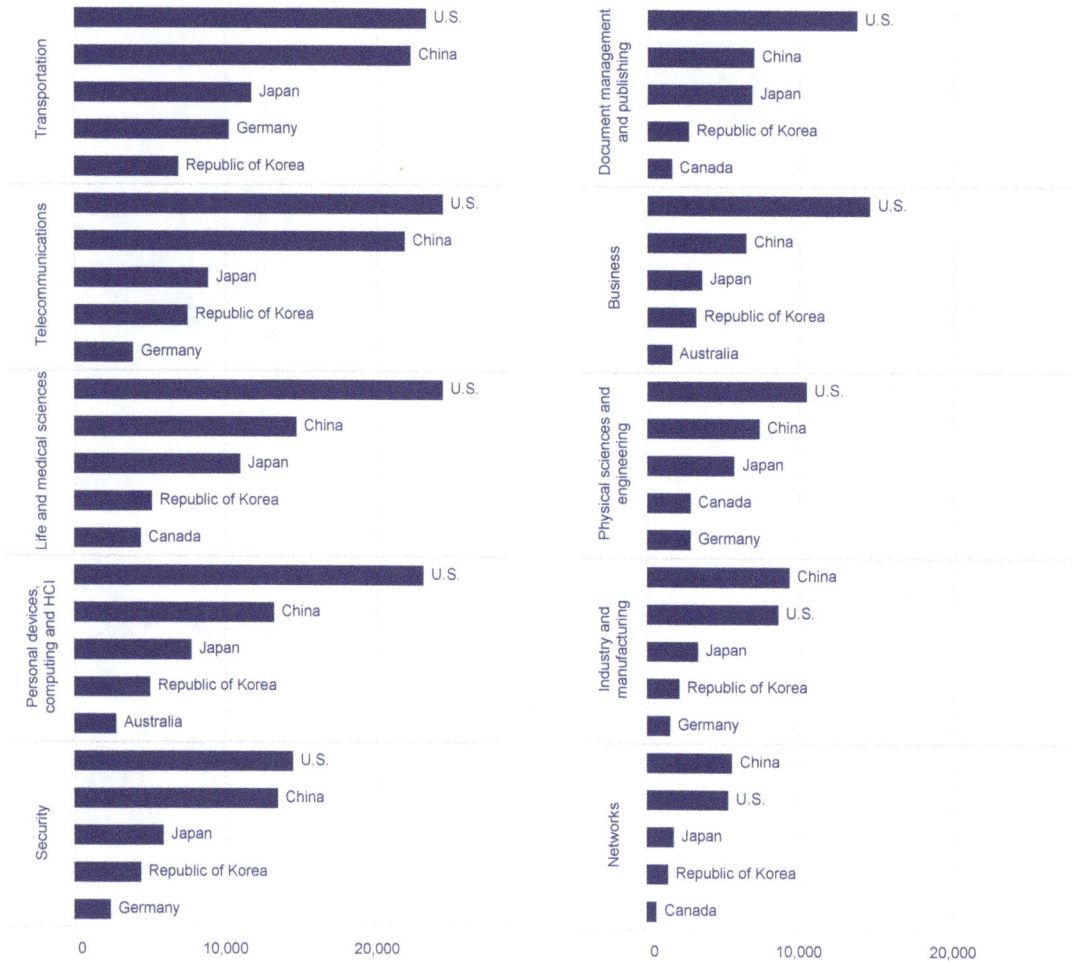

Note: A patent may refer to more than one category

Figure 5.14. Number of patent families by patent office for 20 identified AI application fields (continued)

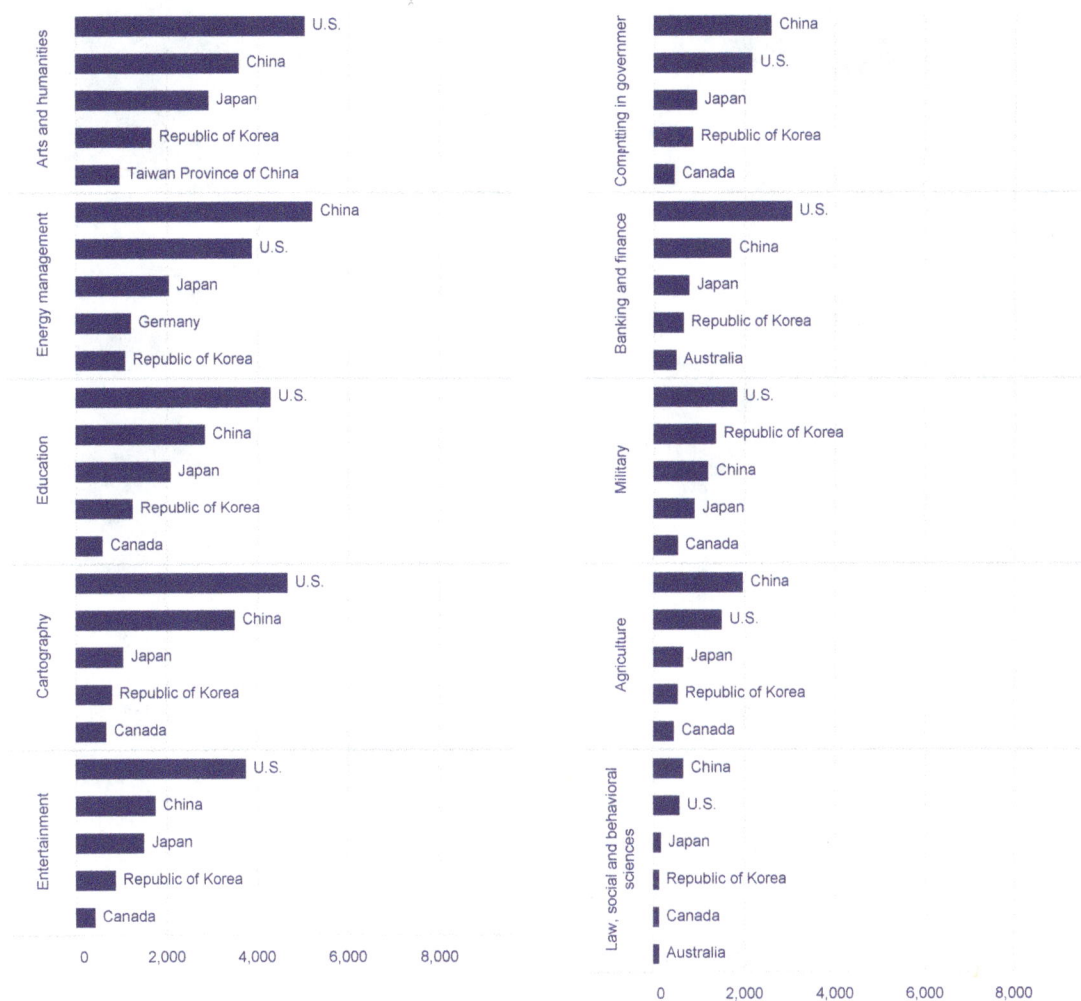

Arts and humanities:
- U.S.
- China
- Japan
- Republic of Korea
- Taiwan Province of China

Energy management:
- China
- U.S.
- Japan
- Germany
- Republic of Korea

Education:
- U.S.
- China
- Japan
- Republic of Korea
- Canada

Cartography:
- U.S.
- China
- Japan
- Republic of Korea
- Canada

Entertainment:
- U.S.
- China
- Japan
- Republic of Korea
- Canada

Computing in government:
- China
- U.S.
- Japan
- Republic of Korea
- Canada

Banking and finance:
- U.S.
- China
- Japan
- Republic of Korea
- Australia

Military:
- U.S.
- Republic of Korea
- China
- Japan
- Canada

Agriculture:
- China
- U.S.
- Japan
- Republic of Korea
- Canada

Law, social and behavioral sciences:
- China
- U.S.
- Japan
- Republic of Korea
- Canada
- Australia

0   2,000   4,000   6,000   8,000

Using AI for lung cancer diagnosis

Our laboratory at the NYU School of Medicine recently launched a new study in which we tested whether we can automate lung cancer diagnosis using AI. We identified a large set of imaging data, made available as a public resource by The Cancer Genome Atlas. These images are typically prepared by pathologists who use microscopes to examine the details of each tumor and deliver a diagnosis. However, this manual process is time-consuming and prone to error.

In our study, we used an AI technique called convolutional neural networks, specifically Inception v3 (a tool made available by Google). Neural networks are shown each image and told what the diagnosis is. To train these networks, we used about 800,000 images obtained from about 1,200 samples from both healthy and diseased lungs. After training was complete – it took about two weeks – we tested the performance of our AI system and found that its accuracy was 97 percent, slightly better than the performance of three pathologists who were independently asked to diagnose the same test set of patients' tumors.

We then explored whether AI can extract additional information from these images: tumor characteristics that human experts cannot discern from images alone, such as genetic mutations. Typically, genetic mutations are determined by a process called DNA sequencing, which allows the reading of the tumor's DNA and comparison with the normal genetic material of the same patient. Intriguingly, AI was able to predict the mutational status of a key cancer-driving gene in lung cancer with more than 80 percent accuracy. The accuracy of the AI models on genetic mutations can be improved if more examples are used for training.

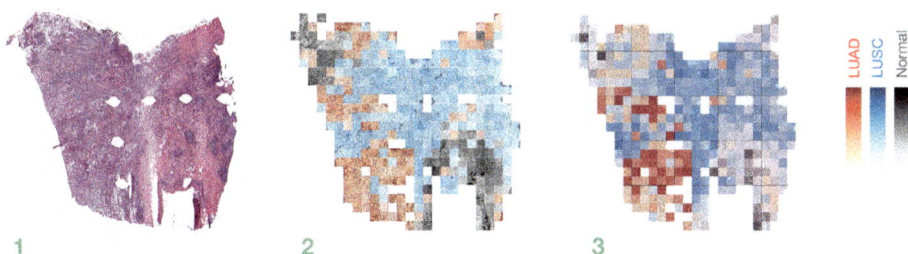

Visualization of images and classification heatmaps: (1) Original whole slide image with lung squamous cell carcinoma (TCGA-LUSC) (2) Aggregated prediction using tiles of the slide for the proposed model (3) Aggregated prediction using tiles of the slide for Inception V3.

Case study by Aristotelis Tsirigos, NYU School of Medicine

6 Market trends related to AI

I predict that in the next five years, AI adoption across multiple industries – especially outside the software industry – will drive massive global GDP growth.

Andrew Ng, Landing AI and deeplearning.ai

Key findings

- 434 companies in the AI sector have been acquired since 1998.
- 53 percent of acquisitions have taken place since 2016.
- The vast majority of acquired companies in the AI field are U.S. (283 acquired companies), while the U.K. ranks second with 25 acquired companies.
- Ten companies have made at least five acquisitions in this field and between them have made 79 acquisitions in total.
- Alphabet, Apple and Microsoft have been the most active entities, with 18, 11 and nine AI-related acquisitions, respectively.
- As of May 2018, based on public information, 2,868 companies active in AI have been identified as receiving funding (44 percent of 6,538 AI companies). This represents about US$46 billion in funding.
- 1,264 patent families are mentioned in litigation cases, corresponding to 0.37 percent of all AI-related patent families; 4,231 are mentioned in opposition cases (equivalent to 1.25 percent of the identified AI-related patent families) and 492 in both types of dispute.
- The top three plaintiffs in litigation cases are Nuance Communications, American Vehicular Services and Automotive Technologies International while Microsoft, Apple and Alphabet are the top defendants.
- The biggest filers of oppositions to AI patents are Siemens, Daimler and Giesecke+Devrient, while the main defendants in oppositions are Samsung, LG Corporation and Hyundai.

Artificial intelligence (AI) is a dynamic field, driven by substantial investment in research and rapid advances in knowledge. It is also a field that will have a significant impact, not only on business, with increased productivity and efficiency, but also on health, transportation, entertainment and agriculture, among other areas. To provide some means to measure impact, the data in this chapter looks at trends in merger and acquisition activity, funding, and statistics on patent litigation/oppositions to the extent that such data is available. While data on patent applications analyzed in earlier chapters provides insight into research and market potential and/or trends, data on litigation and oppositions can provide additional insight into which patents are challenged, where and between which parties. This data may illustrate comparative strengths and weaknesses, as well as which technologies and markets are considered to be commercially important.

Merger and acquisition (M&A) activity in the AI sector

Data on M&A activity in AI was compiled from the CrunchBase database, which includes an AI category. This is a large database, but may not be comprehensive. For example, it may lack information about companies from non-English speaking countries, while these companies may or may not have a patent portfolio. The data was extracted in May 2018.

CrunchBase lists 434 companies in the AI sector that have been acquired since 1998 (figure 6.1), with an acceleration evident in the number of acquisitions since 2012. Moreover, 53 percent of acquisitions have taken place since 2016.

The vast majority of acquired companies (indexed in CrunchBase) in the field of AI are located in the United States of America (U.S.) (283 acquired companies), while the United Kingdom (U.K.) ranks second, with 25 acquired companies (see figure 6.2). All of the top six countries for acquired companies are among the leaders in AI patents and scientific publications (see Chapter 5). However, with the exception of

Figure 6.1. Number of acquisitions in the AI sector by acquisition year

Acquisitions grew by 5 percent on average between 2000 and 2012 and by 33 percent between 2012 and 2017

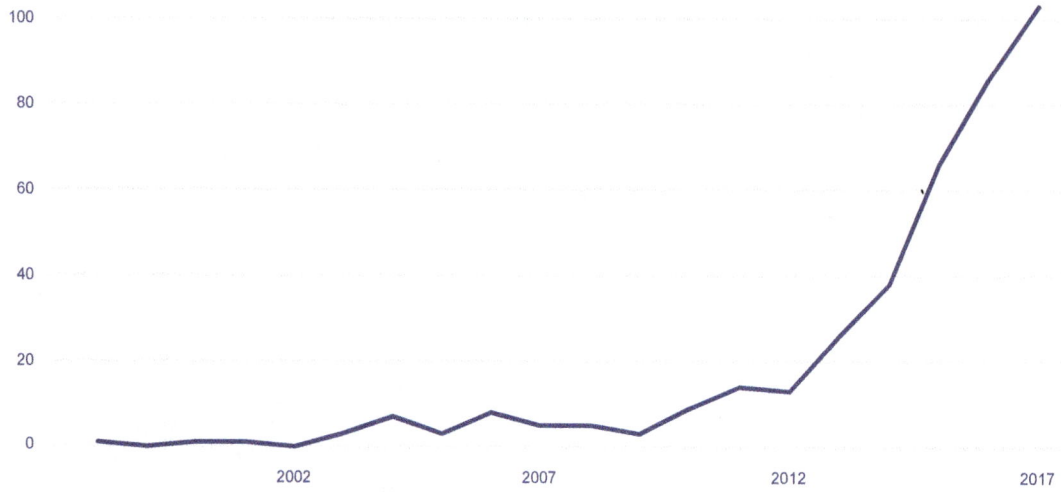

Figure 6.2. Acquisitions in the AI sector by country of acquired company from 1998 to 2018

More than two-thirds of companies acquired since 1998 have been from the U.S.

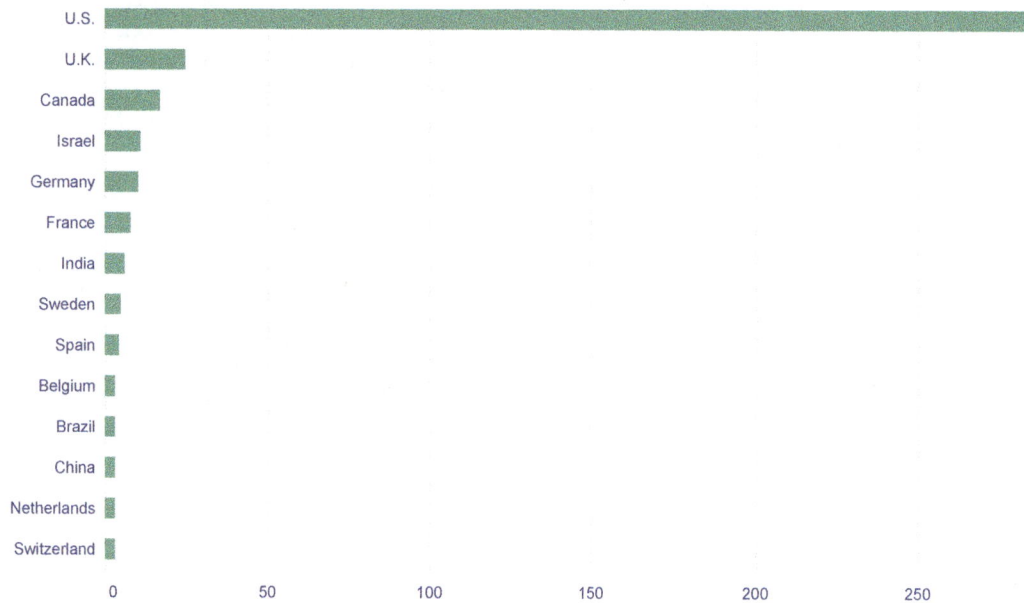

Figure 6.3. Number of companies acquired by top acquiring companies

Alphabet accounts for 4 percent of acquisitions overall

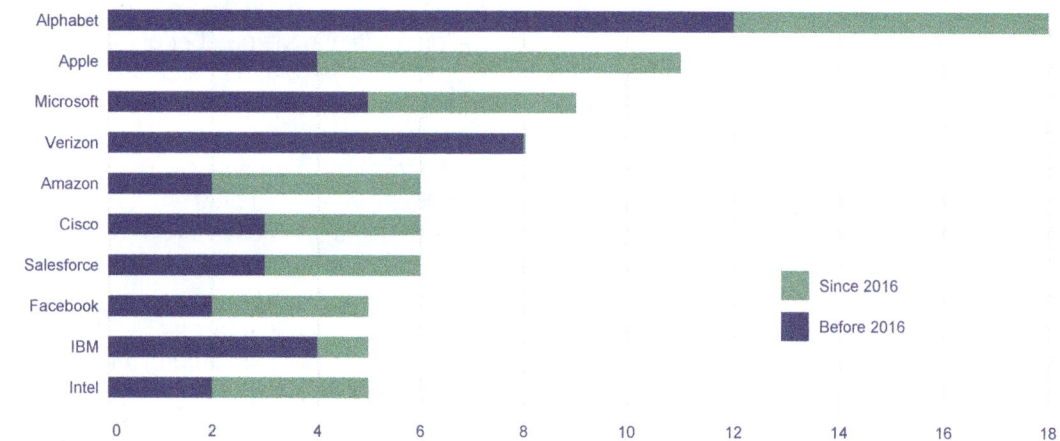

India, Asian countries such as China and the Republic of Korea are far less well represented in acquisitions than they are in the patent/scientific publications rankings. As mentioned above, the coverage of the CrunchBase database may not be as comprehensive in non-English-speaking countries compared with the U.S.

The acquisition price was only disclosed in 85 out of 435 acquisitions, making it impossible to generalize about prices. However, here are some examples of acquisitions with pricing information:

- Orbital ATK (global leader in aerospace and defense technologies) was acquired by Northrop Grumman in 2017 for US$7.8 billion.
- Vivid Smart Home was acquired by Blackstone in 2012 for US$2 billion.
- DeepMind was acquired by Google in 2014 for US$500 million.
- Movidius was acquired by Intel in 2016 for US$400 million.

_____ Top companies for acquisitions

Ten companies have made at least five acquisitions in this field and between them have made a total of 79 acquisitions (18 percent of the total number of acquisitions in the AI field). Moreover, there has been an acceleration in the past two years, with 34 acquisitions since 2016 (see figure 6.3).

All these 10 companies are big tech multinationals from the U.S. Alphabet, Apple and Microsoft have been the three most active entities, with 18, 11 and nine AI-related acquisitions, respectively. Apple has acquired seven AI companies since 2016, while Alphabet, the parent company of Google, has acquired six. However, Verizon has not acquired any AI companies since 2016. Data for Verizon is an aggregation of acquisitions made by recently acquired Yahoo and AOL. Most of these companies also feature prominently among patent assignees in the AI field, with three of the top 10 listed among the top 10 patenting companies. It is worth noting that Alphabet is among the top patent applicants to have decreased their patent filing activity in the last several years (see Chapter 4).

A strong VC ecosystem

Kai-Fu Lee, Sinovation Ventures

You need a strong venture capital (VC) ecosystem to drive the technologies to the right application areas and relentlessly focus on user needs and use that to push the scientists to improve the technologies. Aside from the U.S. and China there are no other countries with such an ecosystem. Israel to some extent has one, but I don't think many countries are aware of that. Most countries are focused on technologies targeting their own industries and that is where they are going wrong.

There are certain trends that can be observed in acquired companies:

- The vast majority of acquired companies are startups (median age: three years old), although a few players tend to acquire more mature companies (for IBM and Intel the median age of acquired companies is 10 years old).
- Technological trends are similar to those observed in the patents and scientific publications analysis: a large majority of the acquired companies (53 out of the 79 that disclosed information) specialize in machine learning. Various functional applications are seen in the acquired companies and the dominance of computer vision technologies is less marked than in the patent collection: 17 specialize in computer vision, 14 in natural language processing, 14 in information extraction and eight in predictive analytics.
- While the acquired companies are diverse, some applications occur frequently. The majority of the top 10 companies have acquired startups specializing in virtual assistants, big data analytics for recommendation systems (advertising and entertainment, for example) and image recognition (photos, etc.).
- Most of the acquired companies (46 out of the 79) are young startups with no patent portfolios. But two of the acquired companies have larger patent portfolios (37 patent families for DeepMind, 38 for DemandTec). While some companies tend to acquire significant patent portfolios through the acquisition process (such as Microsoft), others seem more interested in integrating

Challenges for startups

Petr Šrámek, AI Startup Incubator

The current trend is in AI technologies applied to a niche problem – so-called vertical AI applications – where you take an existing problem requiring human cognition, use a set of AI technologies to create an automated solution, and scale it globally. There are countless opportunities in the world, which translates into a huge opportunity for AI startups. In the short term, industries with the highest potential for gross value added, such as manufacturing, professional services and retail, should be on the startups' radar. The biggest societal impact can then be made in those fields where large populations are affected such as healthcare, education and public services.

Even though AI is over-hyped in the investor community, there is still a lack of AI-specialized funding sources. This is especially true for early stage companies, which constitute the majority of AI startups. Traditional VCs are focused primarily on late seed or A/B round funding stages. Larger corporations have done small AI pilots, mostly without significant success, and are waiting to see what will emerge.

technologies into their products rather than acquiring existing patent portfolios as such (for example, Apple, Verizon and Salesforce).
- As mentioned above, the CrunchBase database does not have full details of acquisition prices. Nonetheless, even if some acquisitions were at the range of billions (such as the cases of Orbital ATK or Vivid Smart Home), most of the public acquisition prices are well above US$100 million, and reach up to half a million dollars in some cases, for example the DemandTec acquisition by IBM or the DeepMind acquisition by Alphabet.

Funding in the AI sector

The CrunchBase database also includes data on funding for companies tagged in the AI category. It shows that, as of May 2018, 2,868 companies related to AI have been identified as receiving a disclosed amount of funding (44 percent of the 6,538 companies related to AI listed in CrunchBase). This represents about US$46 billion in funding.

The amounts of funding range from US$1,000 to US$3.1 billion per company. The largest amount was received by Toutiao, a Chinese company specializing in recommendation system products based on data mining, which received funding from seven investors in seven funding rounds. Seven companies have received more than US$300 million in funding:

- Toutiao
- Wish
- Cloudera (Hadoop)
- Argo AI
- Vivint Smart Home
- ACORN OakNorth Holdings Ltd
- CloudWalk Technology.

These companies, originating from China, the U.S. and the U.K., have all received several rounds of funding, except for Argo AI, which received US$1 billion in just one funding round.

Different types of funding include angel, seed, venture capital (series A to F), grant, debt, private equity and secondary market. Most companies are funded by venture capital or banks. Some receive funding from private companies, such as Ford Motor Company funding Argo AI or Weibo funding Toutiao. Only one of the seven companies listed above has had an initial public offering (Cloudera: NYSE).

Most of these AI companies are mature (i.e., more than six years old in general), with the exception of Argo AI (founded in 2016) and ACORN OakNorth Holdings and CloudWalk Technology (both founded in 2015). They also represent various sectors of applications, from transportation to banking, e-commerce, software and networks.

It is surprising that these funded companies either do not have big AI-related patent portfolios (up to four patent families at the most), or have none at all, except for

CloudWalk Technology, which already has 22 published patents families despite being founded only three years ago, and Vivint (32 patent families, but created in 1999).

Out of the top 10 patenting companies identified in Chapter 4, five have invested in companies related to AI via venture funding or grants. Certain trends in funding and investment among the top 10 patenting companies can be observed. These include:

- Investments are not only directed toward AI products (through private companies) but also toward AI fundamental research (through investments in laboratories), such as IBM investing in MIT-IBM Watson AI Lab in 2017 (US$240 million) and Alphabet investing in Montreal Institute for Learning Algorithms (MILA) in 2016 (US$3.4 million).
- Pivaclouds has received funding from two of the top patenting companies (IBM and Microsoft).
- Investments are often directed toward foreign companies, such as Samsung in the Republic of Korea investing in both Chinese and U.S. AI companies.

To promote the development of AI, many governments have put in place incentives and established public–private partnerships. Some of these and similar policies are discussed in detail in Chapter 7.

The funding of startups is a particular priority for governments, given their role in developing new technologies and generating jobs. Data compiled by the AI Index report 2018 indicates that the number of active U.S. startups developing AI systems increased 2.1-fold from January 2015 to January 2018, while annual venture capital investment into startups developing AI systems increased 4.5-fold from 2013 to 2017.

Open source

For many developers, open source (or open innovation) approaches provide an effective means of sharing and promoting AI technologies, due either to the cost of filing

Open source at Mila

Myriam Côté, Mila

The research community at the core of our model has a culture of open collaboration, open research, open source code, open libraries and open datasets. This culture is reflected in the general policy of our institute regarding partnerships: We are very reluctant to engage in industry projects with IP constraints, which often jeopardize the free flow of information, preventing open discussions among researchers and limiting the number of publications that can be made available to the community at large. Such constraints are often application-specific and result in tying our innovations to IP that belongs to a specific company. The pace of technological progress in such environments is, inevitably, slower. All players have less to gain, despite the short-term gain that exclusivity may appear to offer.

For this reason, the principal mechanism through which we welcome financial support from research partners is through philanthropic donations. We share all of our code and all of our new algorithmic strategies in the public domain by publishing in a timely manner and refraining from writing patents. This open policy necessarily leads to a healthy and fast-paced research environment, a characteristic of which our partners are increasingly appreciative. They too recognize that players in this disruptive domain need to adopt agile philosophies and question the premises behind traditional models of industrial innovation.

a patent or a lack of awareness of the patent system. Many developers also consider open source activity more appropriate for very fast-paced developments. Open source activity is harder to measure than patenting activity, as the information is spread across different platforms. One of the main collaborative developer platforms, GitHub, allows for some indicative analysis of trends. It shows a constant increase in the number of software projects related to neural networks and deep learning as examples of two areas of AI attracting a lot of interest (see

Figure 6.4. Number of patent families involved in litigation, by litigation jurisdiction

More than 70 percent of litigated patent families originate from the U.S.

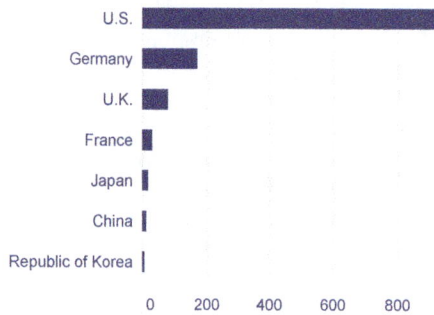

Jurisdiction	
U.S.	
Germany	
U.K.	
France	
Japan	
China	
Republic of Korea	

0   200   400   600   800

Figure 6.5. Top litigation plaintiffs by number of litigated patent families

Nuance Communications, American Vehicular Sciences and Automotive Technologies International account for 4 percent of litigated patent families

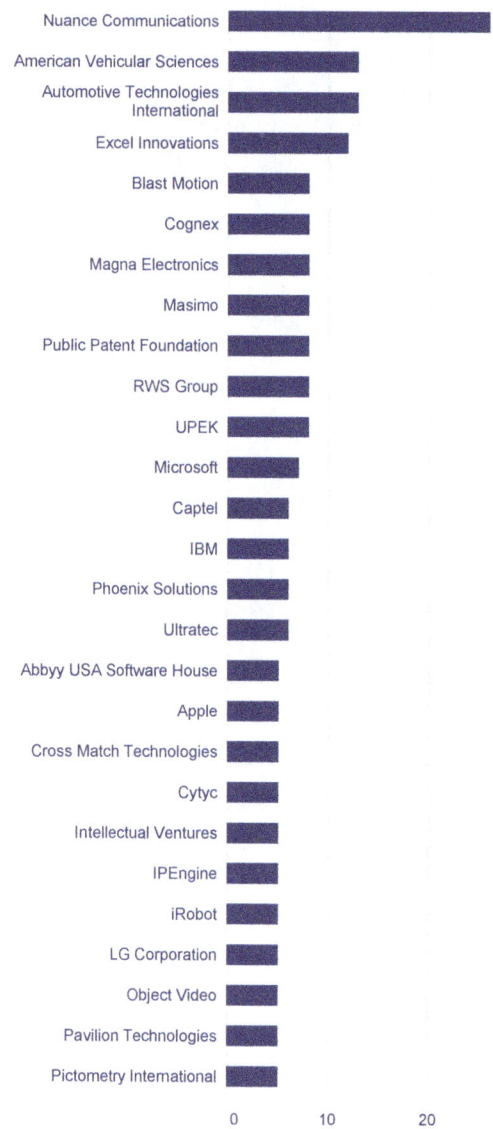

Nuance Communications	
American Vehicular Sciences	
Automotive Technologies International	
Excel Innovations	
Blast Motion	
Cognex	
Magna Electronics	
Masimo	
Public Patent Foundation	
RWS Group	
UPEK	
Microsoft	
Captel	
IBM	
Phoenix Solutions	
Ultratec	
Abbyy USA Software House	
Apple	
Cross Match Technologies	
Cytyc	
Intellectual Ventures	
IPEngine	
iRobot	
LG Corporation	
Object Video	
Pavilion Technologies	
Pictometry International	

0   10   20

Chapter 3). In addition, the AI Index, a project within the Stanford 100 Year Study on AI (AI 100) published in December 2018, measured some software projects by the number of times they were "starred" on GitHub. Each star indicates developer interest and usage of software. The number of stars for the two most popular software packages for deep learning and machine learning, TensorFlow and scikit-Learn, both increased dramatically in the years leading up to 2018.

Litigation and oppositions

Data on litigation and oppositions involving AI patents is drawn from the Darts-IP and Orbit databases. Though not comprehensive, this data reveals 1,264 patent families mentioned in litigation cases, 4,231 mentioned in opposition cases, and 492 mentioned in both types of case. Litigation and opposition information can assist in completing the picture about the IP situation in a given field and the enforcement efforts within a given technology area. Accessing, gathering and analyzing this data is difficult, bearing in mind the limited coverage of various databases (see www.wipo.int/tech_trends/en/artificial_intelligence for more on the methodology), which may be extensive yet not exhaustive, and the differences between legal systems and procedures, issues that are discussed further in WIPO's *World Intellectual Property Indicators 2018*.

_____ Litigation trends

Data on litigation does not include patent oppositions or the appeals arising from them, which are discussed separately below. The patent families involved in the litigation do not necessarily belong to the named player but only to the AI patent collection. Numbers relating to plaintiffs refer only to infringement cases.

Most patent families involved in litigation cases were filed between 1997 and 2007 (775 patent families or 62 percent of the total 1,264 patent families mentioned in litigation). Figure 6.4 shows the most popular jurisdictions for litigation (a patent family may be involved

What are the trends in AI investment?

Frank Chen, Andreessen Horowitz

We're seeing a rapid increase in AI technology investments across the board – from large, public companies, to small startups. If you look at the top 10 auto manufacturers, for example General Motors and Toyota, they're investing large amounts in AI technology. Corporate venture arms, Fortune 500 companies, and venture capital firms are all thinking about AI investments.

in cases in more than one jurisdiction): 73 percent of the identified litigation cases (or 926 cases) were filed in the U.S. Something to bear in mind is that the nature of AI-related technologies may make it very difficult for a patent assignee to identify the infringement of their patent as it may be difficult to identify how it has been embedded in a competitor's product.

Looking at the technology involved in the litigated patent families, machine learning techniques account for 421 of the cases, while logic programming accounts for 96 and fuzzy logic for 59. Ontology engineering and probabilistic reasoning account for just seven and five cases, respectively. Within machine learning, no particular technique stands out, though it is notable that no deep learning patent has been involved in litigation so far, which is probably due to the recent emergence of this technology.

The conclusion is the same when looking at functional applications where the proportion of litigated patent families broadly follows patenting trends. In application fields, however, telecommunications (with 425) has the most cases, followed by personal devices, computing and HCI (with 352), life and medical sciences (with 308), transportation (with 234) and business (with 218). This means that transportation accounts for fewer cases in proportion to the number of patents in this field, perhaps reflecting the fact that most transportation AI (autonomous driving) is yet to be commercialized.

One should also bear in mind that over half of identified patent families are very recent

"Abstract idea" in U.S. jurisprudence

John G. Flaim and Yoon Chae, Baker McKenzie

What precisely constitutes an "abstract idea" in U.S. patent law continues to evolve, and different courts have since invalidated claims of numerous software and business method patents as abstract ideas. Of particular relevance to this report are the courts' invalidations of patent claims for covering subject matter that could be performed through an "ordinary mental process," "in the human mind" or by "a human using a pen and paper" under the *Alice Corporation v. CLS Bank International* test. This creates a tension with patenting AI inventions because the goal of AI is often to automate or better perform human tasks and activities.

As a result, there have been more United States Patent and Trademark Office (USPTO) rejections during patent examination, as well as more court decisions invalidating patent claims on AI, software and computer-implemented inventions. For example, in 2015, the District Court for the Northern District of California invalidated patent claims for being directed to a general-purpose computer implementation of "an abstract idea long undertaken with the human mind," merely seeking to model "the highly effective ability of humans to identify and recognize a signal." In another case in 2017, the Northern District of California also held as invalid patent claims on AI-driven predictive analytics for being "directed to a mental process and the abstract concept of using mathematical algorithms to perform predictive analytics."

and that litigation is linked to the emergence of damages, which usually only arise once a product has come to market. It will thus be interesting to follow the statistics as they evolve in the coming years, when the commercialization of many recently patented inventions will have taken place.

_____Top plaintiffs

The most active companies as plaintiffs in the identified litigation cases are listed in figure 6.5, along with the number of patent families involved in these cases. Companies are listed in order of the number of AI patent families involved in litigation, regardless of whether the company owns the patents. Of course, one case may involve several patent families.

It is notable that entities owned by Acacia Research, a large patent assertion entity, feature prominently among the top plaintiffs in litigation cases. Patent assertion entities

develop and acquire patent portfolios and enforce their patent rights against prominent manufacturers or other downstream businesses. Again, it will be interesting to observe how these AI patent portfolios are enforced in the coming few years.

Looking in more depth at the main plaintiffs:

- Nuance Communications (U.S.) is a plaintiff in cases involving 26 AI patent families. It is a listed company providing speech, imaging and keypad solutions for businesses, organizations and consumers worldwide. The cases comprise four infringement actions against Abbyy, Lexmark (times two) and Tellme Networks and an *ex-parte* reexamination petition against Vlingo. All the cases were initiated between 2008 and 2010. Note that Nuance acquired Vlingo in 2011.
- American Vehicular Sciences (U.S.) is a subsidiary of Acacia Research and owns

more than 180 patent families according to Orbit. It has filed almost 60 suits since 2012. It has launched one case involving a total of 24 patent families including 13 AI patent families, some of which were previously owned by Automotive Technologies International. This was filed in 2013 against several entities, most of them belonging to Toyota. The AI patents are not cited in other cases filed by AVS against Toyota, BMW and other car manufacturers. AVS is also a defendant in 26 *inter partes* reviews involving these 13 AI patent families; some of these cases involve multiple attacks on the same patent.

- Automotive Technologies International (U.S.) is another subsidiary of Acacia Research, and is known for the five infringement actions launched from 2004 to 2011 against automotive companies. It assigned some of its patents to American Vehicular Sciences in 2012. ATI has filed two infringement cases involving 13 AI patent families, the first (dated December 21, 2006) against Hyundai, Elesys, Kia, Honda, BMW and General Motors, and the second (dated February 1, 2008) against Hyundai, Kia, Nissan, Siemens, TRW and TK Holdings. As with AVS, these actions involve quite large patent portfolios: 14 patents in the 2006 case and six in the 2008 case. ATI is also defending these 13 patents in numerous cases.
- Apple is involved as a plaintiff in seven cases involving five patents belonging to the AI collection, six of them being infringement actions against competitors (Samsung, Motorola, HTC) filed between 2011 and 2018. Except for one case, Apple's actions involved only three to four patents at a time, making the AI-related patents major technological items in these cases. These five AI patent families are also involved in eight cases in which Apple is a defending party.
- Microsoft is named as a plaintiff in one declaratory action for non-infringement, involving several patents belonging to Phoenix Solutions and filed in 2010. (Phoenix's patent portfolio was reassigned to Nuance Communications in 2013.) Microsoft's relative inactivity in litigation reflects its company-wide strategy: the

Darts-IP database includes only 25 cases for its entire patent portfolio.

Top defendants

A ranking of entities involved as defendants in litigation cases is shown in figure 6.6, based on the number of patent families involved in the cases (regardless of whether they belong to the company named). The main players as defendants are:

- Microsoft: a defending party in 31 cases involving 55 AI patent families. These cases have been filed by diverse parties, including inventors, large manufacturers and non-practicing entities (NPEs), from 1998 to 2018. The 55 patent families involved in these 31 cases are mentioned in 161 cases in total. Microsoft has also filed *inter partes* review actions against companies that have attacked it.

Figure 6.6. Top litigation defendants by number of litigated patent families

Microsoft, Apple and Alphabet account for 12 percent of litigated patent families since 1960

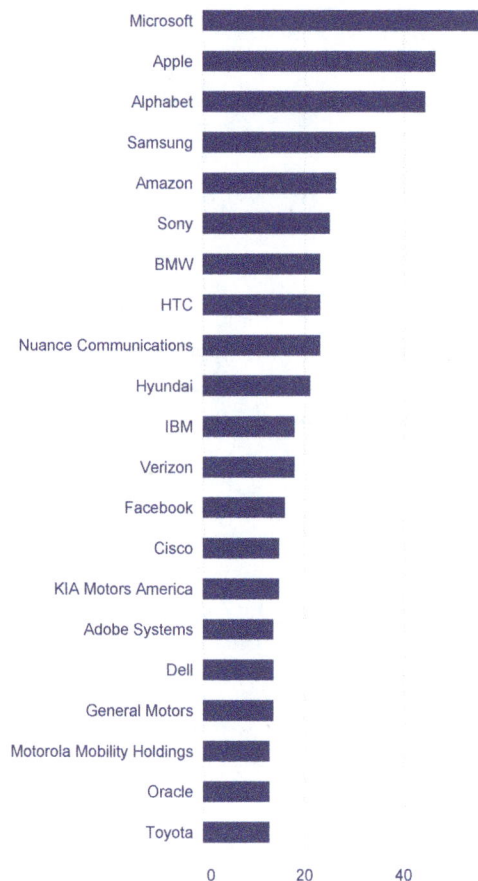

Microsoft	
Apple	
Alphabet	
Samsung	
Amazon	
Sony	
BMW	
HTC	
Nuance Communications	
Hyundai	
IBM	
Verizon	
Facebook	
Cisco	
KIA Motors America	
Adobe Systems	
Dell	
General Motors	
Motorola Mobility Holdings	
Oracle	
Toyota	

0   20   40

Figure 6.7. Number of opposed patent families by patent office

Half of opposed patent families have been filed at the Korean patent office (KIPO)

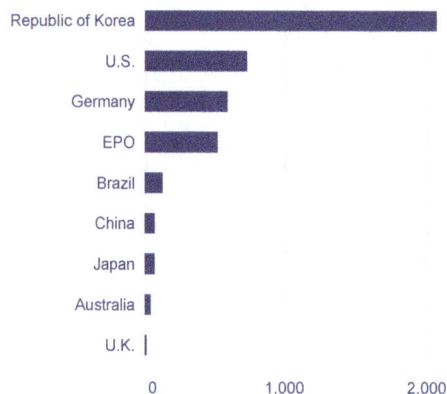

Republic of Korea	
U.S.	
Germany	
EPO	
Brazil	
China	
Japan	
Australia	
U.K.	

0   1,000   2,000

Figure 6.8. Top opponents by number of opposed patents for selected patent offices

Siemens filed oppositions for more than double the number of patent families of other top opponents

Opponent	
Siemens	
Daimler	
Giesecke+Devrient	
Alphabet	
Apple	
Continental	
Interessengemeinschaft für Rundfunkschutzrechte	
Samsung	
Octrooibureau Van der Lely	
Oticon	
Valeo	
ZF TRW Automotive Holdings	
Amazon	

0   20   40

- Apple: mentioned as a defendant in 23 cases involving 46 AI patents: 21 infringement actions, one *ex partes* reexamination petition and one administrative hearing, filed between 1999 and 2017. Of the 20 identified plaintiffs, 12 are NPEs and eight are operating companies. The same patent families are also mentioned in 47 cases where Apple is a plaintiff (including *inter partes* reviews).
- Alphabet: cited as a defendant in 24 cases involving 44 AI patent families, including 22 infringement actions and two *inter partes* reexamination petitions. Out of the 22 infringement actions, 16 were brought by NPEs. As a plaintiff party, Alphabet is mainly involved in actions such as *inter partes* reviews or *inter partes* reexamination petitions against NPEs.

Oppositions

Many patent systems allow third parties to file oppositions against granted patents in procedures normally conducted in the relevant IP office. Decisions in these cases may also be appealed in some jurisdictions. Certain rules generally apply to oppositions. For example, it may be possible to cite other patents in the opposition procedure and to file oppositions anonymously. It may also be possible for the patent holder to modify the claims to avoid the opposition; for the purposes of this research, it has been assumed that when a patent is not fully revoked it is a win for the patent holder.

_____ Global dynamics, geographical and technological aspects

The number of oppositions filed over time has increased consistently since the late 1980s, but the proportion of opposed families per year remains constant (1.2 percent of the yearly AI patent filings on average). In the AI field, most of the oppositions have been filed at the KIPO, the German patent office, the European Patent Office (EPO) and at the United States Patent and Trademark Office (USPTO). Decisions to revoke patents can be made on one ground only or on more than one ground. The Chinese

and Japanese offices are also frequently used for oppositions in the AI field (see figure 6.7).

_____ Top opposing parties

The main organizations to have filed oppositions against the largest number of AI patents are shown in figure 6.8, indicating the number of patent families for which these players are identified as opposing parties. The main companies for filing oppositions to patents are:

- Siemens (Germany): filed 47 oppositions covering 48 AI patent families from 1991 to 2017. Of these, it has won eight cases, lost 37 and three remain undecided. Siemens has been filing oppositions non-anonymously in the AI field since 1991. Of the 47 oppositions, 46 were filed before the EPO and one in Germany. In its successful cases, where information is available, three decisions in its favor were based on inventive step – non-obviousness and two on ascertaining differences – no novelty.
- Daimler (Germany): filed 22 cases involving 22 AI patent families (21 before the EPO and one in Germany). It was won four, lost 16 and two remain undecided. In successful cases, where information is available, the reasons given for the decisions in its favor were inventive step – non-obviousness in two cases and ascertaining differences – no novelty (in one case). Daimler mostly attacked patents owned by competitors (Audi, Nissan, Toyota, Volkswagen, Volvo) and concerning directly applicable technologies (road signals recognition, object detection or parking assist, for instance).
- Giesecke+Devrient: a technology firm that provides payment, secure communication and identity management solutions to clients. It has filed 17 cases, all brought before the EPO, involving 22 AI patent families, winning nine, losing seven, with one undecided. Few decisions are available, but there were two reported cases of inventive step – non-obviousness and one ascertaining differences – no novelty. Most of the oppositions were filed from 2001 to

Figure 6.9. Top opposition defendants by number of opposed patents for selected patent offices

The Korean company Samsung was defendant in more than double the number of opposed patents of any other top defendant

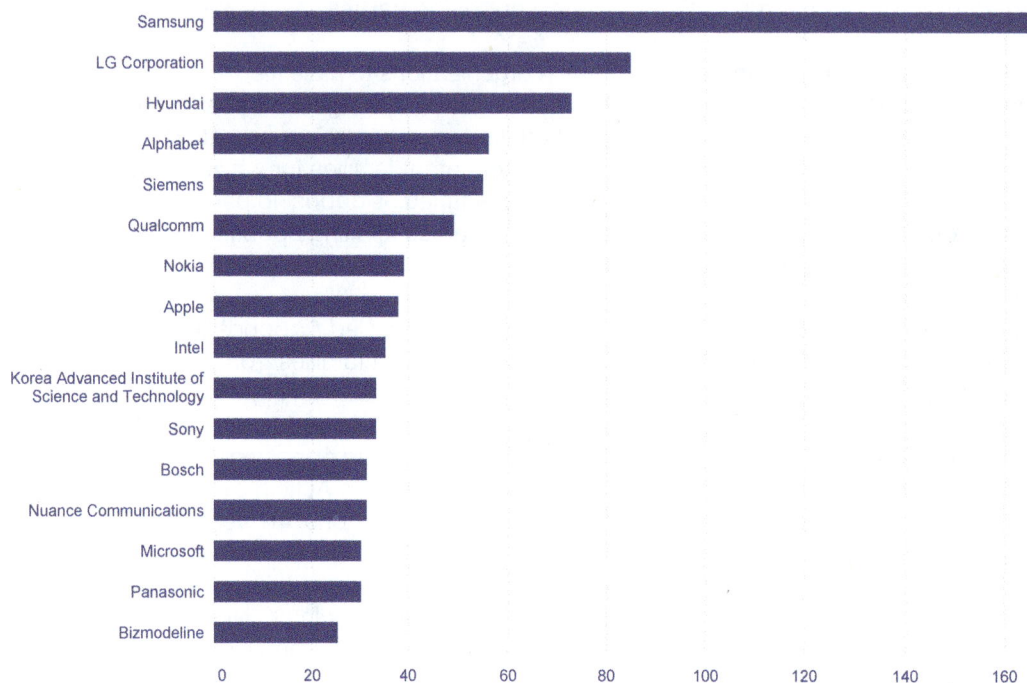

Samsung	167
LG Corporation	86
Hyundai	73
Alphabet	57
Siemens	56
Qualcomm	49
Nokia	40
Apple	39
Intel	36
Korea Advanced Institute of Science and Technology	34
Sony	34
Bosch	32
Nuance Communications	32
Microsoft	31
Panasonic	31
Bizmodeline	26

The biggest filers of oppositions to AI patents are Siemens, Daimler and Giesecke+Devrient, while the main defendants in oppositions are Samsung, LG Corporation and Hyundai.

2004 and involved technologies that included manufacturing an electronic card, a bill serial number reading device and method, fingerprints (times 2) and security devices (times 2).

Top defending parties

The top defending parties in oppositions involving AI patents are shown in figure 6.9, ranked by counting the number of patent families in their portfolio that have been involved in patent opposition cases. The main players are:

- Samsung (Republic of Korea): a defendant in 50 cases from 2005 to 2017, involving 167 AI patent families. It has won 12 cases, lost 30 and eight are undecided. Of the 50 cases, 37 oppositions were in Korea, seven in Japan, four before the EPO and two in China. The oppositions/considered portfolio proportion (50/167) is quite high compared with other players, indicating that Samsung is quite often a target in opposition procedures. When a Samsung patent is revoked or refused, the main causes are classified as a general issue for inventive step assessment (24 times), inventive step – non-obviousness (four times), and novelty – global assessment asserting differences as well as sufficiency of disclosure – clarity of claims (two times). It is worth noting that not all of these 167 patent families were used in infringement actions; the only other legal action involving Samsung's portfolio concerned a cancellation proceeding filed by Huawei Technologies against a Chinese patent.
- LG Corporation (Republic of Korea): a defendant in 11 cases (eight in Korea, two in Brazil and one before the EPO), involving 85 AI patent families. It has won one, lost nine and one remains undecided. Where decisions are available, they are based on general issue for inventive step assessment (eight times) and completeness of disclosure and sufficiency of disclosure – clarity of claims (once). None of the patents at stake was the subject of other legal cases, such as infringement actions.
- Hyundai (Republic of Korea): a defendant in nine cases, all in the Republic of Korea, involving 73 AI patent families. It was won

zero and lost five cases, while four are undecided. These cases are relatively recent, with the first being filed in 2014. Where available, the decisions were based on general issue for inventive step assessment (five times) and inventive step – invention by combination (twice). None of the patents at stake was the subject of other cases.

Seizure-detection algorithm

Imagine you have a neurological condition that can be life-threatening. When this condition occurs, it can cause you to stop breathing. If somebody is there to stimulate you (flip you over, give you a gentle shake; things that no comfortably-wearable technology can do yet), then you are more likely to start breathing again and to recover completely. One day, you have just such a neurological attack and your smart watch, continuously running AI, detects the attack and calls your caregiver list and shows them on a tiny map on their smartphone the location of where you are. Quickly, your nearest friend rushes to your dorm room to check on you and finds you face-down in bed, blue and not breathing. She flips you over. She shakes you gently and says your name. You can't speak but you take a breath. And, …, another breath, …, and then you recover and are fine. Your friend, helped by the AI running on your wrist, probably just saved your life!

Sudden unexplained death in epilepsy (SUDEP) is the number two cause of years of potential life lost out of all the neurological diseases, and kills someone every seven to nine minutes. The wearable described here is the Empatica Embrace, the first smart watch running AI to detect potentially life-threatening convulsive seizures. It was approved by the FDA (U.S. Food and Drug Administration) in January 2018, and has already been credited with helping save lives. Inside, the watch is continuously running a seizure-detection algorithm, built using machine learning. The AI algorithm within the watch at the time of the FDA's acceptance was a support vector machine, a form of supervised learning that is trained by collecting lots of wearable data and asking an expert neurologist to provide a medically accurate label for each time chunk of the data. The labels and data are used to train the support vector machine, enabling it to learn a mathematical function that maps data sensed from the wearer's wrist to labels likely to be given to the data by an expert human.

The resulting trained support vector machine is programmed into every watch, where it runs continuously, looking for events that might be a dangerous seizure. When it detects such an event, it communicates with another piece of software (perhaps on a paired smartphone) that issues alerts and makes calls and text messages. In addition, the additional software logs the data and event timing, so it can be reviewed later by a medical professional. Whereas today the wearable can only detect and alert to seizures as they happen, future wearables and machine learning are active areas of research and development, aimed at being able to give people advance notice of a seizure.

Case study by Rosalind Picard, MIT Media Laboratory

7 Key issues arising from AI and policy responses

It is important that the various regulatory and other governance mechanisms are thought about now; the fast pace of change in this technology is such that we cannot wait.

Kay Firth-Butterfield, WEF

The impact of AI

The spread of low-cost graphic processors allowing the performance of huge computational loads is extending the AI revolution to beyond the big multinational companies and impacting businesses and academic organizations the world over.

In particular, AI is expected to have a fundamental impact on the Fourth Industrial Revolution (4IR), a term coined by Klaus Schwab in his book of that title. Schwab sees the 4IR being characterized by a number of emerging technologies – including AI, robotics, the Internet of things (IoT), 3D printing and autonomous vehicles – which are fusing the physical, digital and biological worlds, and affecting all disciplines, economies, industries and governments.

Ultimately, almost every activity and sector will benefit from the use of AI. The impact of AI can already be seen in applications that people use every day, in transport, health, finance, law and other areas. AI will also transform productivity, with some studies estimating it could reduce conversion costs in industrial operations by up to 20 percent.

As with every new technology, AI offers advantages to early adopters. However, it also poses many challenges. AI is affecting the workplace, replacing skills and so threatening jobs and incomes. Concerns around data are myriad, and include ethical questions, from the fear of security breaches and hacking, to issues around privacy and consent, to potential bias in algorithms and the evaluation of data.

Policies and regulation: some perspectives

A number of writers and thinkers have recently addressed the likely impact of AI technologies on business, the economy, education and leisure, and commented on the role of regulation and private actors. By no means exhaustive, a selection of perspectives is presented below to illustrate the complexity of the landscape.

_____Employment

Some commentators, such as Martin Ford, author of _The Rise of the Robots_, foresee a dramatic impact on jobs and have argued for governments to provide a basic income guarantee to mitigate its effects. He explains: "It's not just about unemployment. It's also about inequality. There's a debate about whether this technology will substitute for people, or is it more about augmentation, where new technologies work with people? My belief is that both of those things will happen, but many people are too sanguine about this augmentation story. That is often a de-skilling effect. Once you had a good job that required training and education, and it turns into something anyone could do – a minimum wage job. It doesn't require training, so people are easy to replace. That is what fast food has looked like for a number of years. This technology will apply that dynamic to more areas and that will increase inequality. The number of those people in good jobs as a percentage of the workforce will shrink. People will either be replaced or wages will be driven down. There's also the globalization effect: these technologies also mean people in low-wage countries can compete."

Like Ford, Kay Firth-Butterfield, Head of AI and Machine Learning at the World Economic Forum (WEF), already sees an impact on jobs: "Socially conscious companies wish to find a way to minimize that disruption to their workforce and to the political stability of the area. In many areas of the world, job loss which

AI startups in Europe

Petr Šrámek, AI Startup Incubator

The accelerating progress of AI technologies means startups need to mature within months, not years. This requires a tremendous concentration of activities – attracting funding, attracting AI software engineers. It's a race not seen before. It is very challenging for B2B AI startups to have to deal with corporations with a slow decision/solution adoption process. Often this can – and does – spell the end for many young companies. Data protection rules in the European Union also play against AI projects because companies are afraid to give access to data. Startups are therefore forced to seek pilot projects outside of the EU. Politicians talk about AI as a priority topic, but there is a lack of real action. Regulation ought lower barriers and improve quick access to funding. A special agency with a more open policy to the funding of AI projects would be very useful.

has not been mitigated by retraining has led to geo-political change, and instability in markets is not generally useful to businesses." She also warns that companies need to be aware of the potential problems when using AI in the area of human resources: "These problems fall into four broad main categories; bias, transparency, accountability and privacy. Substantial brand value can be lost if the wrong decisions are made about the use of AI. Therefore, it is important that the various regulatory and other governance mechanisms are thought about now; the fast pace of change in this technology is such that we cannot wait."

_____Security

Others have sought to identify some of the key security risks posed by radical advances in technology. Nick Bostrom of Oxford's Future of Humanity Institute sees both risks as well as benefits in present and near-term applications of AI technology: "We see this in military applications, such as drones, and in visual recognition systems that can be used for surveillance. On a smaller level, there are concerns about autonomous cars and cyberattacks and creating mischief."

Four views on superintelligence

Nick Bostrom, Future of Humanity Institute: Superintelligence is any intellectual system that greatly outperforms the cognitive performance of the best human minds in virtually all domains of interest. Machine superintelligence would be a watershed moment: it would be the most important invention ever. For that reason, I think we have to be very careful. There are a variety of ways it should be associated with risks.

Martin Ford, futurist: I take that issue seriously. The danger is that worrying about this distracts us from the more immediate concerns in the short term, such as the impact on labor, the potential for unemployment and inequality, as well as privacy and surveillance. There's also risk of bias in the data, around gender and race for example, which will become an issue in the next 10 to 20 years. The threat of truly intelligent machines is not something to laugh at, but it's not an immediate concern.

Frank Chen, Andreessen Horowitz: Most intelligence is orthogonal: some people who have very high IQs may have low EQs [emotional quotient]. It's too easy to label intelligence as a single-dimensional thing. The reality is there are a thousand intelligences, and each requires its own AI techniques. At the core of human intelligence, there's a "you." AI may have super-sophisticated algorithms, but what's fundamentally different from human intelligence is that there are no implicit set of desires.

Kay Firth-Butterfield, WEF: There are many who worry about controlling artificial general intelligence and superintelligence and are, rightly, working on this area. Additionally, we need to be concerned about narrow AI and the issues of bias, privacy, accountability and transparency.

These four problem areas are seen time and again in the use of narrow AI, be it in predictive policing and sentencing, an individual's ability to obtain jobs and loans and, as more AI-enabled objects such as cars and robots come to market, we will see these issues multiplying. This is why the need for governance to be thought through at this stage is so necessary.

Kai-Fu Lee, author of the recently published *AI Superpowers: China, Silicon Valley, and the New World Order*, stresses the threat posed by security breaches and hacking: "AI is also a bunch of numbers that are undecipherable, multiplied together in ways inexplicable to humans. If someone hacked in and changed a thousand numbers, how would people know? What would it cause? These are all questions that will need new ways of security." He observes also that AI technologies in social media can unwittingly reinforce or even exacerbate undesirable behavior and prejudice.

_____ Data privacy and ethics

While many express concerns about data privacy, Frank Chen, partner at the venture capital firm Andreessen Horowitz, suggests that some people may be prepared to give up some of their privacy in order to get the services they want, now that 40 percent of Gmail replies are now auto-replied. "Here's a speculation: we upload a ton of photos to Facebook and Instagram. If they told us that they would scan our photos for skin irregularities and early signs of skin cancer, would we want that? I think eventually we might. But we don't want these companies to be dishonest about what they're capturing and we don't want them selling our personal information. If you could opt in or opt out of this, I think a lot of people would say: Why wouldn't I do that? That's free cancer screening!" One solution, suggests Chen, is greater transparency in AI applications, including explanations as to why a machine is making a particular recommendation.

Eleonore Pauwels, Research Fellow of United Nations University (UNU), describes AI as a "glorified data optimization process." She sees the challenge of developing fair and accurate AI as tied not only to algorithmic design, but also to the datasets used to train it: "When embodied in ubiquitous facial recognition systems, criminal justice predictions, job selection, or in the functioning of hospitals and financial markets, data quality and integrity risks are amplified. One example of this challenge is the use of facial recognition and predictive policing algorithms by law enforcement – when trained on historical crime data, platforms like PredPol and Palantir create negative feedback loops that recommend disproportionate surveillance in low-income and Black communities."

Kai-Fu Lee addressed similar concerns when interviewed for this report. He predicts that each country could develop its own data protection and data privacy laws in line with its own culture. For example, China has strict laws on selling and using data without consent, with the possibility of imprisonment for such offences, while the European Union (EU) has recently implemented the General Data Protection Regulation (GDPR).

Lee welcomes the effort made in passing the GDPR, but questions whether it is an effective model in practice: "The government is playing product manager. It's doing the brute force – let's give every user the choice of every permutation for every website. These pop-up windows keep coming up; people get sick and tired and just click 'yes'. A very tiny percentage of people will clock 'no' a lot and miss out on the convenience while a large number of people will just get annoyed with the pop-up windows."

There is a concern that there will be a race to the bottom whereby countries will compete to implement liberal data privacy regimes as these are more likely to enable the development of AI. In the medium term, this would pose a threat to individuals in those countries. But Lee believes that this may not be the case: "More data collection involves the highest risk of damaging individuals, which will then damage corporations which will in turn force countries to adopt stricter laws. It's like capital punishment: you could argue that countries with the strictest laws have the least crime, but there are side effects to that."

_____ Superintelligence

A lot of the concerns about AI are linked to a lack of specific regulations addressing legal and ethical questions, uncertainty around how an AI-enhanced future will look and whether more optimistic or more pessimistic

National solutions

Kai-Fu Lee, Sinovation Ventures

The entire ecosystem is different in different countries – users, language, expectations, how you build and advertise a product and acquire users. Even assuming no regulatory issues, it's hard to succeed. The U.S. by default exports its products to developed countries so those products are standardized.

AI policy in China

Haifeng Wang, Baidu

AI has been included in the national strategic plan since 2016. The government has issued numerous policies to support the development of AI, covering capital, IP protection, human resources development and international cooperation. Besides the emphasis on the theoretical studies, these policies also leverage resources on the integration of AI into the real economy.

scenarios are likely to materialize. One of the most widely discussed concerns is linked to the development of superintelligence – in other words, the question of what happens when machines exceed the ability of human brains in general intelligence. Superintelligence goes beyond AI taking care of individual tasks (so-called "narrow AI"), which is what current technological developments allow and what is described in the patent documents captured by the current report.

Taking all these concerns related to AI and its future impact into account, another question is who will lead or be a catalyst in the process? As we have seen, the experts contributing to this report have differing views about the roles that governments and private sector organizations should play in the development and regulation of AI. In Bostrom's words: "The more active governments become, the more we have an arms race dynamic. So I think this will be dominated by the private sector." Andreessen Horowitz partner Frank Chen agrees, pointing to the example of autonomous cars: "Regulators who expect it has to be perfect will hold back progress. Cities and countries will make their own decisions – those who regulate technology less will likely attract companies who want to develop using that technology. We're seeing this with the use of autonomous vehicles in the U.S., specifically Arizona and Florida. They took a leap to allow driverless cars on the road while other cities are waiting to see how it plays out.

Boi Faltings of EPFL argues that change will come from big corporations: "There is a lot of potential to positively influence people's lives, for example in medicine, resource sharing and access to information. However, the overwhelming majority of research goes into digital marketing, surveillance and robot weapons. I am not optimistic and I think the development will be toward monopolization of AI by large corporations to control and manipulate society, as only they have access to the data required to develop the technology."

Although striking a more positive note than Faltings, Firth-Butterfield agrees that the implications of AI for business will be profound. In particular, companies in whatever field will need to develop an AI strategy as AI technology becomes ubiquitous in robots, cars, home healthcare, entertainment and other areas: "Currently companies are not investing as much in research and development (R&D) and AI as they probably should be doing. The causes for that are principally in three areas: a lack of understanding of the technology and what it is capable of, some of the technology is still in its

EU policy framework

Paul Nemitz,
European Commission

With the dawn of artificial intelligence, many jobs will be created, but others will disappear and most will be transformed. This is why the European Commission is encouraging Member States to modernize their education and training systems and support labor market transitions, building on the European Pillar of Social Rights. The Commission will support business–education partnerships to attract and keep more AI talent in Europe, set up dedicated training schemes with financial support from the European Social Fund, and support digital skills, competencies in science, technology, engineering and mathematics (STEM), entrepreneurship and creativity. Proposals under the EU's next multiannual financial framework (2021–2027) will include strengthened support for training in advanced digital skills, including AI-specific expertise.

Regulation around the world

Frank Chen, Andreessen Horowitz

We will likely get to a point where regulators who expect that regulation must be perfect to deploy will hold back progress. Those with less regulation, who aren't afraid to push the envelope, will usher in the next generation of AI-backed technologies. Take drones as an example. Today, most drone deployments happen in countries that are less regulated. Andreessen Horowitz invested in a company called Zipline that collects and drops blood to medical facilities in Rwanda, rather than relying on public infrastructure and roads, which can take longer. As new technologies thrive in welcoming regulatory environments, other regions will follow suit.

A lot of AI is very nationalized – the US, Canada, China, and now France, all have national strategies around how to encourage and stimulate the AI economy in their countries. I can't remember the last time technology got this national. China is making direct investment from the government down to city level. It will be interesting to see how that plays out. It's been a while since we had such a national battle over technology.

---

infancy and not yet generally useful, and a lack of understanding about where regulation will come from and which developments it will hit. As a result, we can see some businesses that are forward looking trying to use AI in places where it really is not necessary to use it, for example facial recognition in air conditioning, and other businesses holding back until they see what the innovation space is and how governments may support it."

National and regional responses to AI

Given the questions about AI outlined above, governments will face a dilemma: on the one hand, there will be pressure to promote scientific development and economic progress; on the other, they will be expected to address people's concerns. It is therefore incumbent on governments to adopt public policies that foster competitiveness while at the same time protecting citizens and their rights.

As is often the case with emerging technologies, technological advances may be faster than the frameworks that seek to

regulate them. It could also be that, instead of playing catch-up, policy and regulation try to anticipate the possible yet unknown implications of technology, leading to either too much or too little regulation.

Various policies, regulations and initiatives reflect the optimism around AI and its potential benefits and try to incentivize AI research and encourage the investment or adoption of AI or address the legal and ethical concerns linked to AI. The latter include the transparency, verifiability and accountability of AI, the right to privacy, the right to equal treatment and avoidance of bias, and the mitigation of negative impacts on employment.

In the light of these challenges, it is crucial that policy decisions are based on evidence. The data and analysis presented in this report can contribute to discussions about appropriate

Adding anticipative reflection

Konstantinos Karachalios, IEEE

To mitigate risks, we have to add a layer of anticipative reflection to the traditional technical skills of the involved techno-scientific communities. Goodwill alone will not suffice to achieve this cultural transformation against the prevailing spirit of techno-solutionism. We need concrete, practical assets, such as educational material, guidelines, standards and codes, and we need them now, not tomorrow. To address this singular challenge, we need processes that are universally open and inclusive, are based on robust rules and transparency, and are capable of producing a broad consensus among a great variety of actors. Some standardization ecosystems come close to this, but even they have still to evolve significantly, almost to reinvent themselves, because this challenge cannot be reduced to a matter among technicians. A conscious effort has to be made to attract and include human science experts, lawyers, political actors, sociologists, philosophers, and yes also artists. An image or a story well told may help convince and drive home the message about what we need to do for humans and machines to be able to co-exist and serve humanity as a whole, not only to make ever smaller groups ever more powerful and more dominant over all others. The IEEE Standards Association has been engaging and investing in all these areas, through activities such as the Global Initiative on Ethics of Autonomous and Intelligent Systems, the Global Council on Extended Intelligence and the Open Community for Ethics in Autonomous and Intelligent Systems (OCEANIS).

policies and regulation in this area. This chapter now presents a number of the issues that arise from AI, along with examples of the policies, laws, strategies and other initiatives trying to address them. It also indicates differences in the approach taken by several countries.

Responses to AI can be of a general, declaratory nature, indicating an intention at the national or regional level to invest in AI or highlighting the importance of AI for the country through its inclusion in a related strategy or plan.

The **European Commission (EC)**, for instance, issued in April 2018 a Communication on AI for Europe, announcing among other things its aim to increase investment in AI research and innovation by at least €20 billion from now until the end of 2020. To support this effort, the EC is increasing its investment dedicated to AI to €1.5 billion for the period 2018–2020 under the Horizon 2020 research and innovation program. The EU Member States also signed a Declaration of Cooperation on Artificial Intelligence in 2018 in which they agreed to work together on the most important issues raised by AI, from ensuring Europe's competitiveness in the research and deployment of AI, to dealing with social, economic, ethical and legal questions. Moreover, the EC has established a High-Level Expert Group on AI to make recommendations on policy and investment, and set guidelines on the ethical development of AI. It also issued in December 2018 a Coordinated Plan on the Development and Use of Artificial Intelligence Made in Europe, which states "the ambition is for Europe to become the world-leading region for developing and deploying cutting-edge, ethical and secure AI, promoting a human-centric approach in the global context." The EC report, *Artificial Intelligence: The European Perspective*, published in the same month, provides an overview of European policies, AI challenges and AI opportunities, and aims to support the development of European action in the global AI context.

In the **U.S.**, the White House, acknowledging the growing role of AI for the future, released three reports in 2016: *Artificial Intelligence, Automation, and the Economy*; *Preparing for the Future of Artificial Intelligence*; and *The National Artificial Intelligence Research and Development Strategic Plan*. In May 2018, the establishment of a Select Committee on Artificial Intelligence was announced to advise the White House on interagency AI R&D priorities and to support the Government in achieving its goal of maintaining U.S. leadership in AI.

In **France**, the Government published its France IA (France AI Plan) on March 21, 2017, which included about 50 recommendations. This was followed by a report, *For a Meaningful Artificial Intelligence: Towards a French and European Strategy*, delivered in March 2018, promoting better access to data with a focus on health, transport, ecology and defense.

In **China**, the State Council issued in 2017 the Next Generation AI Development Plan, setting as a goal for the country to become the world's primary innovation center by 2030, with the output of AI industries passing RNB 1 trillion. This is supplemented by local government policies designed to promote different regions and provide incentives to AI companies to base themselves in respective provinces. In November 2017, the Ministry of Science and Technology convened a meeting to mark the official launch of this Plan, setting up a special Promotion Office involving 15 governmental entities, and in December 2017 the Ministry of Industry and Information Technology released a Three-Year Action Plan to Promote the Development of New-Generation AI Industry.

In the **United Arab Emirates (UAE)**, in October 2017, Sheikh Mohammed announced the UAE Strategy for AI as a major part of the country's Centennial 2071 objectives. This strategy aims to make the UAE first in the world in the field of AI investment in various vital sectors, as well as create a new vital market with high economic value. The first Minister of State for Artificial Intelligence was also appointed.

AI plans are expected to be published soon in **Germany** and **Finland**, while the **Nordic-Baltic states** made a joint statement on AI collaboration in May 2018 to enhance access to data for AI, while developing ethical and transparent guidelines, standards, principles and values, enabling interoperability, privacy, security and trust. The signatories stated a wish to avoid any unnecessary regulation that could get in the way of this fast-developing field.

_____AI and public research/funding

A number of policies aim at supporting research and development in the field of AI.

Multilateral solutions to developing responsible AI

Eleonore Pauwels, UN University Center for Policy Research

Multinational corporations such as Google, Intel, Microsoft, and IBM are releasing their own sets of principles for developing responsible AI – but this challenge can't be overcome in institutional silos. With artificial general intelligence (AGI) on the horizon, standardization and regularization should be informed by inclusive foresight to anticipate potential risks and future unknowns. Citizens, private industry, national governments and international institutions must work together to collectively establish standards for training datasets and auditing procedures that require the perspectives of diverse disciplines and coalitions.

In a world where data ownership will determine who will be the leaders in AI innovation, collaborative national policies or even a multilateral treaty may be necessary to combat the global scale of potential disruption. The EU's General Data Protection Regulation (GDPR), the most holistic and comprehensive national data protection legislation to date, came into effect in May 2018, but its efficacy remains untested. Never before has our species been equipped to monitor and sift through human behaviors, physiology and biology on such a grand scale. Geopolitical tensions might rise when states that have the know-how to harness AI commodify, for a very high value, the data of other countries' populations and ecosystems.

In **China**, the Next Generation AI Development Plan proposes strengthening research on the framework of AI standards to cooperate with the world's top universities and public research organizations. Based on the strategy of One Belt One Road, it seeks to encourage the setting up of international science and technology cooperation centers and joint research centers to promote and apply AI technology.

In **India**, the 2018 *Report of the Artificial Intelligence Task Force* focuses on public

Data and information

Herbert Zech, University of Basel

Data can be understood as information encoded in a way that can be processed by machines comprising software and application data alike. Data as property can be found in the area of intellectual property, personality protection and other property rights.

Data and information are widely regarded as key concepts of modern society. Their production, distribution and use have become key aspects of modern economies. Driven by technological progress, information has become a tradeable good in its own right. This has established an information economy and challenged the law to provide a framework suitable to promote the production of data, enable its distribution and efficient allocation, and deal with the risks and benefits inherent in AI and other new information and communication technologies (ICT).

Data concerns being addressed

Miguel Luengo-Oroz, UN Global Pulse

To date, no standards exist for the anonymization and sharing of insights from big data in priority industries such as financial services, e-commerce or mobile telecommunication. New frameworks are needed that go beyond privacy and also ensure accountability and the responsible use and re-use of data for the public good. A recent example in which ethics and the moral obligations of data handling were included in an official UN document is the Guidance Note on Big Data for the achievement of the 2030 Agenda adopted by the UN Development Group (UNDG 2017). This Note, the first official document in the UN on big data and privacy, stresses the importance of ensuring that data ethics is included as part of standard operating procedures for data governance.

Data privacy and the common good

Frank Chen, Andreessen Horowitz

I think all companies who have aggregated personal data need to do a better job at being transparent with their intentions to use that data. What upsets people is when they don't realize their data is being collected by a company. That's what happened when Equifax got hacked in the US. The root of anger is: "I didn't know you were doing that." Companies need to be more open about what data they're collecting and what they're using it for so we can all make a judgment call in the trade-off between privacy and usefulness.

An open source privacy tool

Ben Lorica, O'Reilly Media

In many settings, business intelligence relies on a database. A collaboration between Uber and UC Berkeley's RISE Lab has resulted in an open source tool that lets analysts submit queries and get results that adhere to state-of-the-art differential privacy (a formal guarantee that provides robust privacy assurances). Their open source tool paves the way for privacy-preserving business intelligence within many organizations. More impressively, differential privacy can scale to millions of devices that generate data in real-time. Apple, Microsoft, and Google have built privacy-preserving business analytics for services that support mobile phones and smart meters.

Consumers and data

Kai-Fu Lee, Sinovation Ventures

Eventually every country will have different data laws. China has strong data laws, not with respect to individual privacy, but with respect to companies that sell and use data without user consent, such as in the Facebook-Cambridge Analytica case which would have been punished by imprisonment. The EU has the GDPR and the U.S. is figuring something out.

We are in uncharted waters in figuring out how to deal with individual data management and privacy and what is legal and what is not. I doubt there is one answer that is valid for every country, given the different cultures and user expectations. I think we are at the beginning of a crowdsourcing project. The GDPR is one of the first efforts. I don't think it's a very good design, but I think we will tweak it. Maybe we will have three sets of data laws – EU, China and U.S. – and there will be some commonalities, but also differences.

A fair return for data

Seth G. Benzell and Erik Brynjolfsson, MIT Initiative on the Digital Economy

If AI faces decreasing returns from additional data, or if data from different individuals are close substitutes, then ordinary individuals have little market power in negotiating a price for the use of their information. Governments can empower citizens by either enabling or directly collective bargaining on their behalf.

Anonymized data

Boi Faltings, EPFL

One area in which we have made major contributions is finding mechanisms for multi-agent optimization that preserve the privacy of the participating agents, and more recently mechanisms for artificial data for machine learning that allow learning from the same models as the original data but give no information about this original data (with the guarantees of differential privacy). These techniques can enable AI techniques to work while preserving the privacy of the underlying data, for example to develop models of diseases based on sensitive medical records. The tools and methods in this area have not changed very much over the past 20 years; however, due to the current large interest in machine learning, the focus of interest has shifted to such problems.

Data in the EU

Paul Nemitz, European Commission

The European Commission will continue to create an environment that stimulates investment. Because data is the raw material for most AI technologies, the Commission is proposing legislation to open up more data for re-use and measures to make data sharing easier. This covers data from public utilities and the environment, as well as research and health data.

research, including the funding of an Inter-Ministerial National Artificial Intelligence Mission to coordinate AI-related activities. The *National Strategy for Artificial Intelligence Discussion Paper* also recommends funding for centers of research excellence.

The **EU** Horizon 2020 (2014–2020) project provides European funding for the creation of a platform to host the European AI ecosystem that allows available knowledge, algorithms, tools and resources to be combined. Scientists have drawn up ambitious plans for a vast, multinational European institute devoted to world-class AI research designed to nurture and retain top talent in Europe. This institute is to be called "Ellis."

In the **U.K.**, the *Growing AI in the UK* report recommends establishing the Alan Turing Institute as a national institute for AI and data science to work together with other public research entities or councils to coordinate demand for computing capacity for AI research and to negotiate on behalf of the U.K. research community.

In **Japan**, the Japan Revitalization Strategy has engaged the AI Technology Strategy Council to draw up a roadmap defining objectives for R&D related to AI technologies and their commercialization conducted through cooperation between the Government, industry and academia.

In **France**, proposals in the France AI Plan include promoting a support policy for discovery research and transfer to industry over the long term, identifying key technologies and creating a French "Center for AI" which could host public–private projects. In June 2017, the world's largest incubator for startups opened in Paris. The Station F campus covers 34,000 square meters, can accommodate up to 3,000 workstations available to 1,000 startups, and directly integrates venture funds and other services.

In the **Republic of Korea**, the leading defense business, Hanwha Systems, and the state-run science research university Korea Advanced Institute of Science and Technology (KAIST),

have launched a project to co-develop AI technologies to be applied to military weapons. The two parties recently opened a joint research center at KAIST where researchers from the university and Hanwha will carry out various studies into how technologies of the Fourth Industrial Revolution can be utilized on future battlefields.

In **Saudi Arabia**, the megacity project known as the "King Abdullah Economic City" is being engineered to accommodate autonomous vehicles and the Internet of things. It is expected to be finished by 2020. Similarly, in the **UAE**, the Smart Dubai strategic plan is transforming Dubai into a smart city.

In **Israel**, the Government has authorized a five-year program worth about ILS240 million (US$66.2 million) to promote smart transportation in Israel.

In the **U.S.**, the FY2019 Budget Request was the first in history to designate AI as an Administration R&D priority. In October 2018, the Massachusetts Institute of Technology (MIT) announced a new US$1 billion commitment to addressing the global opportunities and challenges presented by the prevalence of computing and the rise of AI. This initiative marks the single largest investment in computing and AI by a U.S. academic institution. At the heart of this endeavor will be the new MIT Stephen A. Schwarzman College of Computing.

_____AI and jobs

Experts have voiced a concern that AI systems will not only enhance and support human skills, but will to some extent replace them, posing a threat to jobs and income. This issue is being addressed at the national level by a range of policies, aimed either at creating new skill sets in AI to mitigate job losses or preparing for the new jobs that might be created through AI.

Several national strategies address the question of AI and jobs.

In the **Republic of Korea**, the 4th Industrial Revolution Commission, which is directly answerable to the President, considered in May 2018 an AI R&D strategy to train 5,000 AI personnel over the next five years with a fund of US$2.04 billion. The Commission also plans to establish six AI graduate schools from 2019 to 2022, and nurture 1,400 students by strengthening support for AI research at existing university research centers.

In the **UAE**, there are plans to replace immigration officers at airports with an AI system by 2020, and the Ministry of AI is working with other ministries to include AI in the national curriculum. In January 2018, the Government announced its plan to train 500 Emirati men and women in AI.

In **Israel**, in early 2017, the Government passed a resolution to implement a national program for increasing the number of skilled personnel in high-tech industry. Well-known universities, including the Open University of Israel, and private platforms are offering AI training.

In the **U.S.**, in September 2017, a Presidential Memorandum was signed which prioritized high-quality science, technology, engineering, and math (STEM) education, with a particular focus on computer science education.

Germany's Ethics Commission on Automated Driving principles is addressing the need for a "people-centered" AI development, proposing to observe the impact of automated driving on employment and design a national strategy aimed at retraining to reduce the negative effect of AI on the workforce.

_____AI development and issues around data

Data plays a central role in the development of AI. Data is fed into AI systems to train and support them in grouping information, identifying patterns, grouping results and in providing more accurate forecasts, recommendations and decision-making when new data is presented. AI systems tend to perform better the more the data used to train them, and the more relevant that data is to the intended final use.

AI transforming jobs

Martin Ford, futurist: Job creation since the financial crisis has been weighted toward less desirable jobs, including in fast food restaurants and Amazon warehouses. A lot of these jobs involve robots and workers together, but I expect within the next five years robots will have the dexterity to do all of the job, and Amazon has run competitions to achieve exactly that. The nature of those warehouses will be transformed over the next three to five years. When it does change, the dynamic could be quite different.

Kai-Fu Lee, Sinovation Ventures: If AI takes away all the entry-level jobs, how do people get to the higher jobs? How do we promote people in the future?

Frank Chen, Andreessen Horowitz: AI will create a lot of opportunities and new jobs. It will also augment current jobs so that humans can be more accurate and efficient, and keep us safer. AI will augment our doctors, to ensure they're giving accurate diagnoses. AI will help machines perform dangerous tasks once done by humans. The flip side of this is that some jobs, such as truck driving, will cease to exist. And we've got to do a better job of explaining what those truck drivers will be doing instead.

Empathy, curiosity, collaboration, understanding people – those things are going to be hard to automate so let's re-emphasize those.

Owning and accessing data is thus of paramount importance for the development of AI and will be at the core of many of the biggest challenges in AI. There are different types of data, some of which are public, and some of which are private.

Their use creates concerns related to which data may or may not be used, possible violations of privacy and to what extent the subjects of the data know about and consent to its use for certain purposes. Examples include patient information collected by public or private health service providers, and geospatial information that may involve personal or sensitive data. Another issue that arises is the risk that those companies which own large amounts of data gain a dominant position, thereby excluding smaller players (e.g., universities and startups) from equal opportunities in the development of AI and the question as to how this risk could be mitigated.

Some regulation has already been developed to address privacy. There are ongoing discussions about the development of a specific regulatory framework, such as an IP instrument, to address the legal nature and regulation of data, datasets and database ownership. Another debate is whether data owned by bigger players should be shared with public sector institutions to provide more equal opportunities in AI research and development. Some experts believe that the answer to data and privacy concerns can come from technological solutions, mostly related to anonymizing data, to create a win-win situation both for AI developers and subjects of the data.

The GDPR at the European level addresses the right to privacy, the need for transparency, information and control by citizens about the personal information to be used and in what way, and the need for explicit consent. Consumers have become concerned about the tradeoff between gaining useful services and giving up personal information. These are likely to be compounded, especially given the large amounts of personal data that will be generated by new applications such as autonomous vehicles, smart meters and e-commerce.

_____AI and ethics

Further concerns are linked to a series of ethical questions, including the grouping and interpretation of data by machines which may lead to undesired and biased results and discrimination, for example in assessing for health insurance or profiling a subject in the area

The Internet of Bodies

Eleonore Pauwels, UN University Center for Policy Research

We may soon unwittingly surrender to algorithmic networks, giving them unprecedented access to our bodies, genomes and minds, setting the stage for social and bio-control. Networks of biosensors and algorithms will capture and analyze an ever more refined record of our biometrics, vital signs, emotions and behaviors – we call this set of networks the Internet of Bodies (IoB). If the data within the IoB is not given context, then we may fall prey to a lack of the trans-disciplinarity necessary to ward off bad AI design and deployment. When AI-enhanced medical diagnostic platforms are trained on poorly curated data, it can result in unsafe treatment interventions that no doctor would ever recommend. We will go from the predictive power of one algorithm to the next, making data quality standards and AI auditing procedures of the utmost importance.

of criminal justice. Moreover, concerns have been expressed about the use of AI which as a tool and can be used both to benefit and to harm human life and well-being, and the related issue of accountability and liability for AI decisions and actions. Strategies to address these concerns include using a human-centric AI framework, embedding ethical values into algorithms, making sure unconscious biases are removed in the evaluation of data and ensuring transparency in the way AI systems reach a conclusion.

Ethical issues are addressed to some extent in many policies. In **France**, the France AI Plan stresses transparency, information and awareness. The AI for Humanity Plan also formally noted its desire to lay the foundations for the ethical development of AI and promote debate on this issue within society at large and through training.

In the **Republic of Korea**, the Regulatory Reform Plan raises questions about ethics and trust and concerns about the possible unethical use of AI. It established an ethics charter with respect to intelligence information technology and a study of standards and procedures for

Providing an ethical and legal framework

Paul Nemitz,
European Commission

As with any transformative technology, AI may raise new ethical and legal questions, such as those related to liability or potentially biased decision-making. New technologies should not mean new values. The European Commission asked a high level group on AI to present draft ethical guidelines on AI development by the end of 2018, based on the EU's Charter of Fundamental Rights, taking into account principles and existing laws such as those on data protection and transparency, and building on the work of the European Group on Ethics in Science and New Technologies. To help develop these guidelines, the Commission brought together all relevant stakeholders in a European AI Alliance. By mid-2019 the Commission will also issue guidance on the interpretation of the Product Liability Directive in the light of technological developments, to ensure legal clarity for consumers and producers in case of defective products.

It is clear that in the geostrategic positioning of European AI, ethics and law will be key factors in ensuring the sustainable use and profitability of AI investments. This differentiates Europe from the unsustainable development and use of digital technology and AI for massive surveillance and mass control of people, as it is emerging in the social scoring systems in China, and the equally unsustainable concentration of data and AI development in the hands of a few mega corporations in the U.S., so far without a substantial democratic framing in the public interest.

AI for humanity

Myriam Coté, Mila

We are part of the first major wave in an AI revolution. Soon, we will see more and more impacts of this technology on our lives. Now is the time to forecast the changes appearing on the horizon. As part of its core values, Mila is concerned by these important issues and is willing to take action to promote the ethical and socially responsible application of AI. At the same time, it will be increasingly important for research institutes such as ours to contribute to the elaboration of rules, governance guidelines and best practices by providing the technical background and context necessary to validate the coherence and feasibility of possible legislative actions and recommendations. Through dialogue and cooperative projects, we intend to increase the general level of awareness and understanding of these problems in the members of our local communities and with our international allies. This is an urgent and essential prerequisite to the intelligent development of guidelines for ensuring that the technology is used in humane and ethically responsible ways that improve the conditions of human life on a global scale.

data collection and algorithm development. The co-development of AI technologies applied to military weapons mentioned above led the KAIST president to state that the university had no intention of engaging in the development of lethal autonomous weapons systems (LAWS).

In **Saudi Arabia**, Sophia, a humanoid robot designed by the company Hanson Robotics, became a full citizen in October 2017.

In **Japan**, the Ethics Committee of the Japanese Society for Artificial Intelligence (JSAI) was established in 2014 and is exploring the relationship between AI research/technology and society, and striving to effectively communicate it to society at large. These discussions were summarized in a draft Code of Ethics during the first half of 2016 and soon became open to online feedback. This now constitutes the Japanese Society for Artificial Intelligence Ethical Guidelines, approved in 2017.

The **European Commission (EC)** presented in December 2018 a draft of the AI Ethics Guidelines produced by the European Commission's High-Level Expert Group on Artificial Intelligence (AI HLEG), including a set of ethical guidelines considering principles such as data protection and transparency. This forms part of the EC's proposed three-pronged strategy to increase public and private

Technology solutions to privacy

Ben Lorica, O'Reilly Media

Researchers and entrepreneurs are building privacy-preserving methods and tools for AI. The machine learning community has long acknowledged that simple data anonymization techniques can place users' privacy at risk (an early example is the de-anonymization attacks on the Netflix Prize). Here are some recent privacy-preserving techniques in machine learning:

- Federated Learning: introduced by Google, it allows for training a centralized machine learning model without sharing data, and thus fits nicely into services on mobile devices.

- Differential privacy: the interplay between differential privacy and machine learning continues to be an active research area and researchers are beginning to examine deep learning models that adhere to differential privacy.

- Homomorphic encryption: this is an emerging area whose goal is to develop a class of tools that allow computation of complex models over encrypted data. There has been preliminary work done in computer vision and speech technologies.

- Decentralization: this is an area driven mainly by startups who are looking to use blockchains, distributed ledgers and incentive structures that use cryptocurrencies. For example, Computable Labs is building open source, decentralized infrastructure that will allow companies to securely share data and models. They want to "make blockchain networks compatible with machine learning computations."

Governments, standards and regulation

Kay Firth-Butterfield, WEF

There are many forms of governance and regulation by government is only one of them. So often it lags behind fast-paced technologies such as AI because it takes so long to regulate, especially in democratic countries. At the WEF we know that in some cases regulation is necessary; however we believe that the best way of succeeding in governance of AI is to use agile governance measures. These include: the development and use of standards (IEEE and WEF Protocols), the emergence of social norms which constrain or endorse, private incentive schemes, certification, oversight by professional bodies, industry agreements and policies that organizations apply voluntarily or by contract within their relationships with competitors, suppliers, partners and customers. As such the work of the Global Initiative on Ethical Considerations in Artificial Intelligence (AI) and Autonomous Systems (AS) is of great importance as part of these agile governance initiatives.

These guidelines will empower governments to responsibly deploy and design AI technology for the benefit of citizens. At the same time, governments' significant buying power can drive private-sector adoption of these standards even for products that are sold beyond government. And, as industry debates setting its own standards on these technologies, the government's moral authority and credibility can help set a baseline for these discussions. These indirect methods of influencing the trajectory of AI provide a softer alternative to regulation, particularly needed in an arena where traditional governance measures are too slow in the face of fast-paced technological change, especially in AI.

investment in AI, prepare for socio-economic changes and ensure an appropriate ethical and legal framework.

Germany has an Ethics Commission on Automated Driving that has published principles dealing extensively with AI accountability and allocation of liability, and acknowledged the need to avoid bias and discrimination when AI is applied to public decision-making, stressing the importance of the protection of citizens and citizens' rights in the public use of AI.

Two other initiatives linked to ethics are worth noting. First, the **IEEE Global Initiative on Ethics of Autonomous and Intelligent Systems** published *Ethically Aligned Design: A vision for prioritizing human well-being with autonomous and intelligent systems*, the result of input from several hundred participants across six continents representing academia, industry, civil society, policy and government. *Ethically Aligned Design* aims to advance public discussion about how best to establish ethical and social implementations for intelligent and autonomous systems and technologies, aligning them to defined values and ethical principles that prioritize human well-being in a given cultural context.

Second, the **Partnership on AI** is a technology consortium in which the biggest companies active in AI (identified as top players in this report), academic institutions, AI experts and some United Nations (UN) agencies participate. Its stated aims are "studying and formulating best practices on AI technologies, advancing the public's understanding of AI, and serving as an open platform for discussion and engagement about AI and its influences on people and society."

_____AI and open innovation

The development of AI often takes place in an open source environment and certain policies aim at encouraging this as a path to AI-related innovation.

In the **Republic of Korea**, the Government announced in March 2018 that the Ministry of Science and ICT and the National IT Promotion Agency are to promote the development of AI and big data, notably through the application of open software to traditional industries and the development of application software for open operating systems. Financial support is to be given to software companies to commercialize services and products related to AI and other core technologies and support given to the opening of source codes by companies with IP rights.

Also in March 2018, **India** launched a Plan to have enabling policies for socially relevant projects, especially a data policy to include ownership, sharing rights and usage policies, as well as tax incentives for income generated through the adoption of AI technologies and applications. This was followed by a Discussion Paper (National Strategy for AI) in June 2018, recommending a data protection framework, sectoral regulatory guidelines and the creation of open platforms for learning.

In the **U.S.**, at the May 2018 Summit on AI for American Industry, the Government announced its objective to enable the creation of new American industries, by removing regulatory barriers to the deployment of AI-powered technologies. Other recent U.S. initiatives include an update to the 2016 Federal Automated Vehicles Policy; various strategies in the 2016 Big Data Plan devoted to open innovation; while the 2016 report *Preparing the Future of AI* included an Open Data for AI initiative.

Wide engagement

The policies outlined above are just a few examples of the ways in which governments and legislators are responding to the need to provide frameworks for the promotion and regulation of AI applications. The next few years are likely to see many more similar initiatives. It is incumbent on all stakeholders in this field to engage in this process and provide informed input as policies are developed to ensure they balance the many interests and concerns in this field.

Speech recognition and text-to-speech facilitating access to information

One application where recent AI techniques have outperformed the preceding generation is the facilitation of the real-time translation of more and more of the world's languages. This provides the possibility of giving a voice to those not always heard. Together, UN Global Pulse and the Stellenbosch University in South Africa built speech recognition technology that converts public discussions in radio broadcasts into text that can be read in several of the languages spoken in Uganda, including Luganda, Acholi, Lugbara and Rutooro. Monitoring public conversations allows for the understanding of public concerns on subjects ranging from education to corruption and the provision of early warnings of epidemics or low-scale natural disasters.

AI as augmentation rather than substitute for human intelligence

A key characteristic of AI tools is the possibility to automatize certain tasks. However, the errors inherent in any automated method might be unacceptable in certain scenarios. For instance, an estimate of the size of a displaced population is key to allocating sufficient resources and assistance during an humanitarian emergency. The manual analysis of satellite imagery has thus far been the most reliable method for mapping structures in settlements built to house displaced populations. Although automated methods exist, they have proven inadequate for the accurate mapping of structures in different conditions and locations. When dealing with conflict and humanitarian scenarios, precision in satellite image analysis is key to supporting critical operations on the ground. In one project, an iterative human-centered AI system is proposed in order to increase analysts' performance when assessing humanitarian and conflict satellite imagery. The key is that AI augment human intelligence rather than be a substitute for it.

Case studies by Miguel Luengo-Oroz, UN Global Pulse

8 The future of AI and the IP system

The focus of this report has been the analysis of current and recent trends in AI-related technologies, as measured by statistical data on patents and scientific publications. In this final chapter, the future of this technology is reviewed, including the opportunities that the next generation of AI might bring and the interaction between AI and the intellectual property (IP) system. As with previous chapters, it draws on comments and contributions from a range of international AI experts.

The big question may not be what the next breakthrough will be, but rather how existing emergent technologies will be applied across different areas.

The future of AI and the opportunities it brings

Although the nature of AI does not allow for the forecasting of what the next big thing will be, based on the analysis of patent data, scientific literature and business information related to AI, a number of trends have been identified which could provide an indication of the direction in which the field is heading.

- It is clear that we are going through a renaissance of AI and this is also reflected in the increasing numbers of scientific publications and patent applications, with half of the patenting activity in AI having taken place since 2013. This boom in AI patenting activity, combined with growth rates across different AI technologies over the period 2013–2016 which are much higher compared with those observed in general in all fields of technology, clearly indicate that this trend can be expected to continue.
- The analysis shows that most patent applications have a commercial application focus, as they refer to an AI functional application or are combined with an AI application field. This report identifies 20 fields/industry sectors that patent documents refer to, ranging from entertainment to education to banking, indicating that sectors across the board are exploring the application of AI technologies.
- The fields with the most patent applications are the ones which have already attracted a lot of media attention and have been linked to AI such as transportation, including self-driving cars, drones and airplanes, or life and medical sciences with applications such as collection of medical data and related medical diagnostics and predictions. However, growth rates in other fields show the potential for nearly all areas to benefit from the use of AI. At the same time, the analysis suggests that the combination of AI technologies with other emerging technologies, such as robotics, the Internet of things and cryptography used for blockchain, means AI can revolutionize other areas and lead to further developments in combination with them.
- Companies feature as top patent applicants in the vast majority of AI techniques, functional applications and industries. There are, however, certain areas where the top players are mainly populated by public research institutions. These include support-vector machines, bio-inspired approaches, unsupervised learning and instance-based learning for AI techniques; distributed AI for functional applications; and neuroscience/neurorobotics and smart cities for application fields. It will be interesting to observe how cooperation between industry and universities may develop, or whether there will be further acquisition of related technologies or AI talent by industry.
- Building AI talent is a concern for a lot of governments, as seen through the recent adoption of a number of AI-related policies. This may be linked to an identified need to develop skills in AI at a national or regional level to prepare society to match demand and to allow for the democratization of AI so that everyone can benefit from its use.
- A number of experts raise the issue of the importance of accessibility to and availability of large amounts of data, in view of their importance in the context of the dominant deep learning and neural networks, and this is addressed through some government policies. Some of the

What will be the next big thing in AI?

Haifeng Wang, Baidu: While we may hardly name one next big thing in AI, we may consider where the challenges and opportunities in AI lie: human-like learning mechanisms, functional applications synergized with knowledge, combinations of different functional applications and integration with hardware, AI applications customized with real data and vertical scenarios.

Rosalind Picard, MIT Media Laboratory: Of the areas where I have expertise, we will continue to see huge growth in healthcare (especially AI for imaging/diagnostics/monitoring/alerting/mining the microbiome and combinations for better health, forecasting, etc.) and human–computer interaction (HCI) – especially around interactions in transportation, wearables/smartphones, robots, transactions (financial and other easy-to-describe processes) and IoT devices.

Frank Chen, Andreessen Horowitz: Venture capital firms have been pouring money into AI for the past few years and what you're going to start seeing is the deployment of those funds toward research and development across every industry, and around the globe. Right now, you see AI in your email and on your phone, and little by little, in apps. But soon, you'll see fully autonomous systems – cars, buses, planes, ships, delivery trucks. You'll interact with AI in healthcare, education, legal services and in so many different ways. We've got a ways to go, but this is only just the beginning.

Martin Ford, futurist: I remain convinced there will be an enormous impact from AI. I think it would be a huge mistake to be dismissive of it just because we haven't seen this yet. Self-driving cars are one area. I know of three companies working on the automation of fast food. The same is true in warehouse environments. Technology will come online enabling this to happen. More generally, I believe AI will have an enormous impact across society and will bring entirely new capabilities.

Kai-Fu Lee, Sinovation Ventures: The next breakthrough could come from the combination of neuroscience and AI, connecting something about our thinking and statistical thinking, quantum computing, or semantics or language understanding. Each of these has a chance of making a big difference.

Future of patent protection in U.S.

John G. Flaim and Yoon Chae, Baker McKenzie

The number of AI patent suits filed in the United States and other jurisdictions will likely increase, given the proliferation of AI patent applications being filed and granted. For U.S.-based patent suits, §101 will likely continue to play central roles, especially in contexts of providing prosecution challenges and being raised as an invalidity defense in patent infringement cases. But the status of patent protection on software inventions in the United States is in flux, and like any other statute §101 and its interpretation by the courts is subject to change (see for instance the changes the Alice case law brought, making U.S. practice convergent with the more restrictive European approach). During a USPTO oversight hearing held by the Senate on April 18, 2018, the recently appointed USPTO Director, Andrei Iancu, said: "At a high level, the approach to Section 101 should be technology neutral" and that recent "Supreme Court decisions have introduced a degree of uncertainty into the area of subject matter eligibility, particularly as it relates to medical diagnostics and software-related innovations," that can "negatively impact innovation in these and other areas" if applied in an overly broad manner. His discussions with the senators during the hearing may be interpreted by some as implying a need for a less stringent §101 standard.

Given AI's significant economic and technological effects on companies' competitive advantage, as well as on governmental policies, we will likely be seeing more political and academic discussions and legislative and judicial developments regarding AI patentability in the near future.

AI experts contributing to the report talk about the challenges and opportunities for techniques working and providing results with smaller datasets, which may have implications for data requirements. The lack of access to data, particularly for public research organizations or smaller players, could encourage the development of other AI approaches, or the monopolization of certain approaches by owners of proprietary data.

As has been pointed out by a number of expert contributors, the big question may not be what the next breakthrough will be, but rather how existing emergent technologies will be applied across different areas as we experience what Kai-Fu Lee in Chapter 3 calls the "AI implementation age." Some futurists such as Jay Iorio predict that, thanks to increased interconnectivity, the different emergent technologies, including artificial intelligence,

the Internet of things (IoT), augmented reality and virtual reality, will converge into an interconnected environment, already is indicated by the analysis results which refer to the use of AI specifically for some of these areas. This will complete the digital transformation process underway and will have a great impact on our lives, economies and societies.

Despite concerns about the challenges that need to be addressed with regard to AI technologies discussed in the previous chapter, most experts agree that the possibilities offered by these technologies are immense. Even commentators whose reservations with regard to "superintelligence" are substantial and profound, such as Nick Bostrom and Martin Ford, believe the benefits of AI will outweigh the harm. They foresee AI making us more productive, a trend that has been ongoing for hundreds of years, and as Keynes

Convergence of intelligent systems, IoT and full-time augmented reality into an interconnected environment

Jay Iorio, futurist

Intelligent systems are inevitably going to lead to major changes in society over the next generation – some positive, some perhaps not. Healthcare alone could be transformed positively in many ways, including diagnostics based on mountains of real-time data coming from a patient's smart clothing and elsewhere. But despite the potential importance of all the remarkable vertical applications, perhaps nothing is more central to our lives than what our senses tell us. The convergence of intelligent systems, IoT and full-time augmented reality will splice into those animal connections and could lead to a profound shift in our conceptions of self, identity and reality itself (to say nothing of privacy). There is widespread concern, understandably, about the potential uses of intelligent systems in warfare, law enforcement, crucial decision-making, and other areas. But even more fundamentally disruptive could be an intelligent environment of illusion that, over time, becomes our actual perception of reality.

AI as a general purpose technology

Dominique Foray, EPFL

A recent argument made by scholars in the economics of innovation is that AI has the potential to become a general purpose technology in the foreseeable future, thus bringing about a wave of complementary innovations in a wide and ever-expanding range of applications sectors. This is good news for many less advanced and transitional regions – which cannot lead in the development of core technology. However, these regions will not be out of the game if (a big "if") they can design a smart specialization strategy in which the development of AI applications complements the region's productive assets to create future domestic capability and interregional competitive advantage. Sectors such as healthcare, tourism, agrifood and marine resources (to mention just a few) are natural domains in which the development of AI applications could help trigger structural transformation in regional economies, such as the modernization of a traditional sector, the diversification of industries facing declining markets or the transition of a sector toward more productive activities.

predicted back in the 1930s, it may even lead to a future when there are no dehumanizing jobs, there is more space for leisure, and more people dedicate themselves to the arts or to the community.

Frank Chen embraces the new opportunities that AI promises to bring. He looks forward to augmenting his own intelligence and compensating for his biases. Humans are irrational while AI can help make us become better decision-makers. He foresees AI's

potential to allow us to focus on the things AI is not able to do and emphasize those parts of humanity that are hard to automate, such as empathy. Such a focus on empathy will in its turn have an impact on society, argues Chen, predicting that systems will shift to people with such skills, in turn having a long-term impact on both education and software design.

Such a focus on empathy will in its turn have an impact on society, argues Chen, predicting that systems will shift to people with such skills,

Four areas of patent focus

Kay Firth-Butterfield, WEF

The impact of AI on the patent system could be quite significant. Together with a WEF Centre for the Fourth Industrial Revolution Fellow, Yoon Chae, I authored a white paper on this subject. Our conclusions were that four areas should be considered:

1. Patent-eligible subject matter for AI, including the legal framework for patentability of "software patents."
2. Patentability and inventorship issues for AI-generated inventions.
3. Liability issues for patent infringement by AI.
4. Non-obviousness standard for AI.

in turn having a long-term impact on both education and software design.

AI and the IP system in the future

As seen in the previous chapters of this report, AI is expected to revolutionize processes across a wide range of fields. It is foreseen that AI will also affect intellectual property rights, in particular patent rights, and their management. This is likely to be a two-way process: on the one hand, AI developments will affect and be incorporated into IP rights management; on the other hand, IP policies and practices will interact with the strategy of managing innovation in AI.

Some of the questions likely to arise include:

- **Data and the IP system**: Access to and ownership of data is central to the development of AI. The assessment of what is its legal nature and whether data, datasets and databases form a *sui generis*

right or can be protected through an IP right form, combined with other possible provisions requiring disclosure/sharing of data, will also have an impact on the further development and use of AI and the profile of its future leaders.

- **AI and IP protection**: The way different AI technologies will be treated in the assessment of eligible patent subject matter, how the patentability criteria will be interpreted and applied to AI in patent prosecution across different jurisdictions, and whether there may be further refinements or additions in the patent system and its practice to accommodate AI specificities all remain to be seen and merit further discussion by IP specialists. The impact of any such developments can be measured in particular indicators, namely the number of patent filings in the field of AI, the related geographical distribution of patent protection, and the choice of IP rights to protect AI-related inventions. Other questions regarding current rules related to inventorship and infringement are also relevant if AI further develops.

- **AI technologies for patent administration purposes**: In the patent analysis presented in this report, law, including industrial property, is identified among the fields that patent applications refer to: these documents address AI-based solutions facilitating patent search and examination, construction of claims which can support the work of patent professionals, both on the patent offices and patent attorneys/applicants' side. The presence of patent information providers among the top 20 applicants in this field is confirmation of an intended move toward products and solutions to support different profiles of patent professionals. In addition, patent offices are already exploring, or even using, AI technologies to facilitate services, including patent classification, image recognition, state-of-the-art searches, machine translation and customer service. Various discussions are taking place on how AI-specific provisions should be included in the various IP administration tools and instruments, including patent classification.

In addition, as AI develops, some of the questions that are currently discussed only hypothetically may become real issues. These include the inventorship of AI, patent and more generally IP rights infringement by AI. Such questions may call for related regulation or a certain interpretation of existing regulations to cover possible gaps and answer related questions.

Throughout this report, trends in patent, scientific and business data have been presented to provide fact-based evidence for a meaningful discussion on a broad range of issues about what AI technologies involve. These trends reveal how AI technologies have evolved over time and what are the current and future trends in technologies, target markets and key players within the different segments of AI. This report has also offered different, but important perspectives from experts in the field to contextualize AI, as the further development and adoption of AI will depend on a number of other factors whose implications extend far beyond the technology itself and impact humanity as a whole. We hope the unique features of this publication will add to the existing knowledge base and so contribute to vital discussions on policy relating to AI in both the private and public sector in the next few years.

A time for action

Konstantinos Karachalios, IEEE

The patent system, a pillar of the global knowledge economy, must evolve. The circumstances demand that it rises again to its original promise. We should never forget that "patent" means "open," even though most people now believe it means "private" and "closed", hence the "my house" doctrine. Beyond the specific problems related to who owns an invention produced mainly using algorithmic systems, the most fundamental challenge is how the patent system could promote more of (or at least not kill) the collaboration incentives necessary for software-related innovation ecosystems. Several proposals and scenarios have been proposed in the past, but they now need to be enacted and time is running out very fast. In particular, WIPO could throw its weight into supporting the idea of an Autonomous and Intelligent Systems Commons, similar to existing proposals for an agreement on open access to basic science and technology.

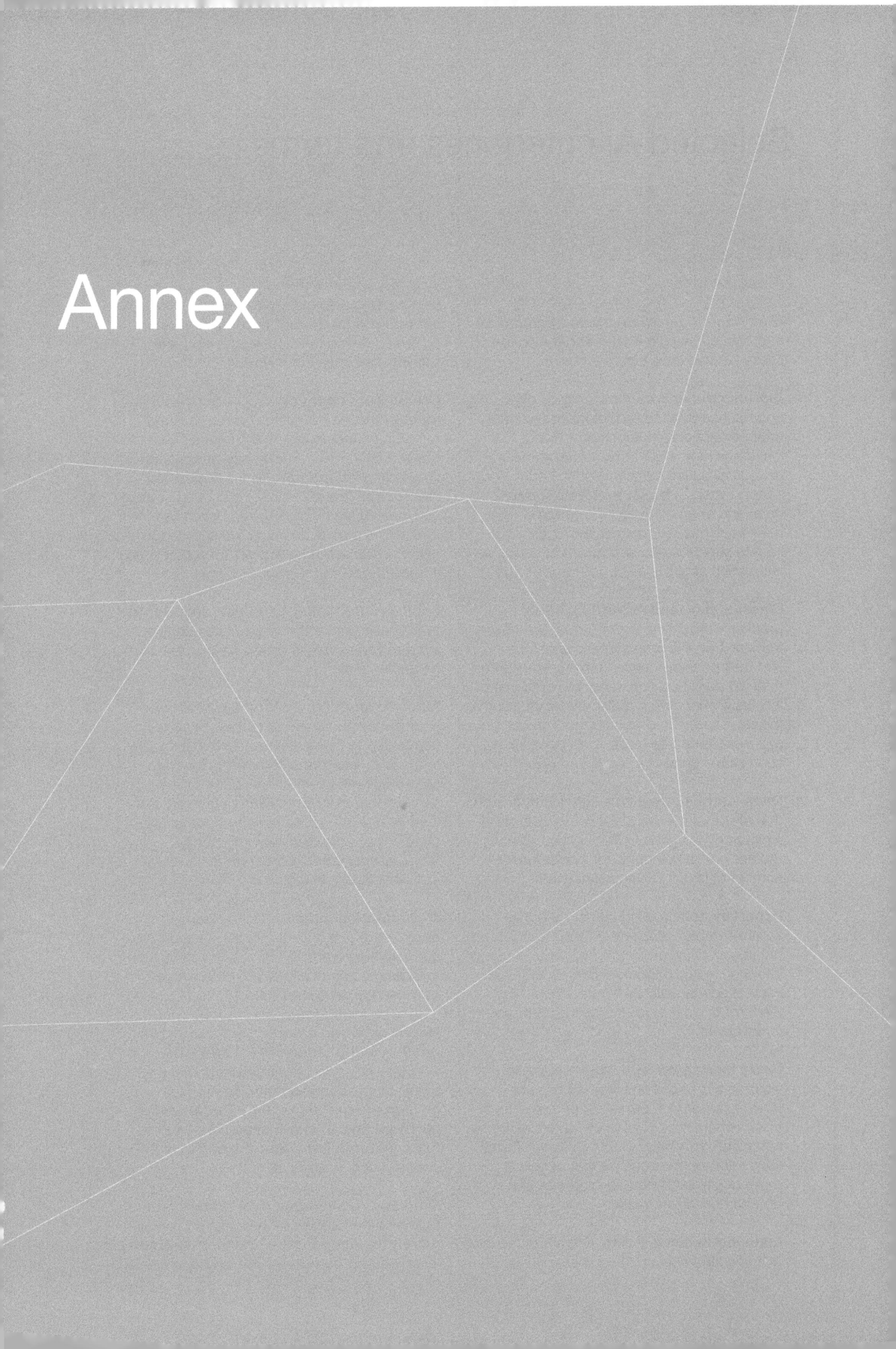

Annex

Selected AI categories and terms

AI techniques

AI techniques are different core algorithmic approaches used to implement AI functions. These techniques are defined below.

Bio-inspired approaches: a family of AI approaches inspired by biological systems, rather than a precise technique. These include genetic algorithms, which mimic genetic evolution mechanisms to better adapt decisions to new problems and new data, and swarm intelligence, where simple rules implemented by individual agents can lead to sophisticated and robust behavior via interaction at group-level.

Classification and regression trees: predictive models to support decision-making that use tree-like representations of facts and their possible consequences, sometimes referred to as decision trees. The outcome of a classification tree is a discrete value, such as the class to which data belongs. The outcome of a regression tree takes continuous values, such as the price of a house.

Deep learning: a machine learning approach that tries to understand the world in terms of a hierarchy of concepts. Most deep learning models are implemented by increasing the number of layers in a neural network.

Expert system: a computer system that solves complex problems within a specialized domain, usually requiring a high level of human intelligence and expertise. This expertise is expressed manually by human experts in the form of a set of rules which are simple logical tests.

Fuzzy logic: a decision-making approach which is not based on the usual "true or false" assessment, but rather on "degrees of truth" (where the "true" value ranges between completely true and completely false). Fuzzy logic relies on the principle that people make decisions based on imprecise and non-numerical information.

Instance-based learning: a family of machine learning algorithms that compare new problem with cases seen in training and can adapt the model to previously unseen data. It is called "instance-based" learning because it constructs hypotheses directly from the training instances themselves.

Latent representation: the mathematical representation of variables that are inferred rather than directly observed. Latent representation is applied in natural language processing, for example, where it is usually inferred from the statistical distribution of words, and in deep learning, where it is often used for performing transfer learning, i.e. knowledge gained while solving one problem and applying it to a different but related problem.

Logic programming: uses facts and rules to make decisions, without specifying additional intermediary steps, in order to achieve a particular goal.

Machine learning: an AI process that uses algorithms and statistical models to allow computers to make decisions without having to explicitly program it to perform the task. Machine learning algorithms build a model on sample data used as training data in order to identify and extract patterns from data, and therefore acquire their own knowledge. A typical example is a program that identifies and filters spam email.

Multi-task learning: a machine learning approach where a single model is used to solve multiple learning tasks at the same time, exploiting commonalities and differences between the various tasks.

Neural network: a learning process inspired by the neural structures of the brain. The network is a connected framework of many functions (neurons) working together to process multiple data inputs. The network is generally organized in successive layers of functions, each layer using the output of the previous one as an input.

Ontology engineering: a set of tasks related to the methodologies for building ontologies, namely the way concepts and their relationship in a particular domain are formally represented.

Probabilistic graphical models: a framework for representing complex domains using distribution of probabilities, where the models use a graph-based representation for defining the statistical dependence or independence relationships between data.

Probabilistic reasoning: an AI approach which combines deductive logic and probability theory to model logical relations under uncertainty in data.

Reinforcement learning: an area of machine learning that uses a system of reward and punishment for learning how to attain a complex objective. This approach seeks to incentivize software agents to learn correct decisions by trial and error and to pursue a long-term reward.

Rule learning: machine learning methods which identify and generalize automatically a set of rules to be used for prediction or classification of new unseen data. These rules are usually simple conditional tests.

Supervised learning: the most widely adopted form of machine learning. In supervised learning the expected grouping of the information in certain categories (output) is provided to the computer through examples of data (input) which have been manually categorized correctly and form the training dataset. Based on these examples of input-output, the AI system can categorize new, unseen data into the predefined categories.

Support vector machine: a supervised learning algorithm that analyzes labeled/grouped data, identifies the data points that are most challenging to group and, based on that, identifies how to separate the different groups and classify unseen data points. The name "support vector machine" comes from the boundary lines that separate the different groups of data.

Unsupervised learning: a type of machine learning algorithm that finds and analyzes hidden patterns or commonalities in data that has not been labeled or classified. Unlike supervised learning, the system has not been provided with a predefined set of classes, but rather identifies patterns and creates labels/groups in which it classifies the data.

AI functional applications

AI functional applications cover the functions performed by AI techniques, independent of the field of application. These functional applications are categorized as follows.

Augmented reality: this computer vision application provides an interactive experience of a real-world environment, where elements from the real-world are "augmented" by computer-generated sensory information and layered over with the natural environment.

Biometrics: deals with the recognition of people based on physiological characteristics, such as face, fingerprint, vascular pattern or iris, and behavioral traits, such as gait or speech. It combines computer vision with knowledge of human physiology and behavior.

Character recognition: the process of reading typed, handwritten or printed text and converting it into machine-encoded text. A subset of image recognition, it is also known as optical character recognition or reader (OCR).

Computer vision: an interdisciplinary field that deals with how computers see and understand digital images and videos. Computer vision spans all tasks performed by biological vision systems, including "seeing" or sensing a visual stimulus, understanding what is being seen, and extracting complex information into a form that can be used in other processes.

Distributed AI: systems consisting of distributed, multiple autonomous learning agents which process independently data and provide partial solutions which are then integrated, through communication nodes connecting the individual agents. Distributed AI systems can by design aim at solving complex learning and decision-making tasks, involving large data sets and requiring high computational power.

Image and video segmentation: the process of breaking down a digital image into multiple segments or analyzing the images constituting a video, assigning a label to every pixel in an image, in order to simplify or change the representation of an image into something that is more meaningful and easier to analyze. This process is typically used to locate objects and boundaries (lines, curves, etc.) in images.

Information extraction: the task of extracting structured information from unstructured or semi-structured textual sources.

Knowledge representation and reasoning: the field dedicated to representing information about the world usable by a computer to solve complex tasks. These representations are usually based on the way humans represent knowledge, reason (for instance through rules and building relations of sets and sub-sets) and solve problems.

Natural language processing: use of algorithms to analyze human (natural) language data so that computers can understand what humans have written or said and further interact with them.

Object tracking: the process of locating one or more moving objects over time in a video.

Planning/scheduling: the realization of strategies or action sequences for execution by intelligent agents, such as autonomous robots and unmanned vehicles.

Predictive analytics: the process of making predictions about future or otherwise unknown events using a variety of statistical techniques to analyze current and historical facts.

Robotics: the design, construction and operation of machines able to follow step-by-step instructions or perform complex actions automatically and with a certain level of autonomy. Robotics combines hardware with the implementation of AI techniques to perform these tasks.

Scene understanding: the process, often in real-time, of perceiving, analyzing and elaborating an interpretation of a scene and objects in context with respect to the 3D structure of the scene, its layout, and the spatial, functional, and semantic relationships between objects.

Semantics: the automatic recognition and disambiguation of topics and concepts in raw text, image or video, and the application of reasoning for further identifying new associations and facts.

Sentiment analysis: the identification, extraction, analysis and categorization of affective state or opinion from text, social media activity, audio, video or biometric sensors information.

Speech processing: systems involving analysis of speech signals, including speech recognition, natural language processing and speech synthesis.

Speech recognition: the process of identifying words in spoken language and of translating them into text.

Speech synthesis: the artificial production of human speech.

Speaker recognition: the identification of a person from the characteristics of their voice.

Speech-to-speech application: an end-to-end systems where the input and output are a raw audio voice signal, which can be different (another voice or another language) or enhanced (de-noised).

AI application fields

AI technologies can be applied to multiple fields, as summarized below.

Banking and finance: Machine learning is already deeply integrated into many aspects of financial systems, from the approval of loans, to the management of assets and the assessment of risks. Automated trading systems involve the use of complex AI algorithms to make extremely fast trading decisions. Modern fraud detection systems actively learn new potential security threats. AI is predicted to have an impact on financial customer services in the future, with specialized chatbots and voice assistants, recommendation systems for financial products and for improving safety by exploiting advances in biometric systems.

Business: AI techniques are already commonly used for improving marketing and advertising, personalization and product recommendations. Many companies rely on AI algorithms to identify trends and insights into customer data and to make faster decisions with the objective of following their impact on the market in real-time.

Document management and publishing: Over the past two decades, AI has been continuously improving automatic data extraction, structuring and conversion of documents (including automatic translation). Improved document clustering and advanced data analytics are expected to better exploit the huge volume of documents that exist. AI-powered document management systems could also enhance security and protect customer data.

Industry and manufacturing: AI is likely to have major impact on industry and manufacturing. Predictive maintenance is expected to limit costs related to unplanned downtime and malfunction. AI algorithms should also help companies to cope with the increasing complexity of products, engineering processes and quality regulations. Improved robots are expected to handle more cognitive tasks and make autonomous decisions. Generative design systems are able to quickly generate, explore and optimize design alternatives from a set of high-level design goals. Continuous monitoring of the market by AI tools could help proactively to optimize staffing, inventory, energy consumption and the supply of raw materials.

Life and medical sciences: Automatic diagnostic systems are a very promising application of new machine learning techniques. Recent results have shown that it is possible to surpass human expert accuracy for several narrow tasks, such as detection of melanoma or risks of atherosclerosis in arteries. Drug personalization is also frequently cited as a key marker of progress driven by AI. The availability of large amounts of clinical data mean AI is predicted to improve drug discovery and reduce development costs by helping select the most promising hypotheses and focus on more targeted research.

Security: Cyber-security (spam filtering, intrusion-detection) has benefited from machine learning since the 1990s. Automated surveillance is developing quickly, sometimes in conjunction with smart city technologies. AI techniques such as face detection, behavior and crowd analysis are mature enough to make surveillance cameras more "active" without the need for human supervision. Predictive policing technology has started to be used in several U.S. states and the U.K. and AI techniques are also integrated in mass surveillance programs. AI is also considered as a new enabler for a vast range of military requirements, including intelligence, surveillance, reconnaissance, logistics, battlefield planning, weapons systems and defense/offense decisions.

Telecommunications: AI is expected to drive new opportunities in telecoms by helping to improve network performance, thanks to anomaly detection and prediction of service degradations, and also by optimizing customer services.

Transportation: Fuzzy logic and other AI approaches have been used in transportation since the 1980s. It is widely predicted that autonomous vehicles will save costs, lower emissions and enhance road safety, and that AI will improve traffic management by reducing traffic jams and make possible crewless cargo ships and fully automated package delivery.

Further reading

Bergstein, B. (ed.) (2017). The artificial intelligence issue. *MIT Technology Review*, 120(6).

Bostrom, N. (2016). *Superintelligence: Paths, Dangers, Strategies*. Oxford: Oxford University Press.

Brundage, M. et al. (2018). *The Malicious Use of Artificial Intelligence: Forecasting, Prevention, and Mitigation*. Future of Humanity Institute; University of Oxford; Centre for the Study of Existential Risk; University of Cambridge; Center for a New American Security; Electronic Frontier Foundation; OpenAI.

Brynjolfsson, E. and A. McAfee (2017). The business of artificial intelligence. *Harvard Business Review*. https://hbr.org/cover-story/2017/07/the-business-of-artificial-intelligence (accessed January 24, 2019).

Bughin, J. et al. (2017). *Artificial Intelligence: The Next Digital Frontier?* Discussion Paper, McKinsey Global Institute.

Cockburn, I., R. Henderson and S. Stern (2017). The impact of artificial intelligence on innovation. *NBER Conference on the Economics of Artificial Intelligence*, Toronto.

DeepAI. *Data Science Glossary*. https://deepai.org/data-science-glossary/a (accessed January 17, 2019).

Deloitte (2016). *Artificial Intelligence Innovation Report*. https://www2.deloitte.com/content/dam/Deloitte/at/Documents/human-capital/artificial-intelligence-innovation-report.pdf (accessed March 29, 2018).

EPO. (2017). Patents and the Fourth Industrial Revolution. Munich: European Patent Office.

Ford, M. (2018). *Architects of Intelligence: The Truth About AI from the People Building It*. New York: Packet Publishing.

Furman, J. and Seamans, R. (2018). *AI and the Economy*. Available at SSRN: https://ssrn.com/abstract=3186591 (accessed January 22, 2019).

Gartner. *IT Glossary*. https://www.gartner.com/it-glossary/ (accessed March 29, 2018).

Ghandeharioun, A. et al. (2017). Objective assessment of depressive symptoms with machine learning and wearable sensors data. *Seventh International Conference on Affective Computing and Intelligent Interaction (ACII)*, 2017. San Antonio, TX: IEEE, 325–332.

Giles, M. (2018). The GANfather: The man who's given machines the gift of imagination. *MIT Technology Review*, 121(2), 49–53.

Goodfellow, I. et al (2016). *Deep Learning*. Cambridge, MA: MIT Press. http://www.deeplearningbook.org (accessed January 17, 2019).

Hoffmann Pham et al. (2018). Data fusion to describe and quantify search and rescue operations in the Mediterranean Sea. *2018 IEEE 5th International Conference on Data Science and Advanced Analytics*. Turin: IEEE.

ITU (2017). *AI for Good Global Summit Report*. Geneva: International Telecommunications Union.

LeCun, Y., Y. Bengio and G. Hinton (2015). Deep learning. *Nature*, 521, 436–444.

Lee, K.-F. (2018). *AI Superpowers: China, Silicon Valley, and the New World Order*. New York: Houghton Mifflin.

Lorica, B. (2018). *Data Collection and Data Markets in the Age of Privacy and Machine Learning*. O'Reilly On Our Radar. https://www.oreilly.com/ideas/data-collection-and-data-markets-in-the-age-of-privacy-and-machine-learning (accessed January 22, 2019).

— and M. Loukides (2018). *Building Tools for the AI Applications of Tomorrow*. O'Reilly On Our Radar. https://www.oreilly.com/ideas/building-tools-for-the-ai-applications-of-tomorrow (accessed January 22, 2019).

— (2018). *What Machine Learning Means for Software Development*. O'Reilly On Our Radar. https://www.oreilly.com/ideas/what-machine-learning-means-for-software-development (accessed January 22, 2019).

Marr, B. (2016). *What Is the Difference Between Deep Learning, Machine Learning and AI?* Forbes. https://www.forbes.com/sites/bernardmarr/2016/12/08/what-is-the-difference-between-deep-learning-machine-learning-and-ai/#707f26da26cf (accessed January 22, 2019).

McAfee, A. and E. Brynjolfsson (2017). Machine, Platform, Crowd: Harnessing Our Digital Future. New York, NY: W. W. Norton & Company.

Ng, A. (forthcoming). *Machine Learning Yearning*. Draft copy available at http://www.mlyearning.org/ (accessed January 24, 2019).

— (2018). *AI Transformation Playbook: How to lead your company into the AI era*. https://landing.ai/ai-transformation-playbook/ (accessed January 24, 2019).

Onorati, F. et al. (2017). Multicenter clinical assessment of improved wearable multimodal convulsive seizure detectors. *Epilepsia*, 58 (11), 1870–1879.

Pauwels, E. and S.W. Denton (2018). Searching for privacy in the Internet of Bodies. *The Wilson Quarterly* (May).

Poole, D.L. and A.K. Mackworth (2017). *Artificial Intelligence: Foundations of Computational Agents*, 2nd Edition. http://artint.info/2e/html/ArtInt2e.html (accessed March 29, 2018).

Quinn, J.A. et al. (2018). Humanitarian applications of machine learning with remote-sensing data: Review and case study in refugee settlement mapping. *Philosophical Transactions of the Royal Society A: Mathematical, Physical and Engineering Sciences*, 376 (2128).

Rotman, D. (2018). Making AI into jobs. *MIT Technology Review*, 121(4), 10–17.

Schwab, K. (2017). *The Fourth Industrial Revolution*. New York: Crown Publishing Group.

Selbst, A. and S. Barocas (2017). *AI Now 2017 Report*. The AI Now Institute (1–2).

Shoham, Y. et al. (2018). *The AI Index 2018 Annual Report*. Stanford, CA: Stanford University.

Stone, P. et al. (2016). *Artificial Intelligence and Life in 2030*. Stanford, CA: Stanford University.

Suhara, Y., Y. Xu and A.S. Pentland (2017). Deepmood: Forecasting depressed mood based on self-reported histories via recurrent neural networks. *Proceedings of the 26th International Conference on World Wide Web*. Perth, Australia: International World Wide Web Conferences Steering Committee, 715–724.

Taylor, S.A. et al. (2017). Personalized multitask learning for predicting tomorrow's mood, stress, and health. *IEEE Transactions on Affective Computing, PP(99)*. https://affect.media.mit.edu/pdfs/17.TaylorJaques-PredictingTomorrowsMoods.pdf (accessed January 18, 2019).

Thurman, D.J., D.C. Hesdorffer and J.A. French (2014). Sudden unexpected death in epilepsy: Assessing the public health burden. *Epilepsia*, 55(10), 1479–1485.

United Nations Department of Economic and Social Affairs (2018). *World Economic and Social Survey 2018: Frontier technologies for sustainable development*. New York: United Nations.

United Nations Global Pulse (2017). *Using Machine Learning to Analyse Radio Content in Uganda*. Geneva: United Nations.

van Duin, S. and N. Bakhshi (2017). *Artificial Intelligence Defined*. https://www2.deloitte.com/nl/nl/pages/data-analytics/articles/part-1-artificial-intelligence-defined.html (accessed March 29, 2018).

Vasisht, D. et al. (2017). FarmBeats: An IoT platform for data-driven agriculture. *14th USENIX Symposium on Networked Systems Design and Implementation*. Boston, MA: USENIX.

WIPO (2018). *World Intellectual Property Indicators 2018*. Geneva: World Intellectual Property Organization.

Wikipedia contributors. *Glossary of artificial intelligence*. Wikipedia, The Free Encyclopedia, https://en.wikipedia.org/wiki/Glossary_of_artificial_intelligence (accessed January 17, 2019).

Policy and regulatory frameworks

Access Now (2018). *Mapping Regulatory Proposals for Artificial Intelligence in Europe*. https://www.accessnow.org/cms/assets/uploads/2018/11/mapping_regulatory_proposals_for_AI_in_EU.pdf (accessed January 17, 2019).

Barton, J.H. and K.E. Maskus (2004). Economic perspectives on a multilateral agreement on open access to basic science and technology. *SCRIPT-ed*, 1(3).

Craglia, M. (ed.) (2018). *Artificial Intelligence: A European Perspective*, EUR 29425 EN. Luxembourg: Publications Office of the European Union.

European Commission (2018). Communication from the Commission to the European Parliament, the European Council, the Council, the European Economic and Social Committee and the Committee of the Regions on Artificial Intelligence for Europe. *Artificial Intelligence in Europe*. Brussels.

European Commission High-Level Expert Group on Artificial Intelligence (2018). *A Definition of AI: Main Capabilities and Scientific Disciplines*. Brussels.

Finnish Government (2017). *Finland's Age of Artificial Intelligence Turning Finland into a Leading Country in the Application of Artificial Intelligence Objective and Recommendations for Measures*. Publications of the Ministry of Economic Affairs and Employment Ministry, 47/2017.

Foray, D. (2015). *Smart Specialisation: Opportunities and Challenges for Regional Innovation Policies*. London: Routledge.

Foray, D., P.A. David and B. Hall (2009). Smart specialisation: The concept. *Knowledge for Growth*. Brussels: European Commission.

Nemitz, P. (2018). Constitutional democracy and technology in the age of artificial intelligence. *Royal Society Philosophical Transactions A*, 376: 20180089.

Nordic Council of Ministers (2018). *AI in the Nordic-Baltic Region*. https://www.regeringen.se/49a602/globalassets/regeringen/dokument/naringsdepartementet/20180514_nmr_deklaration-slutlig-webb.pdf (accessed January 23, 2019).

République Française (2017). *France Intelligence Artificielle (FIA) Rapport de synthèse*. https://www.economie.gouv.fr/files/files/PDF/2017/Rapport_synthese_France_IA_.pdf (accessed December 13, 2018).

United States National Science and Technology Council (2016). *Artificial Intelligence, Automation, and the Economy*. https://www.whitehouse.gov/sites/whitehouse.gov/files/images/EMBARGOED%20AI%20Economy%20Report.pdf (accessed January 22, 2019).

— (2016). *National Artificial Intelligence Research and Development Strategic Plan*. https://www.nitrd.gov/PUBS/national_ai_rd_strategic_plan.pdf (accessed January 22, 2019).

— (2016). *Preparing for the Future of Artificial Intelligence*. https://info.publicintelligence.net/WhiteHouse-ArtificialIntelligencePreparations.pdf (accessed January 22, 2019).

Employment and productivity

Autor, D. and A. Salomons (2017). Robocalypse now: Does productivity growth threaten employment? *ECB Forum on Central Banking*, 2142 (June), 1–74.

Benzell, S.G., G. Kotlikoff, G. LaGarda and J.D. Sachs (2015). Robots are us: Some economics of human replacement. *NBER Working Paper No. 20941*. Cambridge, MA: NBER.

Brynjolfsson, E., D. Rock, and C. Syverson (2017). Artificial intelligence and the modern productivity paradox: A clash of expectations and statistics. *NBER Working Paper No. 24001*. Cambridge, MA: NBER.

Dauth, W., S. Findeisen, J. Suedekum and N. Woessner (2018). Adjusting to robots: Worker-level evidence. *Federal Reserve Bank of Minneapolis Working Paper No. 13*. Minneapolis, MN: Federal Reserve Bank of Minneapolis.

Ford, M. (2016). The Rise of the Robots: *Technology and the Threat of Mass Unemployment*. New York: Oneworld Publications.

Frey, C.B. and M.A. Osborne (2013). The future of employment: How susceptible are jobs to computerisation? *Oxford Martin Programme on Technology and Employment Working Paper*. Oxford: Oxford Martin Programme on Technology and Employment.

Gerbert P. et al. (2015). *Industry 4.0: The Future of Productivity and Growth in Manufacturing Industries*. Boston Consulting Group. https://www.bcg.com/en-gb/publications/2015/engineered_products_project_business_industry_4_future_productivity_growth_manufacturing_industries.aspx (accessed January 18, 2019)

Kahn, J. (2018). *Just How Shallow Is the Artificial Intelligence Talent Pool?* Bloomberg. https://www. bloomberg.com/news/articles/2018-02-07/just-how-shallow-is-the-artificial-intelligence-talent-pool (accessed January 22, 2019).

Data privacy and ethics

Boucher, P. et al. (2014). *Ethics Dialogues: Experiencing Ethics Through "Things": Open IoT, Civil Drones and Wearable Sensors*. Luxembourg: Publications Office of the European Union.

Cath, C. et al. (2018). Governing artificial intelligence: Ethical, legal and technical challenges and opportunities. *Philosophical Transactions of the Royal Society A: Mathematical, Physical and Engineering Sciences*, 376 (2133).

Council of Europe (2017). *Algorithms and Human Rights. Study on the human rights dimensions of automated data processing techniques and possible regulatory implications*. Committee of Experts on Internet Intermediaries (MSI-NET). Strasbourg: Council of Europe.

IEEE (2018). *Ethically Aligned Design, version 2*. https://ethicsinaction.ieee.org/ (accessed January 17, 2019).

Patent information

Dechezleprêtre, A., Y. Ménière and M. Mohnen (2017). International patent families: from application strategies to statistical indicators. *Scientometrics*, 111(2), 793–828

Fink, C., M. Khan and H. Zhou (2013). Exploring the worldwide patent surge. *WIPO Economic Research Working Paper No. 12*. Geneva: WIPO.

Fujii H. and S. Managi (2017). Trends and priority shifts in artificial intelligence technology invention: A global patent analysis. *Research Institute of Economy, Trade and Industry*, 17-E-066.

Hidemichi, F. and M. Shunsuke (2017). Trends and priority shifts in artificial intelligence technology invention: A global patent analysis. *Research Institute of Economy, Trade & Industry Discussion Paper 17-E-006*. Tokyo: RIETI.

Martínez, C. (2011). Patent families: When do different definitions really matter? *Scientometrics*, 86(1), 39–63.

Motohashi, K. (2018). Understanding AI driven innovation by linked dataset of scientific articles and patents. *Research Institute of Economy, Trade & Industry Discussion Paper 18-P-017*. Tokyo: RIETI.

UKIPO (2015). *The Patent Guide: A handbook for analysing and interpreting patent data*, 2nd Edition. Newport: United Kingdom Intellectual Property Office.

WIPO (2018). *World Intellectual Property Indicators 2018*. Geneva: World Intellectual Property Organization.

— (2015). *Guidelines for Preparing Patent Landscape Reports*. Geneva: World Intellectual Property Organization.

WIPO (1991). *Conference Proceedings of the WIPO Worldwide Symposium on the Intellectual Property Aspects of Artificial Intelligence*, Stanford University, Stanford CA, March 25– 27, 1991.

World Economic Forum (2018). *Artificial Intelligence Collides with Patent Law*. Cologny/Geneva: WEF Centre for the Fourth Industrial Revolution.

Zech, H. (2016). A legal framework for a data economy in the European Digital Single Market: Rights to use data. *Journal of Intellectual Property Law & Practice*, 11(6), 460–470.

Intellectual property

Brynjolfsson, E. (1994). Information assets, technology and organization. *Management Science*, 40 (12), 1645–1662.

Kerber, W. (2016). Governance of data: Exclusive property vs. access. *International Review of Intellectual Property and Competition Law*, 47(7), 759–762.

Ramalho, A. (2018). *Patentability of AI-Generated Inventions: Is a Reform of the Patent System Needed?* Institute of Intellectual Property, Foundation for Intellectual Property of Japan, 1–32.

United States Patent and Trademark Office (2019). *2019 Revised Patent Subject Matter Eligibility Guidance*. https://www.govinfo.gov/content/pkg/FR-2019-01-07/pdf/2018-28282.pdf (accessed January 8, 2019).

— (2017). *Patent Eligible Subject Matter: Report on Views and Recommendations from the Public*. Washington, D.C.: USPTO.

www.ingramcontent.com/pod-product-compliance
Lightning Source LLC
Chambersburg PA
CBHW082311210326
41599CB00030B/5761